COMPOSITE FARMING PRACTICES AND ECONOMIC DEVELOPMENT

Editors

AMOD SHARMA
RAVISHANKAR KUMAR SINGH

ABHIJEET PUBLICATIONS
DELHI 110094

ABHIJEET PUBLICATIONS
2/46 Tukhmeerpur Extension
Delhi 110 094
Phone: (011)-22960492, 65698474
e-mail: abhijeetpublication@gmail.com

COMPOSITE FARMING PRACTICES AND ECONOMIC DEVELOPMENT

First Published 2007

ISBN 978-81-89886-27-1

PRINTED IN INDIA

Published by J.K. Singh for Abhijeet Publications, Delhi 110094, Lasertypeset by Rajesh Data Services, New Delhi and Printed at Himanshu Printers, Delhi.

Foreword

I am very happy to note that the School of Agriculture. Sciences and Rural Development (SASRD) is bringing out the conference proceedings of the seminar on "Technology for Improving Agriculture Productivity in Nagaland" which was held on 11th October 2003 as part of the Silver Jubilee Celebrations of the SASRD, Medziphema.

Our country being mainly focused at agri-business, the efforts of SASRD in providing not only training qualified graduate but also closely interacting with the agricultural farmers for the last 25 years in really praiseworthy.

Our country has tremendous potential in the areas of Animal Husbandry, Horticulture, Floriculture, Fishery and Forestry etc. Even the conventional traditional agricultural practices have been preserved and has not been tampered with chemical pesticides or chemical fertilizers. This is indeed a unique opportunity for SASRD to compare green revolution versus traditional practices in our country. Further it is essential that there should be a balance between traditional practices and implementation of modern technology, so that benefits are more than risks.

I am sure, the readers will be immensely benefited by reading such a publication. I must complement my colleagues at SASRD for being very sensitive to the local needs and doing their best to promote good practices in agriculture.

K. Kannan
Vice Chancellor
Nagaland University

Preface

Nature has been so kind to men. Ever since its appearance on the earth's surface man has been dependent on nature for his subsistence. We needed edible plants and animals, everything that comes from nature but its utilization is possible on the availability of appropriate technology. Keeping in view the squeezing land to man ratio, the food, fibre, fuel and fodder requirements in future have to be met through enhancement of productivity with the efficient use of natural resources. In order to improve production and productivity especially in hilly region the analysis of resources is of utmost importance.

Agriculture and allied activities sector is the most important segment of the economy. Technological progress and introduction of scientific agricultural inputs have made remarkable improvement in agriculture and allied activities. It is technological innovation and efforts of devoted scientists, which enabled us to achieve strategic breakthrough in agriculture. The process of diversification in agriculture, the success of technological breakthrough is area specific as well as crop specific. Some other emerging problems in agricultural sector are—soil degradation, environmental pollution, food security, non-sustainable agricultural practice, credit availability etc.

The rapid growth of population and technological revolution has created a serious concern to the existence of life on earth. Indiscriminate use of natural resources has also posed a serious threat to the environment. Our natural resources will be at increasing risk from soil degradation, deforestation water scarcity and contamination, loss of bio diversity and climatic changes owing to over consumption in our State. The changing agro-system-environment has posed a question mark on the sustainability of the production system.

In the rainfed area where natural hazards have put these areas in situation of production-uncertainties, systems of farming have its own economic significance. Rural people in general are dependent on locally available resources. Therefore, in the rainfed areas, the chances of shifting towards other farming activities like—piggery, fishery, and poultry are more economically viable and socially acceptable.

Our country has immense potential for agricultural development including development of animal husbandry, horticulture, fishery, forestry etc. Present agriculture activities has been found to be labour-intensive. There is great need to have an in-depth knowledge of the production potentialities of the land and its proper management. Most of the existing systems of agriculture in the region are primarily subsistence farming only.

However, due to increasing population, decreasing community participation and local forest products, deforestation and land degradation due to shifting cultivation, productivity of some of these systems is not sufficient to fulfill the needs of the farmer. Agricultural development in our country is constrained by lack of appropriate technology, inadequate infrastructure, poor marketing network etc. Thus, in view of scientific advancement and development, this seminar to discuss the following themes in-depth to generate simple and sound recommendation for environmental conservation and sustainable development.

SUB-THEME

- Natural resource utilization pattern
- Constraints in agricultural production
- Relevance of traditional farming systems in relation to agricultural production
- Dimensions of improved technologies for increased agricultural productivity.

I, take this privilege to thanks all the sponsors of the seminar without which it would not have been possible to organize it. We also place on record our gratitude to all the resource persons of the seminar who had taken utmost pains to go in-depth into issues pertaining to the technology for improving agricultural productivity of the state for resource management and sustainable development. It is because of their sincere effort that the seminar saw its successful completion.

I am very much grateful to Prof. G.D. Sharma, Ex. Vice Chancellor, Nagaland University, Nagaland. I am also grateful to the SASRD Administration, all Convenors and members of the different sub-committee & other staff members, those who's have directly or indirectly provided their timely help and support for this seminar.

This book is the outcome of this very seminar and the fruit of the effort put in by all these people. We hope that this book will serve the very purpose for which it is being published. We wish to encourage our readers to go through this volume with the same zeal and enthusiasm put in by the authors and editors; so that the ideas and suggestions put forth are truly assimilated by the readers. Then only can the true reward of writing and reading of this book can be accomplished. .Last but not the least I am also thankful to Prof. D.P. Sharma and Dr. K.K. Jha who assisted in bringing out this book in this form.

Dr. Amod Sharma
Dr. R.K. Singh

Content

Foreword *iii*

Preface *v*

1. Rain Water Harvesting Techniques for Increasing Crop Production in Nagaland 1
A.K. Verma

2. Prospect and Constraint of Fish Production Under the Rainfed Condition of Nagaland 11
Sharma, A. Kalita, D.C. Singh, A. K. Nakhro, R. & Sharma, V.B.

3. Performance of Tomato (*Lycopersicon esculentum* L.) as Influenced by Transplanting Times and Cultivation Methods 22
Naresh Babu

4. Alternate Cropping System of Nagaland in North East Region of India 27
Sharma, Amod, Sharma, Anamika & Sharma, S.K.

5. Dynamics of Ecosystem and Its Pyramidical System 33
Amod Sharma

6. Impact of Livestock Resources to Uplift the Economy of Rural Dairy Farmers of KOMUL 38
Nizamuddin & Sharma, A.

7. Constraints of Oyster Mushroom Cultivation in Nagaland 52
Sharma, A. Jha, K.K., Kalita, D.C., Nizamuddin & Upadhyay, D.N.

8. "Bukhari" an Alternative to Conventional Method of Brooding in Remote and Rural Areas 58
R.K. Chaurasia, B. Prakash, and V.B. Sharma

9. Comparative Study of Mash vs. Pellet Feeding on the Performance of Broiler Chicken under Cage System 64
Nizamuddin and A.K. Singh

10. Constraints and Prioritization of Strategies of Agricultural Development in Nagaland 71
Kalita, D.C., Singh, A.K., Sharma, A. & Nakhro, R.

11. Crossability Relationships Among Cajanus Species 83
Jogendra Singh & G.C. Bajpai

12. Efficacy of Biocontrol Agents and Chemical Fertilizers for Control of While Mould of French Bean 87
N. Tiameren Ao, K.N. Bhagabati, A.K. Phookan, B.C. Das & M.C. Talukdar

13. Water Management for Effective Crop Production in Northeastern Hilly Region 94
R.C. Nayak and Sewak Ram

14. Variability and Character Association in Various Rice Ecotypes 108
Chaturvedi, H.P. and D.M. Maurya

15. Relevance of Indigenous Farming System in Solving Food Security Problem: A Case Study of Phek District 116
A.K. Tripathi, K.K. Datta, D.K. Sonowal & A.K. Khan

16. Constraints Faced by Lowland Paddy Cultivators in Dimapur District of Nagaland 124
Jha, K.K.

17. Relevance of Jhum Cultivation in Nagaland 130
Jha, K.K.

18. Technology for Improving Agricultural Productivity in Nagaland 137
Dr. Supong Keitzar

19. Effect of Simulated Erosion and Nitrogen Levels on the Uptake of N, P and K and Yield of Upland Rice 143
Manoj Dutta, Zakir Hussain and B.S. Chauhan

20. Constraints of Crop Production in Nagaland 153
M.K. Singh

21. Constraints Faced by the Mushroom Growers of Dimapur District of Nagaland 161
Tzudir, Bendangmenla, Sharma, A., Kalita, D.C. & Sharma, Y.K.

22. Soil Conservation and Its Fertility Management Systems Practice of Sloping Land in Northeast India 170
Sapu Changkija

23. Performance of Maize (*Zea mays* L.) Under Various Nutrient Management Practices on Terraced Land 175
Sewak Ram, B.S. Chauhan and Manoj Dutta

24. Integrated Nutrient Management and Sustainable Agriculture—An Overview 189
A.K. Singh, P.K. Singh and S.K. Sharma

25. Zabo and Alder Agriculture—Indigenous Farming Systems of Nagaland 202
S.D. Rao, Anamika Sharma, Chandan Rajkhowa & Joseph Kikon

26. Regulated Market in India 207
Bendangmenla Tzudir

27. Evaluation of fungicides *in vitro* against the growth of *Cercospora capsici* : the casual organism of chilli leaf spot disease 212
Ruokuovilie Mezhatsu; L. Daiho and D.N. Upadhyay

28. Evaluation of fungicides *in vitro* against the growth of *Colletotrichum capsici* : the casual organism of Chilli fruit rot disease 216
Ruokuovilie Mezhatsu; L. Daiho & D.N. Upadhyay

29. Screening of chilli cultivars against leaf spot and fruit rot diseases caused by *Cercospora capsici* and *Colletotrichum capsici* 220
Ruokuovilie Mezhatsu; L. Daiho & D.N. Upadhyay

30. Studies on management of fruit rot of Chilli (*Capsicum annuum* L.) 224
Ruokuovilie Mezhatsu; L. Daiho and D.N. Upadhyay

31. Studies on management of Cercospora leaf spot of chilli (*Capsicum annuum* L.) with systemic and non-systemic fungicides 230
Ruokuovilie Mezhatsu; L. Daiho & D.N. Upadhyay

32. An Analysis of Marketed Surplus of Rice in Assam 236
D.C. Kalita[1], B.C. Bhowmick, R.S. Saikia & C. Hazarika

33. Role of Biofertilizers in Crop Production 243
R.P. Singh

34. Alder-based Jhum Cultivation in Nagaland 249
Sentinungba Longchar

35. Status, Constraints and Prospects of Farm Inputs Marketing in Manipur 254
S.B. Singh and I.M. Singh

36. An Analytical Study of Almond Marketing and Problems of the Almond Growers in Kashmir Valley of J&K 257
Jaspal Singh, Tyagi, D.B. & Sharma, A.

1

Rain Water Harvesting Techniques for Increasing Crop Production in Nagaland

*A.K. Verma**

Meaning of Water Harvesting

To most of the people the term "Water Harvesting" means collection of rainwater in pond and roof top rainwater collection. But water harvesting means the collection of rainwater in many ways. It includes:

i. The collection of rainfall at points where it falls (Example—leveling of land, bench terrace bunding).
ii. Collecting rainwater that flows over the ground (Example—ponds, tanks, reservoirs).
iii. Storing water in Nallas/streams (Example—by checkdam or stop dam).
iv. Collection of water from springs, creeks (Example—through diversion channel).
v. Collecting rainwater from roof top.

---

* Lecturer, Department of Agricultural Engineering, School of Agricultural Sciences and Rural Development, Medziphema, Nagaland.

vi. Conserving rainwater through crop management (Growing cover crops i.e. crops having maximum foliage.

Need of Water Harvesting

Irrigation is a vital factor towards obtaining stabilized and reliable crop yield. Although there has been a rapid growth of irrigation in India, the growth is very skewed in terms of regional distribution (80% in Punjab and 10% in M.P.). This figure is worse in hill areas where the irrigated area is less than 10 % (Shrivastava *et. al.* 1994). In Nagaland the ultimate irrigation potential from all sources is estimated to be 165000 ha when fully developed (Table 1). However the total irrigation potential developed so far is 70379 ha with 41624 ha as utilization comprising of only 2.5 % of the total geographical area (1658000ha). The water resource scenario of Nagaland has been presented in Table 2.

Table 1: Irrigation Potential Areas in Nagaland

Sl. no.	*Location*	*Ultimate Potential, Ha*
1.	Foot hill area around Diamapur	55000
2.	Jalukie valley and surrounding hill slopes	8000
3.	Medziphema Bowl	3500
4.	Foot hill areas, Wokha	7500
5.	Baghty valley, Wokha	2000
6.	Tsurang valley, Wokha	6000
7.	Tsuong valley, Mokokchung	3000
8.	Foot hill areas, Mokokchung	4000
9.	Foot hill areas, Mon	3000
10.	Teru-Safrai and Tizit valley, Mon	8000
11.	Hill sides of varying degrees of slopes in smaller valleys, scattered throughout the state	65000
	Total	165000

Source: Njilo Kemp (2000).

Table 2. The Water Resource Scenario in Nagaland

Particulars	
Annual average precipitation	2150mm
Total Available water	3.56 million ha-m
Net sown area	204000 ha
Gross cropped area	228000 ha
Irrigation potential developed	70379 ha
Total irrigated area	41624 ha

As ground water exploitation in the state is beyond economic level, the irrigation water is received through rainfall only.

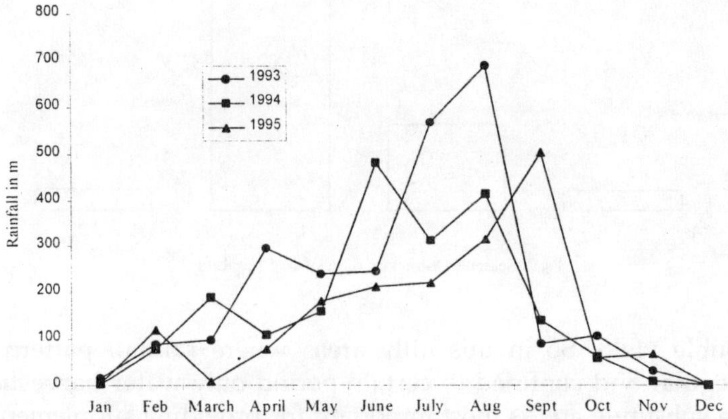

Fig.1 Monthly Rainfall Distribution in Nagaland

Data Source: Meteorological Report, Published by Directorate of Soil And Water Conservation, Kohima

The rainfall pattern of Nagaland has been shown in the Fig. No. 1 and in Fig. 2. From Fig. 1 it is clear that the high amount of rainfall (1700mm-2600mm) received in the Nagaland is unevenly distributed throughout the year. Fig. 2 shows that monsoon season (June-September) account for 68% of total annual rainfall, post monsoon (October-November) account for 22% leaving only 5% each during winter season (December-February) and pre monsoon season (March-May).

Monsoon rain also does not contribute much to meet the total water requirement of various crops because a substantial part of the water is wasted in the form of runoff through nallas and stream due to high intensity of rainfall, undulated topography of the area and negligible ground water recharge. So by harvesting water during rainy season, the irrigation water can be made available to protect Kharif crops and to make Rabi crops more productive. The application of irrigation at appropriate time during Kharif and Rabi season may result in

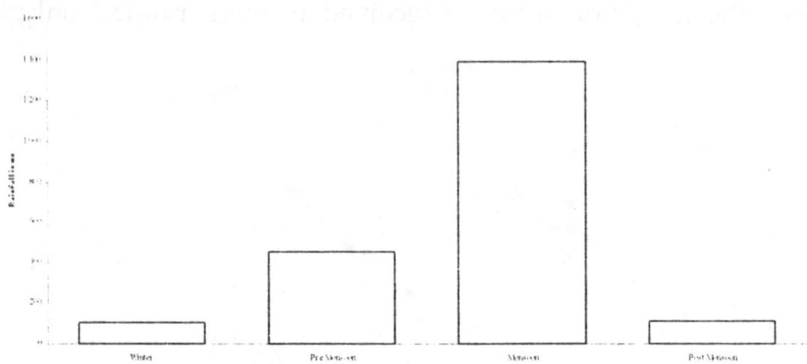

Fig.2. Seasonal Distribution of Rainfall of Nagaland

double yield. So in this hilly areas where rainfall pattern is irregular and confined to certain period only water harvesting is a substitute and is most important for providing supplemental irrigation to the crops.

Different Techniques For Water Harvesting

Water harvesting techniques includes a wide range of methods. A uniform pattern of water harvesting technique is not suited for different places. Depending upon the location, soil, rainfall and socio-economic status different techniques can be adopted for harvesting the rainwater. The following three basic points are considered before adopting a particular technique for water harvesting:

1. Sources of water available.
2. Required storage duration.
3. Intended use of harvested water.

On the basis of above listed points the different harvesting techniques can be enumerated as below:

A. In-Situ Rainwater Harvesting (Harvesting rainwater where it falls).

For this following techniques can be applied:

1. Contour Trenching
2. Land leveling

3. Bunding
4. Bench Terracing
5. Conservation tillage and deep ploughing
6. Cover crops and Mulching
7. Contour farming

B. Rainwater/Direct Surface Runoff Harvesting:

1. Roof top collection.
2. Dug out pond/storage tanks.
3. Diversion channels.

C. Stream Flow or Runoff Harvesting:

1. Nalla bunding
2. Gully control structures
3. Check dams/stop dams
4. Water diversion
5. Percolation tank.

D. Sub-Surface flow harvesting:

1. Sub-surface dams/barriers

E. Micro-catchments/Watersheds:

1. Enter-terrace/inter plot harvesting
2. Micro-watershed.

A brief description of above mentioned techniques are given as below:

1. Contour Trenching: Contour trenching implies excavating trenches along a uniform level across the slope in the top portion of the denuded hilly area. The rainwater is intercepted in the trenches increases the moisture status of the soil and thus provides advantageous site for sowing of grass and planting of trees. In addition to this, the rainwater retained in the trench percolates through the soil slowly and travels down benefiting the land in the middle and lower section of the hilly area.

While excavating the trenches, the soil, boulders and gravels from excavation should be placed on the lower side of the trenches. The shape of the trenches may be rectangular with length not more than 15m and depth and width as 30cm. The interspace between two trenches may be kept as 1m and row to row distance may be kept as 3 to 5m.

2. *Land Leveling:* On sloping land, land leveling eliminates small depressions, cuts and furrows where water would otherwise concentrate and start to run off causing damage by erosion year after year. Further land leveling ensures higher amount of rainfall to infiltrate into the soil and make even distribution of even low amount of rainfall.

3. *Bunding:* Bunding refers to construction of embankment like structure across the land surface having mild slope (Maximum upto 6%). By bunding practice, the entire area is divided into several small parts. Runoff water is collected in the surrounding area of the bund. Bunds of small cross-section ($0.05m^2$) are laid at 0.3 to 10m vertical interval (difference in height between two consecutive bunds) on hill slope. In this system the rainwater impounded in bunded field during monsoon season can be used for growing Rice in *Kharif* and direct sowing of *Rabi* crops can be done after removing the impounded water. For removal of the impounded water proper outlet is provided with each bund at suitable height.

4. *Bench Terracing:* Bench terraces are most effective measure to harvest and utilize the rainwater properly. In bench terracing work step like structure is constructed across the hill slope having embankment at the edge of the step.

Construction of bench terrace is generally started from the highest point of the area and proceeded towards its lowest point. When subsoil in not good, then it is necessary to keep the topsoil part and should be spread on the terrace after construction. The bench terrace areas should have a provision of outlet for safe disposal of surface runoff passing through terraces.

5. *Conservation Tillage and Deep Ploughing:* Conservation tillage refers to the preparation of the field in such a way that maximum moisture can be conserved in the field. In this regard following points may considered for tillage operations:

i. Tillage operation should be done at proper moisture condition.

ii. Excessive tillage of land should be avoided.

iii. Depth of ploughing should be varied.

Deep ploughing of fields after crop harvest have been found to increase infiltration rates (downward entry of water into the soil) of the field which results in more availability of moisture to the plant roots.

6. Cover Crops and Mulching: Cropping pattern for an area should be such that during the rainy season there is vegetative cover over the soil surface. A vegetative cover controls the runoff water and move rainwater is absorbed in the soil. Also roots of vegetation after decay provides numerous cavities, which promotes infiltration.

Mulching is the application any plant residue (stubble, trash or any other vegetation) or other material to cover the topsoil surface for conserving the soil moisture by checking evaporation and to retard runoff. Polythene mulches have also been utilized for water harvesting and control of seepage.

7. Contour Farming: Contour farming consists of carrying out all agricultural operation like ploughing, planting and interculture operation nearly on the contour across the land slope (contour is an imaginary line on land slope having same elevation). The small ridges and plant stems in the contour cultivation area hold rainwater and thus provide maximum moisture to the soil. Crops like maize, sorghum, perl millet which are normally grown in a row are ideally suited for contour farming.

8. Roof top Collection: Roof water harvesting techniques is applied mainly for the domestic purpose. It may be either for short duration or long duration, depending upon the amount of roof water available.

9. Dug Out Pond/Storage Tank: The dugout ponds are constructed by excavating the soil from the ground surface. Thus ponds may be fed by surface runoff. Construction of these ponds is limited to those areas which have land slope less than 4%. The dugout ponds can be recommended on the basis of utilizing their maximum harvested runoff water for increasing the production of some important crops.

Storage tank can be constructed by forming the embankment around the valley or depression of the area. The runoff water is collected into this storage tank and is used when required.

10. Diversion Channel: Use of springs and streams through

diversion is most common procedure for harvesting perennial water. Irrigation on hill slopes and valley lands is common through this procedure. Diversion channel can also be used to intercept surface runoff and convey it safely to an outlet. But there should be a permanent filter strip of close-growing vegetation to catch the silt carried in the runoff from the area.

11. Nalla Bunding: It consists of constructing the bunds of suitable size, across the nalla for intercepting the runoff coming from the hill area to create water storage. These bunds are equipped with surplusing arrangement at suitable point to drain the excess water from the area in a controlled manner. In nalla bunding work, a trench is excavated across the nalla and it is filled with black clay puddle soil to form a core wall. The core wall forms a barrier to check the passing of water from the bund section. Remaining portion of the bund is constructed by filling the locally available earth material. A suitable outlet is constructed and stone pitching is done on the upstream face of the bund to check damage caused by water currents.

12. Gully Plugging: Gully plugging means checking the velocity of runoff water in a gully or small nalla by constructing a barrier across it. Various materials like brush wood, live hedges, earth, sand bags and stone boulders can be used for gully plugging. Gully plugs help in reducing speed of runoff water, redistributing it, increasing percolation and improving moisture regime for vegetation.

13. Check dam/Stop dams: In this methods the small size rock or concrete check dams or stop dams are constructed across the streams to intercept runoff from the hill area and store it for optimum utilization. The stored water behind the structure is used for drinking, irrigation and recharging the downstream wells.

14. Percolation Tank or Dam: These dams or tanks are generally constructed at the valley head without the provision of checking the percolation loss. In this way a large portion of runoff is stored in the soil. The growing crops on downstream side of the dam receive the percolated water for their growths. These structures are also used to recharge the wells or other water harvesting structures situated down side.

15. Sub-Surface Dam: It consists of construction of subsurface vertical barriers across the *nalla* or stream with clay, stone, masonry, concrete or steel materials etc. The water flow through the stream is stored in sub-surface reservoirs created by barriers. The water stored in these dams is utilized by gravity or shallow wells later on according to the need.

16. *Inter-Terrace/InterPlot Harvesting:* In this method runoff water is diverted to the area covered by terraces through diversion channels where crops are irrigated by flooding. This method of harvesting of floodwater is applied for a short duration.

17. *Microwatershed Management Basis:* Microwatershed is a unit of land from where rainwater (runoff water) drains to a common outlet point. Since each field is an integral part of the entire microwatershed, so a particular harvesting techniques will result in limited benefits, will become costlier and may also lead to social and other problems. In microwatershed management, whole area is treated with integral efforts to develop different sectors to get the benefits of interaction. Different suitable water harvesting techniques are adopted from the ridge of the hill area and are culminated at the valley portion.

Conclusion

The rainwater can be controlled, collected and conveyed right from the ridge portion of watershed. At the ridge portion where mostly non-arable land exists, possible water resources can be tapped through contour trenches, contour stone wall, gully plugging etc. The excess water is safely lead through diversion channel to the natural nallas where it will be again harvested for life saving irrigation by construction of farm ponds, percolation tanks, checkdams etc. This will help in groundwater recharge in lower portion of the hill area. The rainwater in cultivable land can be harvested through bench terraces, land leveling, bunding, conservation village, contour farming etc. The excess water will be let out of each filled through suitable outlet to waterways. The water that has entered the waterway will be stored in a farm pond and subsequently used as supplemental irrigation. The excess runoff from the farm pond will be then allowed to enter the natural nalla, which should be fully strengthened through structures like checkdams/stop ams etc.

Thus it is clear that how different water harvesting techniques can be applied from the ridge to the valley portion to ensure maximum rainwater harvesting for supplemental irrigation to get better production.

REFERENCES

1. Srivastava, R.C.; Bhatnagar, V.K.; Bhatnagar, P.R.; Chandra Shubhash and Koranne, K.D. (1994): "Rainwater harvesting and Utilization for sustainability of Hill agriculture in U.P. Hills", Proceedings of the 8th ISCO Conference, 1994, New Delhi India. pp. 354-364.
2. Kemp, Njilo (2000): "Command Area Development in Nagaland- Present Status and Future Prospects". Proceedings of National Semianr on "Resource Management for Self Reliant Economy of N.E. Region, organised by NERIWALM, Tezpur, pp 40/2-47/2.
3. Verma, A.K.; Sharan, V. and Singh, V.B. (2000). "Rain water Harvesting for Increasing Crop Production in Hilly Region". Proceedings of National seminar on "Resource Management for Self Reliant Economy of N.E. Region", pp. 16/1-21/1.

2

Prospect and Constraint of Fish Production Under the Rainfed Condition of Nagaland

Sharma, A. Kalita, D.C. Singh, A. K. Nakhro, R. and Sharma, V.B.[1]*

ABSTRACT

Though in present scenario of green revolution, country has reached to the level of self-sufficiency in food grain production, the rainfed areas, where natural hazards have put these areas in situation of production uncertainties, fish farming have its own economic significance.

Therefore, in the rainfed area the chances of shifting towards the other farming activities like—fisheries, piggery, poultry etc, have much scope. For better utilization of un-culturable wasteland, a fishery is the best option with the farmer.

Nagaland, being a tribal dominated state, consumption of fish in daily diet is a normal routine. Fish farming is not a new

* Department of Agricultural Economics, Nagaland University: SASRD, Campus: Medziphema—797106.

1 Department of Animal Production Management, NU SASRD, Campus: Medziphema —797 106.

practice in Nagaland. Paddy-cum-fish culture is the most common practice. Since long, however, they still lack the scientific knowledge concerning fish farming. Therefore, there is always remains wide gap between demand and supply as most of the varieties of fishes consumed in the state are imported from neighbouring states.

KEY WORDS: Aqua culture, fish species, enterprise, respondents, per cent.

INTRODUCTION

Fishes form one of most important group of vertebrates for men in influencing his life in various ways. Millions of human beings suffer due to hunger and malnutrition and fishes from a rich source of food and provide means to tide over the nutritional deficiencies of man.

The fish flesh is an excellent source of proteins. The percentage of protein present in fish flesh varies from 15 to 20 per cent of their weight, liver oil contains 55 to 75 per cent fat, 5 to 10 per cent protein and rest of water, Fish meal is composed of 60 to 80 per cent protein, 1 to 5 per cent ash and 5 to 6 per cent oil.

In India average size of holdings of the farmers and their income is among the lowest in the world. Disguised unemployment of labour is one of the important factors for low income of the rural people. Rural people constitute over 75.05 per cent of the total population of our country, contributing only 42.8 per cent to the national Income. Therefore, there is need of reducing the pressure of rural population on land either through rural industrialization or providing ways and means to take up allied agricultural enterprises, which certainly will reduce disguised unemployment on the one hand and higher family income on the other.

Nagaland is a land of hilly mountains and evergreen forest. The people living in the state are mostly of the Mongoloid race. It has got the 14 sub-tribes and the four major tribes are the Angami, Ao, Sema and Lotha tribes.

Agriculture is the main occupation of the Naga people living in the villages and rural areas. Fish farming is not a new practice in Nagaland, paddy-cum-fish culture is most common practice, practicing in the villages long before though they don't know the scientific agriculture.

Almost 90 per cent of the fishes consumed by the people of Nagaland are imported from the neighboring states, like A.P., Assam, West Bengal, Bihar etc. The fish production in Nagaland is not at all sufficient for the supplying it all over Nagaland. So there is a lot of progress to be done in this field of fish enterprise in Nagaland.

Some Indigenous Fauna in Nagaland

Since a vast number of areas crossing a number of water bodies is commonly under land region. Numerous species of fishes are naturally presents in all parts of Nagaland and the other seven states. However many number of the fish fauna is commonly found in Indo-gangatic plain where as some of attend are representative of Burma fauna. The incidence of common representative among the Indo-gangatic and the Hill areas fauna can be alternated to the various inter connecting water body of the two regions, namely, major river system and their tributaries. On the other hand the other land valleys system of Manipur and Nagaland express the presence of Burma representative in the Region. In addition to this intermingling population there is certain species, which are restricted to the region only in order or other word they are not repeated either from Indo-gangatic plain or from Burmese water.

Some of the indeginous species of fishes of this region are as under.

1. *Barilius dogarsingis.*
2. *Bainio acutitechla.*
3. *Bainio naganensiy.*

SOME PROBLEMS ASSOCIATED IN FISH-CULTURE

Major problems associated with fish culture in Nagaland are sub marine.

1. *Availability of water:* A good number of naturally occurring Pond in Nagaland are rainfall during the monsoon, there will be enough water. However, with the on set of summer many of them are getting dried up rendering them very

unsuitable for fish culture activities in Nagaland.

2. *Nitrification of lake ponds:* Due to modern agriculture activities involving heavy adulteration of chemical fertilizers the adjoining water body namely ponds and Lakes are getting contaminated Leading to nitrification accumulation of exam nutrient, this result in the promotion of algae-born which will ultimately reduce the dissolved oxygen content of leading to fish death.

3. *Aquatic weeds:* The unwanted aquatic weeds create several problems in fish culture in Nagaland as well as in natural fisheries. The ever growth of this plant limited the space for fishes movement. They compete with phytoplankton for nutrients, leading to the decreased in phytoplankton productivity.

The dissolved oxygen content of the water is reduced due to there over crowding. Over crowding aquatic weeds hampered the mating operation also, further it may harboured unwanted pre-debris organelles.

4. *Predators:* Any invertebrate predator namely carva and adult of a number of aquatic insects and vertebrate predator viz; cariverous wild fishes, pours problems spreading in the nursery ponds. They prey upon hatching fry and finger-link and so on.

5. *Weed fishes:* Weed fishes though not prey upon the culturable spp. but they compete for food and space, thereby adversely affect the fishes. These fishes mainly find their way into the cultural pond through mixed collected from natural water and during rainy season from the adjoining water to body incase of a natural pond a number of weeds fishes can be expected in water body.

6. *Availability of seed or stocking materials:* Irrespective of the advancement of induce breeding technologies we will still depend upon the natural sources of the process of stocking materials from the natural breeding pond. Sufficient supply stocking materials to all the farmers at the right time still remains to be a distant objective in Nagaland.

NEED OF FISH CULTURE

With the increased literacy and improved purchasing capacity, there is increase regeneration of fish as the major sources of animal protein. In addition to this there is rise in quality and quick increase in population throughout the world as well as in Nagaland, growing demand for increasing production resources and enhancing the nutritional values of various food production.

The quantum of fish currently being exploited captured method from one natural body in each other state is in accent to make the demand of over increasing population and also to combat malnutrition. Therefore we, have to catch addition to fishes resources to arrangement the fish supply in this concept the most important of aqua-culture is greatly felt as that of agricultural and animal husbandry. It should be and alternative venture to often protein rich food and at the same time, the means of increase income will be solved.

By this çentury the domestic need for fish in India is about to be 60 to 125 tones lakhs per year. For this only marine catch fish is not sufficient to meet the demand of the consumption, so half of the demand should be filled from the inland water contribute about 14-15 lakhs tones total fishes production, which is not sufficient for the consumer in India. So the most case in Nagaland, also.

The time has come for the people in Nagaland for the cultivation, for fish culture operation has being taken up as a branch of agriculture.

IMPORTANCE OF AQUA-CULTURE

As fish culture technologies is in improving in areas under cultivation and fishes are also increases day by day. Fish farming has been accepted as a branch of agriculture. In application to agricultural development from time to time man changes it habit from simplistic cattle to cultivatable fish farm and other use for agriculture. The importance of aqua-culture as branch of agriculture are as follows:

1. Fishery cultivation water resources are extremely important for agriculture crops especially in acid region using such resources additionally for aqua-culture is one way of increasing profitability.
2. Fishery occupy a major position in the National Economy

as it is not only provide protein, protein rich food supply, to the local people and also, major commodity with time considerably amount of foreign exchange.

3. In India at present out of 7.5 lakhs of pond water available only 20 per cent is being exploited by means of aquaculture. Thus, there still remains vast area to be exploited.
4. It has been estimated that a 'ton' of fish can be raised in the same area that expect to raised a few hundred Kg. of live-stock meats. Therefore, aquaculture has been found to be a very productive when sell where compared with the agriculture, livestock and poultry product.
5. In the traditional extensive fish culture the food consumption ratio is 1.5 times more in fish than compared to poultry. In case of cattle and sheep it is too hard, however in case of intensive aqua-culture, when the adequate supplement seed is prevailed then the concentration ratio in fish is much higher than that of the livestock.
6. Integrated fish farming in with Agriculture and A. H. is known to be more profitable than agriculture alone.
7. Fish protein is not only easily digestible food items, but is also rich in essential amino acid like Vitamin, minerals etc.
8. Aquaculture help in Integrated Rural Development by Employment opportunity generating for many unemployed and under employed persons.

DESIRABLE CHARACTER FOR CULTIVABLE FISH SPECIES

1. The Fish spp. should have fast growth rate.
2. The feed conversion ratio should be high.
3. They should be able to use the natural food of the pond as well as the artificial feed to maximum advantage.
4. They should be resistant to diseases.
5. They should be hard enough to survive in temporary stress condition, hardship and easy to transport.

6. Should not be carnebalistic and predeators in nature and should be accommodated to crowded environment and should not fight with other members.
7. To be valued on a good table fish, the fish should be tasteful and preferably with high nutritive value.
8. The fish inqitient should breeding in confined condition and or by induced breeding.
9. Preferably items should not be any inter space competition for various reasons.

PROSPECT OF FISH PROCUTION AT HIGH ALTITUDE ZONE OF NAGALAND

In Nagaland lakes and the streams are located at 914 meters above the main sea level are generally termed as cold water. The cold-water lake are commonly characterised by the presence of high oxygen, low carbon-di-oxide, inorganic soil of rocky bottom, the less vegetation and high transparency of water. The temperature varies from 0^0–20^0 C, with optimum temperature ranges to 10–12^0 C.

In India major corps and fishes, which are commonly distributed in rivers and lakes of the plain do not survived in high altitude region due to low water temperature. These fishes, which are found in the hilly areas and cold water of this region are adopted for the peculiar condition prevailing in this region.

A large number of fish species occur naturally in the cold water of Nagaland whereas, some other has been transported to this region, out of those cold water fishes, the important one on the cultural point of view are as follows:

a. Trout.
b. Common crop
c. Tinca tinca
d. Cursion crop
e. Mahseer
f. Snow trout
g. Indian trouts
h. Labeo spp.
i. Gana spp. &
j. Glyetophorus spp.

Commercial Cultivable Species of Fish in Nagaland

1. Indian labeo corp.
   a. Catla (*Catla catla*)
   b. Rohu (*Labeo rohit*)
   c. Mirgal (*Cirrhina mirgala*)

2. Exotic corp.
   a. Silver corp (*Hypophthalmichthys molitriu*)
   b. Gran crop (*Ctenopharyngodon idellus*)
   c. Common corp (*Cyprinus capio*)

Composite or poly-culture fish farming: In order to obtain a high production per hectare of water body, fast growing compactable species of fishes of different feeding habits are stocked together in the pond, so that all the available ecologically riches could be exploited by these fishes. This system of pond management is called mixed fish farming or composite fish culture. Fish production by all traditional method give a low yield. Yet, it is favorably fishes having different feeding habits are stated together. All the available food material in the pond have been effectively used by them. The compatible fishes do not harm each other on the other hand may have beneficial effect on the other.

The different spp. usually stock together in composite fish culture are in the ratio of combination of different spp. of fish culture.

Indigenous	*Feeder*	*Exotic spp.*
Catla catla	Surface feeder	Silver corp
Rohu	Bottom feeder	Common corp
Mirgal	Column feeder	Gram corp

The recommended ratio for various fish culture varies from place to place and pond to pond. The generally followed pattern of different combination is as follows:

1. 3 Catla: 3 Rohu: 3 Mirgal.
2. 3 Catla: 4 Rohu: 1 Mirgal: 2 Common corp.
3. 2 Catla: 3 Rohu: 4 Mirgal: 4 Common corp: 1 Silver corp.
4. 4 Silver corp: 4 Gram corp: 4 Common corp &
5. 3 Silver corp: 3 Gram corp: 2 Common corp: 2 Rohu.

These ratios are out of the total number of finger-link stored or stock. The number of spp. as well as the number of individual of the singles spp. May be increase or decrease depending on the surface namely availability of the species among of food available in the pond, types of food available in the pond etc.

Stocking density: The generally recommended stocking density for composite fish culture is 5000 to 10000 finger-link per hectare. However depending on the fertility of the water body, level of feeding availability of fish finger-link and experience of the farmer the stocking density may be altered for the optimum utilization of pond.

Management of Composite Fish Farmer in Nagaland: The management activities involved rational manuring and fertilization of pond, supplementary feeding, quality water requirement. Supplementary food include powdered oil-cake, groundnut and rice bran together made in the small ball, silk warm purpose weed fish etc. Grass corp. is feed twice a day with coarse vegetation @ 100 kg/ha in the first month per day at any forth night or month (according to demand) till the month of harvesting. The food of the grass corps normally place on floating pen made of bamboo poll, about 80 per cent of the daily food taken by grass corp. is desiccated in semi digested condition which intern fertilized the water body as for manure. Thus benefiting the fish species.

To ascertain the constraints in fish production, some farmers were asked few questions with regards to fish farming which are given in the table no. 1. Also, it gives clear picture of sever ness of various problems but most important one was of timely marketing of fish, 20 per cent of the farmers were facing the problems of availability of water is the main problem faced by them.

Table 1: Total Number of Respondents

S. No.	*Particulars*	*No's of respondents*		*% to total.*
		Yes	*No*	
1.	Lack of proper supply of inputs	22 (73.33)	8 (26.67)	30 (100.00)
2.	Lack of water availability	18 (60.00)	12 (40.00)	30 (100.00)
3.	Proper selling of the produce is a main problem	25 (83.33)	5 (16.67)	30 (100.00)

4.	Lack of finance & recovery of loan	20 (66.67)	10 (33.33)	30 (100.00)
5.	Lack of proper transportation and good remunerative prices	24 (80.00)	6 (20.00)	30 (100.00)

Table 2: Cost of Cultivation and Net Income per quintal of Fish

S. No.	*Particulars of cost*	*Quantity*	*Total (in Rs.)*
1.	Total cost of cultivation	(Rs./ha./annum)	19611.20
2.	Yield	(Ha./qtls.)	7.21
3.	Cost of production	(Rs./qtls)	2720
4.	Net Income	(Rs./ha./annum)	2364.80
5.	Input-output	(Rs./ha./annum)	1: 2.206

Yields: In general an average individual growth rate of 0.8 to 1 kg/10-12 month and a yield of 10 time par hectare per year from composite fish culture system. However, in the case of grass corp. the faster growth rate and attainment of 3 kg weights in one year has also been reported.

CONCLUSION

The most important observation of this study reveals that training in fish production technology & level of skill on the one hand and of aquatic weeds presents in the ponds on the other hand till date no fish farmers was managing his fishponds on scientific lines, so as to generate more income and employment from this enterprise. Moreover, fish propagation can be intensified in the area with the help of proper water storage in fishpond and popularizing co-operative marketing system.

Government also provides necessary infra structural technical backup, supply of inputs to the farmers at subsidized rate, which is available at village level. In this context, Nagaland has great potential for the development of fisheries. Which can help to improve socio-economic situation of the farmers.

As the demand for fish is increasing day by day in Nagaland and India as a whole there is lot of scope for the fish farming, which can be made successful only through the join effort of the government fishery department and the local fishery owners.

ACKNOWLEDGEMENT: *The Senior author's is grateful to the Prof. G. D. Sharma, Vice Chancellor, Nagaland University for constant encouragement for carried out this research work. The author's is also thankful to Editorial committee members for their co-operation.*

REFERENCES

1. Anonymous, "Fish farming and inland fisheries management in rural economy", F.A.O.
2. Draft of Eighth five year Plan (1990): Govt. of India.
3. Dhandyal, S.P. and Singh, G.N. (1968): "Benefit cost ratio in fish culture", *I.A.J.E.* Vol. XXIII. Oct-Dec. No. 4. p. 235.
4. Francis, C. (1985): *Fishery and Botany of Eastern India*, Oxford Univ. Press, New Delhi.
5. *India* (1992): Government of India.
6. Jhingran, V. G. (1978): *Fish and Fisheries of India*, Hindustan Publishing, New Delhi.
7. Leys, C. (1970): *Fish Farming, Land Owning in Scotland*, pp. 28-30.
8. Singh, S.K., Pathak, M.P. and Tiwari, P.P. (1991): "Scientific techniques of aquaculture". Monthly report. '*Purvanchal Kethi*'. Dec. No. 12, pp. 19-20.
9. Srivastava, V.K. (1983): *Fisheries Development in India*, Concept Publishing Company, New Delhi.
10. *Times of India* (1990): "Directory".

3

Performance of Tomato (*Lycopersicon esculentum* L.) as Influenced by Transplanting Times and Cultivation Methods

Naresh Babu*

ABSTRACT

Performance of tomato to different date of transplanting (2nd and 3rd week of August, 2nd and 3rd week of September and 2nd week of October) with 4 methods of cultivation viz. plain bed, plain bed with staking, raised bed and raised bed with staking were studied on sandy loam soil during 2002-2003. Transplanting done in second week of August recorded highest yield (317.49q/ ha), followed by third week of August (304.67 q/ha) which significantly superior as compared to second and third week of September transplanting (290.32 and 282.16q/ ha, respectively). Late transplanting significantly reduced fruit weight, number of fruit, whereas crop stand showed improvements. In both plain and raised bed with staking

* ICAR Research Complex for NEH Region, Nagaland Centre, Jharnapani, Nagaland- 797 106.

significantly reduced the unmarketable yield thus producing higher yield. Cultivation methods had no influence on crop stand and number of locule/ fruit. Raised bed with staking recorded maximum plant height (93.69 cm), fruit (46.32) and yield (286 17 q/ ha) which were significantly superior as compared to plain bed.

Introduction

Tomato (*Lycopersicon esculentum* L) is one of the most popular vegetable grown in India due to its special nutritive value high productivity, great processing potentiality and wide ecological amplitude (Singh *et al.*, 2000 and Babu *et al.*, 2001). Cultivation of tomato in monsoon season is assuming great importance in the North–Eastern region in general and in Nagaland in particular owing to high prices of produce obtains from other part of the country during this period. For popularize of tomato cultivation among the local farmers requires standardisation of agro- techniques. Though the agro- climatic condition of Nagaland is quite favourable and there is tremendous scope for taking up commercial cultivation of this vegetable crop, the standardisation of horticultural practices has not been done so far under local agro- climatic condition for its profitable cultivation. The present paper gives the information about the planting time and cultivation system of tomato for obtaining higher yield under foot- hill condition of Nagaland.

Material and Methods

The field experiment was carried out at ICAR Research Complex for NEH Region Nagaland Centre, Jharnapani during 2002-2003 on a sandy loam soil, having pH 5.6, organic carbon 0.79% and available NPK 56.40, 37.76 and 147.08 kg/ha, respectively. The experiment was laid out in a split- plot design with three replications, having transplanting times in the main plots and cultivation methods in sub- plots of 3.0 mt x 3.0 mt. A plant spacing of 60 cmx 60 cm was followed. The treatment consisted of 5 transplanting times i.e. second and third week of August, second and third week of September and second week of October with 4 cultivation systems viz. plain bed, plain bed with staking, raised bed and raised bed with staking. A uniform dose of well decomposed farmyard manure @ 20t/ha was applied 15 days before transplanting. A fertilizer dose of NPK @ 80: 60: 60 kg/ha was also applied. Half dose of nitrogen and full dose of phosphorus and potassium were applied a day before transplanting and remaining half dose of nitrogen were supplied in two splits. Recommended cultural practices were followed. The observations on growth, yield and yield parameters were recorded and statistically analysed.

Results and Discussion

The vegetative growth and fruit yield of tomato were significantly influenced by planting time (Table 1). Plant height was maximum (87.69 cm) under third week of August planting followed by second week of August planting (81.45 cm). Lowest individual plant height was recorded by second week of October transplanting (66.72 cm). Significantly more fruits were observed in third week of August planting (46.21), followed by second week of August planting (41.36). Lowest fruit/plant was recorded in 3rd week of September planting (32.75). Transplanting of tomato in second week of August gave significantly greater fruit weight (63.12 g) as compared to September and October planting. Fruit weight again improved when the planting was done in October. Transplanting done in the middle of September (81.36%) was recorded significantly higher stand of crop at final harvest compared to second and third week of August (49.35 and 70.17%, respectively) and second week of October planting. This may be due to favorable weather conditions prevailing in second week of September for planting tomato. Number of locules/fruit was not significantly affected by time of planting. Observations revealed that tomato yields were significantly influenced by time of planting. Maximum yields were recorded with second week of August planting (317.49 q/ha) followed by third week of August planting (304.67 q/ha) which significantly higher as compared to second and third week of September planting which were at par with each other. Delaying planting of tomato resulted in significantly reduced yield (256.47 q/ha). This was due to heavy rains adversely affecting the growth, flowering and fruiting (Rao, 1986). A positive effect of delayed planting was observed in unmarketable yield. A significantly lowest unmarketable yield was obtained in second week of October (17.41%) as compared to 2nd and 3rd week of August (29.63 and 26.18%, respectively) and 2nd week of September (23.63%). Delaying of planting up to second week of September decreased number of marketable fruits (23.49/m^2) but a significant effect was recorded only in case of 3rd week of September planting (17.10 fruit/m^2). Further delay in planting showed a significant increase in the number of marketable fruits.

Data revealed that plant height was significantly affected by cultivation systems. Highest plant height was recorded by raised bed with staking (93.69cm) which significantly superior than other cultivation systems. Lowest plant height was observed under plain bed (70.15 cm). Maximum fruits/ plant was recorded by raised bed with staking (46.32) which significantly higher as compared to plain bed and raised bed (34.72 and 37.51, respectively) systems but at par with plain bed with staking (40.13). Cultivation systems had no significant effect on fruit weight and number of locules/ fruit. The highest individual fruit weight was recorded in plain bed with staking (68.31 g) followed by raised bed with staking (66.02 g). However, lowest fruit weight was obtained in plain bed (56.25 g). A similar trend was also observed in case of locules. Further cultivation system did not significantly affect the crop stand. Maximum crop stand (72.12%) at final harvest was recorded in raised bed with staking and minimum crop stand was found in plain bed (63.24%). System of cultivation significantly influenced total yield, the least being recorded with plain bed system (237.12 q/ ha), which significantly improved with staking the plants (270.63 q/ ha). The results are in agreement with the findings of Olasantan (1985), Kimoto *et al.*, (1984), Narayana and Rama Rao (1981) and Singh (1994) in tomato. The highest fruit yield in staking system might be due to the availability of more spacing, receiving more sun light and aeration for the promotion of photosynthesis and plant metabolism for assimilation of nutrients and food reserve for higher yield. Staking of plants significantly reduced the unmarketable yield in both plain bed (21.40%) and raised bed (18.17%) as compared to plain bed and raised bed which at par with each other. Staking either with plain bed or raised bed system recorded significantly more marketable fruit. Highest marketable fruit/ m^2 was recorded in raised bed with staking (30.12) followed by plain bed with staking (28.49) which at par with each other but significantly superior than other cultivation systems. Lowest marketable fruit/ m^2 was obtained in plain bed (22.01).

REFERENCES

Babu, Naresh, P. Venkateswarwlu and R.C. Verma (2001). Performance of tomato cultivars in foot-hills of Nagaland. *Indian Journal of Hill Farming*. 13 (1&2): 98-100.

Kimoto, T., A.C.W. Zanin and F.A.D. Conceicao (1984). Alternative plant support systems and mulching for tomato (*Lycopercicon esculentum* Mill.) cultivars of determinate growth. *Cientifica* 12 (1, 2): 111-6.

Narayana, N. and M. Rama Rao (1981). Improvement of yield in tomato through staking and nutrient applications. *Indian Journal of Horticulture*. 38 : 207-10.

Olasantan, F.O. (1985). Effect of intercropping, mulching and staking on growth and yield of tomatoes. *Expl. Agric.*, 21 (2): 135-44.

Rao, N.K.S. (1986). Growth analysis and differentiations of flowering and fruit setting behaviour in relation to planting season in tomato. *Singapore J. Primary Indus*. 14: 75-81.

Singh, R.V. (1994). Performance of kharif tomato as influenced by cultural practices. *Indian J. Hort.*, 51 (2): 192-96.

Singh, R., U.K. Kholi and S.K. Sharma (2000). Effect of nitrogen, phosphorus and potassium combin..tions on yield of tomato hybrids. *Annals of Agri. Research* 21 (1): 27-31.

4

Alternate Cropping System of Nagaland in North East Region of India

Sharma, Amod*, Sharma, Anamika ** & Sharma, S.K.***

ABSTRACT

The most of the existing system of agriculture in the hilly areas especially in the North east region are primitively subsistence farming. There are different cropping pattern are in vague in the North east region. The most popular among them is the shifting agriculture also causing the great ecologically balanced, socio-economically viable agricultural system/pattern. This is possible only by adopting judicious blends of different agro-rotation and or cropping pattern.

KEY WORDS: - *Alternate cropping, Cropping system, Agro-forestry,* Shifting cultivation.

---

* Department of Agricultural Economics, Nagaland University: SASRD Campus: Medziphema, District Dimapur—797106.

** Horticulturist, ICAR Research Center for NEH Region, Jharnapani, Medziphema (N.L.).

*** Reader & Head, Dept. of Agricultural Chemistry, SASRD, NU, Campus: Medziphema (N.L.).

Introduction

The alternatives to shifting cultivation should be socially acceptable, economically feasible and environmentally sound besides being area specific. These should be based on either biological or physical methods of erosion control or a combination of the two. The alternatives, which could be based on physical methods of erosion control are obviously expensive and therefore are beyond the economic reach of the rural peasants. However, the alternatives based either on biological or a combination of both biological and physical methods of erosion control are expected to have leader acceptability among the rural peasants as these would be neither their economic reach.

Crop cultivation based on improved cropping patterns is expected to increase crop production per unit area and time by increasing cropping intensity and utilizing resources more efficiently. This may increase the income from small farms to a certain extent. Traditional agriculture can not develop the region economically. The present agriculture needs to be both diversified and intensified by introducing remunerative alternate agricultural crops and by adopting suitable cropping patterns. These would not only intensify cultivation, but it would also align the same to local needs and market and demands.

Methodology Opted

This study is completely based on primary data collected through simple and well designed questionnaires by an extensive field data collected through simple and well designed questionnaires by an extensive field survey of the sample villages of the state. Kohima and Dimapur district were selected randomly for the present study. While, total number of sixty-(60) household was selected from two villages of each district for thew present study.

Scope of Alternate Cropping

1. Though alternate cropping specific agro-forestry systems in which field crops and high value annual crops like—ginger *(Zingiber officinale)*, turmeric *(Curcuma longa)* etc; could be cultivated with woody perennial trees can be developed and

evaluated for different parts of the region.

2. Similarly, through various combinations of two story plantations. In which high value perennial crops like—cardamom *(Elettaria cardamomum)*, black pepper *(Piper nigrum)*, dalchini *(Cinnapromum zeylanicum)* and paan *(Piper betel)* could be cultivated either with timber trees like Gomari or with any other trees cultivated locally can be evaluated and recommended for different parts of the region.

3. The local forest trees could be successfully used as woody perennial component to train local variety of pan for its cultivation in agro-forestry system.

For example, in Arunachal Pradesh, the betel vine is trained on *Dipterocarpus macrocarpa* trees growing in the forest. The local variety of betel vine in Nagaland and Meghalaya has been successfully trained on mango and jackfruit *(Artocarpus heterophyllus)*. Betel vine can also be trained on *sesbania* sp. (Legume plant). Black pepper can be trained on Gomorra and other timber trees. Similarly, other vines can also be trained on local or exotic plant species.

4. In alternate cropping medicinal and aromatic plants could also be used as a component of agro-forestry systems and two story plantations, cultivation of aromatic plants on hill slopes would be a viable alternate to shifting cultivation.

5. The agro-technology for cultivation of *Citronella jaya* and *Dioseorea floribunda* has already been standardized for northeast region. These alternatives would not only diversify the present agriculture by integrating cultivation, non-conventional plants either as pure crop or as a component of agro-forestry and two story plantations, but would also play an important role in breaking the subsistence syndrome and consequently the economy of the rural peasant would improve.

6. The impact of agriculture based economic development on the prosperity of common man would not be visible unless socially relevant and acceptable agro-technologies are made available.

Some of the alternate cropping patterns suitable for different agricultural lands in Nagaland as well as some part of the north east region, which are conducive for enlarging the scope.

1. Irrigated foothills, valleys and terraced land:

Maize/Paddy	-	Wheat /Potato
Cowpea/Moong	-	Wheat/Potato/ Sugarcane
Sesamum/Groundnut	-	Potato/Mustard/Barley
Paddy/Maize	-	Cole crops (Cauliflower/ Cabbage /Turnip/Knol khol)
Maize/Ragi	-	Tomato/Lahipatta/Spinach
Sorghum	-	Pea/Lentil/Gram
Maize+Soyabean	-	Wheat/Cole crops
Maize+Soyabean	-	Maize+Soyabean
Maize+Moong/Cowpea	-	Pea+Mustard/Wheat+Gram
Maize+Guar	-	Pea+Mustard/Wheat+Gram
Sugarcane+Moong/Cowpea	-	Ratton+Mustard

Spices/Vegetables

Medicinal and Aromatic plants.

2. Un-irrigated foothills, Valleys and Terraced land:

Paddy/Maize/Job's tear	-	Safflower/Sunflower/Linseed/ Mustard
Paddy/Maize/Ragi	-	Pea/Gram/Lentil
Cowpea/Moong/Jowar	-	Safflower/Sunflower/Linseed/ Mustard
Cowpea/Moong/Ginger	-	Wheat/Potato/Barely
Cowpea/Moong/Sesamum	-	Cole crops
Cowpea/Moong/Groundnut	-	Sugarcane
Tapioca		Pea/Gram/Lentil

Groundnut + Maize

Seasamum + Soyabean/Groundnut

Pegeon pea + Jowar

Pigeon pea + Maize

Paddy + Soyabean/Groundnut

Cotton

Pigeon pea

3. Mild slopes:

Paddy
Job's tear + Rice bean
Maize + Soyabean
Soyabean
Sesamum
Tapioca
Cotton
Pigeon pea
Ground nut
Medicinal and Aromatic plants
Agro-foresrty
Two story plantations.

4. Medium and Higher slopes:

Tapioca
Fodder grass
Pineapple + Guava / Papaya / Litchi
Pineapple
Kiwi fruit
Arecanut
Coconut
Coffee
Tea
Fruits
Medicinal and Aromatic plants
Agro-forestry
Two story plantations
Timber plantations
Fast growing multipurpose indigenous trees.

5. Mild, Medium and Higher slopes of Shallow depth:

Fast growing multipurpose indigenous trees
Indigenous timber tree plantation

6. Steep slopes and Hill top:

Forestry

Conclusion

Cultivation systems like agro-forestry and two story plantations are ecologically sound, environmentally correct, economically viable and socially acceptable and assimilable. These alternate cropping patterns are also expected to provide effective vegetative cover to the soil against erosive forces of water. Such system, which combine tradition with modernity hold promises and undoubtedly these would forms the backbone of future agriculture in northeast region. The technology for some of these, system has successfully been introduced in the agro-climatic conditions of Nagaland (NEPED and IIRR, 1999) and may also be successful for other parts of the region. The alternate cropping patterns suitable may be adopted to make farming system more resource efficient and remunerative.

Acknowledgement

The Authors are grateful to the Vice chancellor, Nagaland University, Nagaland for constant encouragement for carried out this work.

REFERENCES

1. Borthakur, D.N. (1976): 'Agriculture of North-east region with special reference to Hill Agriculture'.
2. Chauhan, B.S. (2000): 'Shifting cultivation in Perspective'. Nagaland University Publication, Nagaland.
3. Kerenyi, Attila and Szabo, Gyorgy (2000): 'Environmental Pollution of a modern plant cultivation of Agricultural Farmers a Hungarian Example'. pp. 225-235.
4. NEPED & IIRR (1999): Building upon - 'Traditional Agriculture in Nagaland', IDRC, New Delhi.
5. Sharma, A. & Singh, M. (2001): 'Cropping Pattern/System for North-east region'. Workshop: 'The impact of Agricultural infrastructures on the Economic Development of a state', NERIST, Itanagar (A.P.), pp. 46-49.
6. Souvenier (2000): International Workshop – 'Agroforestry & forest Products. NEHU, Aizawl.

5

Dynamics of Ecosystem and Its Pyramidical System

*Amod Sharma**

Introduction

Living organism and their environment are inter-related and interact with each other in such a way that they are inseparable. Each community has its own developmental history. It has its origin and developmental stages. It virtually develops as a result of a directional change in it with time. This directional change, ecological succession has been referred to as ecosystem development.

Although a typical community maintains itself more or less in equilibrium with the prevailing conditions of the environment, in nature this is hardly true because communities are never stable. They are dynamic changing more or less regularly over time and space. The environment always keeps on changing over a period of time due to: - Variation in climatic and physiographic factors and the activities of the species of the communities themselves.

---

* Nagaland University: SASRD, Campus: Medziphema—797106.

This, influence bring about marked changes in the dominants of the existing community, which is thus sooner or alter replaced by another community at the same place. This process continues and successive communities develop one after another over the same area, until the terminal final community becomes more or less stable for a period of time. This occurrence of relatively definite sequence of communities over a period of time in the same area is known as ecological succession. Clement (1916), while studying plant communities defined succession, as "the natural process by which the same locality becomes successively colonized by different groups or communities of plants".

The dynamics of large complex systems are of three types. With a given time and space scale as a reference point, one can think of the system as being compared of:

(a) Mechanisms: These parts of the system have rapid responses and behaviour, which are often used as a basis for understanding the system.

(b). Constraints: This parts of the system respond slowly with respect to the time scale of interest and are essentially non-dynamic within this time frame. Constraints represent environmental factors or boundary conditions that govern the behaviour of the mechanisms.

(c) Phenomena: This system behaviour is dynamic in the time frame of interest. The behaviour of the components has their origins in the interactions of the mechanism, as modified by the system constraints. Consideration of scale necessarily originates in hierarchy theory. The space and time domain of several different phenomena involved in the dynamics of forests one sees the scale of exogenous factors, the biotic responses of ecological systems and the domain of vegetation patterns.

Causes of Succession

Since succession is a process, more properly a series of complex processes, it is natural that there may not be a single cause for this. Generally, there are three types of causes:

i) Initial or initiating causes: - These are climatic as well as biotic. The former includes factors, such as erosion and deposits, wind, fire etc., caused by lightning or volcanic activity and the latter includes the various activities of organisms. These causes produce the base areas or destroy the existing populations in an area.

ii) Excess or continuing cause: - These are the processes as migration, crisis aggregation, competition, reaction etc, which cause successive waves of populations as a result of changes, chiefly in the edaphic features of the area.

iii) Stabilizing causes: - These cause the stabilization of the community. According to Clemens, climate of the area is the chief cause of stabilization; other factors are of secondary value.

An ecological succession proceeds along the following four lines: - *a)* A continuos change in the kinds of plants and animals, *b)* A tending increase in the diversity of species, *c)* An increase in the organic matter and biomass supported by the available energy flow and *d)* Decrease in net community production or annual yield.

General Process of Succession

The whole process of a primary autotrophic succession is actually completed through a number of sequential steps, which follow one another. These steps in sequence are as follows: -

1. *Nudation:* This is the development of a bare area without any form of life. The area may develop due to several causes such as - landslide, erosion, deposition or other catastrophic agency. The cause of nudation may be due to the – i) Topographic, ii) Climatic and iii) Biotic.
2. *Invasion:* This is the successful establishment of a species in a bare area. The species actually reaches this new site from any other area. This whole process is completed in the following three successive stages: i) Migration, ii) Excises (establishment) and iii) Aggregation.
3. *Competition and coaction:* After aggregation of a large number of individuals of the species at the limited space, these develops competition (inter as well as intra-specific) mainly for space and nutrition. Individuals of a species affect other's life in various ways and this is called coaction.
4. *Reaction:* This is the most important stage in succession. The mechanism of the modification of the environment

through the influence of living organisms on it is known as reaction. As a result, changes take place in soil, water, light conditions, temperature etc, of the environment.

5. *Stabilization (Climax):* Finally, there occurs a stage in the process, when the final terminal community becomes more or less stabilized for a longer period of time and it can maintain itself in equilibrium with the climate of the area. This final community is not replaced and is known as climax community and the stage as climax stage.

Sometime due to changes in local conditions as soil characteristics or micro-climate, the process of succession becomes deflected in a different direction than that presumed under climatic condition of the area. Thus, the climax communities are likely to be different from the presumed climatic climax community. This type of succession is called deflected succession.

Ecological Pyramids

Tropic structure, i. e; the interaction of food chain and the size metabolism relationship between the linearly arranged various biotic components of an ecosystem. The tropic structure and function at successive tropic levels, viz.

Producers →Herbivores → Carnivores

May be shown graphically by producer level constitutes the base of the pyramid and the successive levels, the tiers making the apex. Ecological pyramids are of three general types:-

1. Pyramids of members: They show the relationship between producers, herbivores and carnivores at successive tropic levels in terms of their number. In grassland the producers, who are mainly grasses are always maximum in number. This then shows a decrease towards apex, as the primary consumers like rabbits, mice etc; are lesser in number than the grasses, the secondary consumers, snakes and lizards are lesser in number than the rabbits and mice, finally, the top (tertiary) consumers hawks or other birds, are least in number. Thus the pyramid becomes upright. Similarly, in a pond ecosystem the pyramid is upright. In a forest ecosystem, however, the pyramid of numbers is somewhat different in shape. The producers are mainly large-sized thus are lesser in number and from the base of the pyramid. The herbivores are more in number than the producers. Then there is gradual decrease in the number of successive carnivores, thus making the pyramid again upright. However, in a parasitic food chain the pyramids are always inverted.

2. **Pyramids of biomass**: They show the quantitative relationships of the standing crops. They are comparatively more fundamental instead of geometric factor. In grasslands and forests, there is generally a gradual decrease in biomass of organisms at successive levels from the producers to the top carnivores. Thus pyramids are upright. However, in a pond as the producers are small organisms, their biomass is least and this value gradually shows an increase towards the apex of the pyramid, thus making the pyramid in shape.

3. **Pyramids of energy**: Of the three types of ecological pyramids, the energy pyramids gives the best picture of overall nature of the ecosystem. Here, number and weight of organisms at any level depends not on the amount of fixed energy present at any one time in the level just below but rather on the rate at which food is being produced. In shape it is always upright as in most of the cases there is always a gradual decrease in the energy content at successive tropic levels from the producers to various consumers.

6

Impact of Livestock Resources to Uplift the Economy of Rural Dairy Farmers of KOMUL

Nizamuddin & Sharma, A.*

ABSTRACT

Despite many obstacles and pitfalls, the KOMUL has strategically manoeuvred to achieve its goals. The total procurement exceeds 5000 LPD, thereby marketing liquid pasteurised milk in addition to lassi, misti dahi and ghee extending to the neighbouring state of Assam. The progressive trend in respect of acquiring infrastructures and input services to farmers, if. not spectacular is moderately increasing to the satisfaction of the farmers. The KOMUL has been instrumental in inculcating changes in the attitude of the people towards milk in a society where flesh of animals constituted a basic element of food. The awareness of the nutritive and commercial value of milk and acceptance of the Anand Pattern Cooperative Societies by the people is an innovation through the organisation to bring about socio-economic advancement.

KEYWORDS: KOMUL, DCS's, LPD, Member, Non-member.

* Nagaland University; SASRD, Campus: Medziphema, District: Dimapur — 797106.

Introduction

Dairy industry in India has assumed a role of economic importance. The estimated total milk production of about 74.3 million metric tonnes in 1997 has ranked India, first in the milk production scenario of the world. Milk has thus emerged as the single largest agricultural product-output in India.

The development of dairy industry was possible through the Dairy Co-operative movement as initiated in the Country, basically aims at protecting the average milk producers in the rural areas from the unscrupulous milk vendors and middlemen. This was first evolved in the district of Kaira in Gujarat by a group of farmers in 1946, who revolted against exploitative practices and formed the Kaira District Co-operative Milk Producers' Union, Anand, which is also popularly known as Anand Milk Union Limited (AMUL).

The principle, philosophy and sense of direction have subsequently guided the policy makers in formulating and launching a nation wide project known as the 'OF' programme under the aegis of NDDB in 1970.

The 'OF' programme has been undoubtedly instrumental in bringing about phenomenal growth in milk production in India and clearly is a pace maker for dairy industry anywhere in a developing society.

Dairy as a concept and practice however, is relatively new to the Nagaland State as compared to the other parts of mainland India. With a milch animal population of 42,080 the state has produced 47,000 tonnes of milk (1999), contributing an insignificant 0.063 per cent only to the National Production. The per capita availability of milk in Nagaland is also only 104 gm/head/day vis-a-vis against the World Health Organisation's recommendation of 220 g per day.

Nagaland has also stepped forward along with the rest of the states of the Indian Union in implementing 'OF' programme and as a result of that, Kohima District Co-operative Milk Producers' Union Limited was formed in line with the APC system and made functional in 1986. The Department of Veterinary and Animal Husbandry has made every effort to develop dairying in Nagaland by initiating intensive cross breeding programme to upgrade the local indigenous cattle population for enhanced milk production.

Dairying in Nagaland is still in its infantile stage and is a marginalised activity to the main agriculture. However, it is blessed with bountiful agro-forest natural vegetation, which provide advantages and incentive for dairying to thrive and prosper.

With the introduction of the 'OF' programme in the state through the Kohima District Milk Producers' Co-operative Union Ltd., Dimapur in 1986, the Union has travelled by the distance through various ups and downs. The major drawback was the cattle were kept mostly for beef and to a lesser extent for draft purposes. Secondly, whatever milk was produced in the 1980 were from the 'Khutias' or the Nepali community taking milk production as their livelihood: However, with the establishment of Dairy Co-operatives in rural areas the benefits of 'OF' programme when understood by the local farmers, more Naga farmers have joined the Milk Producers' Societies and accrued benefits out of this programme.

The primary objective of the APC is basically to build up self-sustaining primary DCS' s through its operations and consequently a viable Milk Union as the district apex body. With this in view, DCS's were organised and made functional in areas or villages where potential milch herd were located and the producers willing to form Co-operative Society.

The essential feature of a DCS's is its autonomy, where democratic principle of election is followed to elect its managing committee and chairman. A secretary is appointed to look after the daily business transactions. Milk being a highly perishable commodity, requires a capable and dedicated secretary who will test the milk and maintain books of records.

Milk is procured twice daily involving a two-tier system; namely, member to DCS and DCS's to Union, the price of milk being strictly based on quality, namely, the fat and solid-not-fat (SNF) content and not the quantity, the importance of milk testing in Dairy Co-operative Society and at the Union level is indispensable.

The Milk Union is fully responsible to provide transportation facility to collect milk at DCS level or delivery to the milk plant. Milk vans are employed for collecting the milk wherever road communication is available and from the more inaccessible areas bicycles or head load services are generally used.

To achieve long-term productivity of milk producers, provision of stable and remunerative price is not particularly helpful unless supported by comprehensive packages of extension services technical inputs and marketing infrastructure. The Milk Co-operative Union has the distinctive role in not only arranging balanced cattle feed for its producers but it provides subsidy for every kilogram of feeds purchased and delivers the same to the doorsteps of the members through its organised transport network. Technical assistance for cultivation of good quality fodder, provision of improved fodder seed, are other input *to* producers. Extension activities including seasonal film shows, printing and distribution of news bulletin, training of farmers on different topics, seminars etc; are essential features of the Dairy Co-operatives.

Type and productivity of dairy animal is inherent in its genetic make-up, improvement of which can be realised through cross breeding either by A.I. or N.S., which are essential features of the APC system.

With the above in view, a through survey has been planned to record, evaluate the extent of incentives provided to the farmers and in turn, the extent of farmers participation in the KOMUL, Dimapur, to bring prosperity to farmers and also to success of the organisation.

Results and Discussion

should have emphasized on A.I. programme over the implementation of Rural DailY Development Scheme.

In regards to supply of balanced concentrate feed, it was observed that the performance of the member producers reflected on many possible factors, such as lack of awareness, rigidity of members or failure to respond to innovation, inefficient extension activities, pricing policy of the Union, etc. The performance of members in utilising the facility remained low.

The implementation of fodder development programme in the entire operation area is in the initial stages and the area under cultivated fodder is only 31 acres in the selected DCS' s. Cultivation of fodder should be encouraged in the all DCS's through motivation programme from the Union since variety in the diet, supplemented by high nutritious fodder (legumes and non-legumes) would induce economic production.

Provision of timely extension of Vetetinary aid to the ailing or distressed animals and prevention of outbreak of any viral or contagious diseases, is mandatory on the part of the Union. Thus the Union is responsible for preservation of health of dairy animals within its operation area. From the records it was observed that provision of this input needs review and satisfactory programme may be initiated in all the societies. Appropriate steps may be made to educate the farmers by organising Veterinary Health Cover Camps in each of the Societies for prevention of various diseases like Mastitis, *diarrhoea*, Dyspepsia etc.

The provision of transport facility in the operation area of KOMUL was not as per desire; since, delay in transportation resulted in economic loss. Special attention is necessary in maintaining time factor for efficient execution of this input In regards to mode and regularity of payment to Society and member producers, observation made was conflicting. Reports indicated regular payment only to some societies while it was found to be delayed in some Societies which contributed towards disposal of milk to vendors resulting in lower collection of milk from the Societies. It is suggested that mode and regularity of payment of milk bills to Societies and member producers should equally be looked into, to avoid discrepancy in this regard.

KOMUL has taken bold step in matters of marketing of milk and milk products. In addition to pasteurised milk the KOMUL has introduced its brand of *ghee, lassi* and *misti dahi* which have become popular not only amongst the consumers in the state of Nagaland but also in nearby district headquarters of the state of Assam. It is hoped that KOMUL will keep this spirit of marketing strategy in days to come.

Maintenance of accounts (auditing of the Societies) needs careful velification and auditing should be regular. The KOMUL should strepgthen its efforts to improvise the prevailing system in some societies, and so that producers are not deprived of their dues.

In the matter of emolment, training of member producers and office bearers of the Societies, it was encouraging to note that the members emolment increased from 100 odd members in 1986 to 2100 in 1999. In regards to training of member producers and office bearers, so far, 52 members from 13 Societies have been trained under farmers Induction Programme, 18 members members on EVF A, 4 members on VDC Secretary, 14 members on MCM orientation Programme, and 32 members on Dairy Animal Management programme. Beside this, the KOMUL has so far organised 4 dairy melas. The input, training of member producers, office bearers of the DCS' s has been handled carelessly as selection of members for various training programmes was not uniform. Therefore, it is suggested to allow equal exposure to all the members of the Societies.

From the constitution of the Board of Directors of KOMUL, it has been observed that out of 13 member Board of Directors, only 5 member producers have been inducted selecti vely and therefore the democratic character of the Union has not been maintained. To ensure equal participation and balanced contributory role from evelY Society, the KOMUL should try to adhere to the spirit of cooperation based on which the Union is formed.

Table 1: Dairy animal population in operation area and selected area in KOMUL

KOMUL	*Population*		*% Cattle*		*% Buffalo*
Operation area	13 193	54.25	44.82	99.07	0.93
Selected area	2136	52.99	45.59	98.58	1.40

Table 2: Percent distribution of different type of dairy animals in selected area of KOMUL

Type	*%*	*Wet (33.09)*	*Dry (26.32)*	*Heifers& Calves (34.64)*	*Bulls (6.23)*
Local non-de script	52.99	41.72	59.86	59.05	50.38
Jersey crossbred	33.43	43.71	29.39	26.89	32.06
Holstein friesian crossbred	11.10	12.45	9.86	10.25	13.74
Brownswiss crossbred	1.08	1.83	0.89	0.54	0.76
Local buffaloes	1.40	0.20	—	3.24	3.05

Figures in parenthesis indicate percentage to the total.

Name of DCS,	*1998*		*1999*		*% of Dairy Cows/Member*
	Dairy Cows	Bulls	Dairy Cows	Bulls	
Valley DCS,	—	1	—	—	—
Bhola DCS,	40	1	—	—	0.75
Everest DCS,	—	1	—	—	—
Dairy farm DCS,	10	1	—	—	0.40
Kyong DCS,	2	—	—	—	0.11
Dzevi DCS,	—	1	1	—	0.02
Krotho DCS,	—	—	1	—	0.04
Kikhru DCS,	—	1	—	—	—
Medziphema DCS,	—	1	12	—	1.33
Mugashe DCS,	—	—	—	—	—
N.C. DCS,	—	1	12	—	1.09
Tukikhe DCS,	—	—	10	—	0.62
Lucky DCS	—	—	10	—	0.59
Niuto DCS	—	—	—	—	0.15
Total	52	8	64	—	

Year	*A.I.*	*N.S.*	*No. of A.I.*	*No. of N.S.*	*No. of confirmed pregnancy*	*No. of confirmed pregnancy*
1998	182 (6)	141	1443	1203	(60%)	(83.36%)
1999	95 (7)	57	1816	1551		(85.40%)
Total	277	198	3259	2754	(53.74%)	(73.19%)

Year	*Total Quantity (Tonnes)*	*Members Other DCS's*	*14 DSC's*	*Total*	*Non-members*
1998	125.628	35.381 (28.16%)	54.933 (43.73%)	90.314 (71.83%)	35.314 (28.11%)
1999	190.592	18.193 (9.55%)	47.763 (25.06%)	65.956 (34.61%)	124.636 (65.39%)
Total	316.22	53.574 (16.94%)	102.696 (32.476%)	156.27 (49.42%)	159.95 (50.58%)

DCS's	*Total* (Acre)	*1998*		*1999*	
		No. of Beneficiaries	*Subsidy (Rs.)*	*No. of Beneficiaries*	*Subsidy (Rs.)*
Valley	3	4	5,680	5	7,100
Bhola	5	7	9,940	8	11,360
Everest	1.33	2	2,840	2	2,840
Dairy farm	1.33	2	2,840	2	2,840

Dzevi	4	6	8,520	6	8,520
Krotho	4	6	8,520	6	8,520
Kikhru	—	—	—	—	—
Medziphema	1.33	2	2,840	2	2,840
Mugashe	—	—	—	—	—
N.C.	1.33	2	2,840	2	2,840
Tukikhe	4	5	7,100	7	9,940
Lucky	1.33	2	2,840	2	2,840
Niuto	2.67	3	4,680	4	5,680
Kyong	1.67	3	4,260	2	2,840
Total	31	45	63,900	48	68,180

S.N.	*Name of the Societies*	*Registered members*	*Pouring/ members*	*% of active members*	*Non-members pouring milk*
1	Valley DCS, Seitheikima	89	52	58.43	25
2	Bhola DCS	107	53	49.53	19
3	Everest - I, DCS, Chumkedima	27	20	74.07	—
4	Dairy Farm DCS, Kushiabil	32	25	78.13	—
5	Dzevi DCS, Chumukedima Village	36	36	100	14
6	Khrotho DCS,	36	25	69.44	14
7	Kikhru DCS, Chumukedima Village	31	26	83.87	45
8	Medziphema	10	9	90	—
9	Mugashe DCS, Lotovi Village	30	7	23.33	—
10					
11					
12					
13					
14.					

Table 3: Distribution of genetic groups (types) of dairy animals in selected DCS's

S.No.	DCS	Total	Genetic Groups		Daily Groups			
			Local	Crossbreed	Wet	Dry	Heifers & Calves	Bulls
1.	Valley CDS, Sethikiema	327	133 (40.64)	194 (59.32)	124	50	135	18
2.	Bhola DCS, Singrijan	161	—	161 (100.00)	89	25	41	6
3.	Everest DCS, Chullukedima	131	(100.00)	(100.00)				
4.		105	(100.00)	(100.00)				
5.		236	(100.00)	(100.00)				
6.		269	(100.00)	(100.00)				
7.		90	(100.00)	(100.00)				
8.		82	(100.00)	(100.00)				
9.		24	(100.00)	(100.00)				
10.		190	(100.00)	(100.00)				
11.		59	59 (100.00)	—				
12.		44	(100.00)	(100.00)				
13.		334	(100.00)	(100.00)				
14.	Kyong DCS, Dumukhya	81	(100.00)	(100.00)				
	Total							

Table 4: Lactation length and lactation yield of different genetic groups/types of dairy animals in KOMUL

Type	*Average lactation Length (days)*	*Average lactation yield (litres)*	*Average **milk** yield per day (litres)*
Local non-de script.	183.01:6.39 (112)	499.59 (160)	2.37
Jersey Crossbred	258.01:8.98 (157)	1179.06 (190)	4.57
Holstein Friesian Crossbred	312.3 1: 9.76 (46)	2801.33 (56)	8.97
Brown Swiss Crossbred	295.3 1: 7.85 (20)	1948.98 (20)	6.6

Figures in parentheses in indicate number of observations

Table 5: Distribution of dairy cattle in different DCS's under rural dairy development programme in the study area

Name of DCS,	*1998*		*1999*		*% of*
	Dairy Cows	*Bulls*	*Dairy Cows*	*Bulls*	*Dairy Cows/Member*
Valley DCS,	—	1	—	—	—
Bhola DCS,	40	1	—	—	0.75
Everest DCS,	—	1	—	—	—
Dairy farm DCS,	10	1	—	—	0.40
Kyong DCS,	2	—	—	—	0.11
Dzevi DCS,	—	1	1	—	0.02
Krotho DCS,	—	—	1	—	0.04
Kikhru DCS,	—	1	—	—	—
Medziphema DCS,	—	1	12	—	1.33
Mugashe DCS,	—	—	—	—	—
N.C. DCS,	—	1	12	—	1.09
Tukikhe DCS,	—	—	10	—	0.62
Lucky DCS	—	—	10	—	0.59
Niuto DCS	—	—	—	—	0.15
Total	52	8	64	—	

Table 6: Number of A.I. and N.S. done with per cent successful conception in the study area

Year	*A.I.*	*N.S.*	*No. of A.I.*	*No. of N.S.*	*No. of confirmed pregnancy*	*No. of confirmed pregnancy*
1998	182 (6)	141	1443	1203	(60%)	(83.36%)
1999	95 (7)	57	1816	1551		(85.40%)
Total	277	198	3259	2754	(53.74%)	(73.19%)

Figures in parentheses indicate number of DCS 's and percentage.

Table 7: Cattle feed manufactured and distributed amongst registered members and non-members in KOMUL

Total Quantity (Tonnes)	*Other DCS's*	*Members 14 DSC's*	*Total*	*Non-members*
125.628	35.381 (28.16%)	54.933 (43.73%)	90.314 (71.83%)	35.314 (28.11%)
190.592	18.193 (9.55%)	47.763 (25.06%)	65.956 (34.61 %)	124.636 (65.39%)
316.22	53.574 (16.94%)	102.696 {32.476%)	156.27 (49.42%)	159.95 (50.58%)

Fig. 1 Freuqncy of Occurrence of various diseases in study area (1998 & 1999)

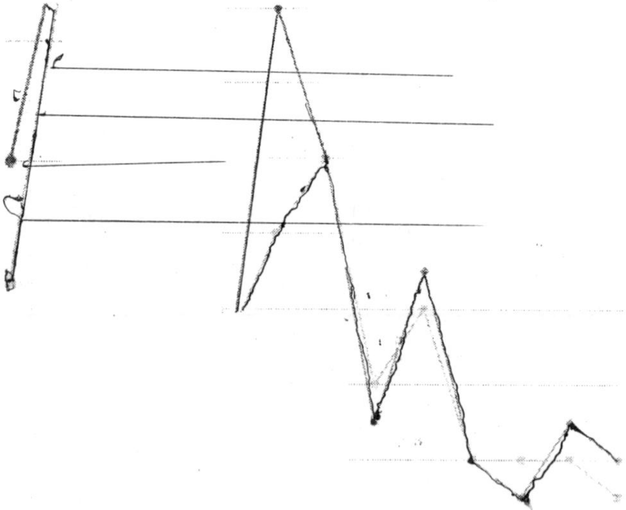

Table 8 : Bonafide registered members of the selected DCS's in KOMUL

S.N.	Name of the Societies	Registered members	Pouring/ members	% of active members	Non-members pouring milk
1	Valley DCS, Seitheikima	89	52	58.43	25
2	Bhola DCS	107	53	49.53	19
3	Everest – I, DCS, Chumkedima	27	20	74.07	—
4	Dairy Farm DCS, Kushiabil	32	25	78.13	—
5	Dzevi DCS, Chumukedima Village	36	36	100	14
6	Khrotho DCS,	36	25	69.44	14
7	Kikhru DCS, Chumukedima Village	31	26	83.87	45
8	Medziphema	10	9	90	—
9	Mugashe DCS, Lotovi Village	30	7	23.33	—
10.	N.C.DCS New Chumukedima	19	11	57.89	—
11.	Tukikhe DCS, Xukiye Village	54	16	29.63	4
12.	Lucky DCS, Zani Village	25	17	68	—
13.	Niuto DCS, Vihokhu Village	66	66	100	20
14.	Kyong DCS, Dumukhya	30	18	60	—
	Total = 128 members				

Summary

A study was conducted on The Livestock Resources and Provision of Inputs in the operation area of the Kohima District Milk Producers' Co-operative Union Ltd., (KOMUL), Dimapur.

A total of 65 DCS' s were organised out of which only 14 DCS' s were selected based on proper records for 1998 and 1999, by which years, one 20,000 LPD capacity milk processing unit and one 1.0 tonne capacity per day feed processing unit were commissioned and operated. Data on Dairy animal resources in the operation area, specifically on population pattern, type and lactation length and yield of each type were collected from the selected DCS's. Alongwith, information were also collected on provisions of inputs with special pointers to implementation of Rural Dairy Development Scheme, provision of A.I. and N. S., supply of balanced Concentrate feeds, implementation of fodder development programme, provision of veterinary aids, provision transport facility, mode and regularity of payment, marketing strategies, maintenance of accounts and auditing, enrolment of membership, training of member producers, office bearers and fanners parlicipating in management.

Out of 13,193 heads of dairy animals available in the operation area of KOMUL, the study was confined to 2136 dairy animals available in the 14 selected DCS's. The percentage of cattle and buffaloes within the selected area were 98.59 and 1.40 respectively. Of the cattle population, local nondescript and cross-bred cattle constituted 52.99 per cent and 45.59 per cent. Amongst the crossbred dairy cattle, Jersey crossbred accounted to 33.43 per 49 cent, Holstein-Friesian Crossbred 11.01 per cent, Brown Swiss Crossbred 1.08 per cent and local buffaloes 1.04 per cent. It was further categorised into dairy cows (33.09%), city cows (26.12%), heifers & calves (34.640/0) and breeding bulls (6.13%). The percentage of wet cows during the period of study was highest among the Jersey Crossbreds (43.71%), where as in case of dlY cows, heifers & calves; and breeding bulls, the local non-descript animals were prominent with 59.86 per cent, 59.05 per cent and 50.38 per cent, respectively. It has been observed that the member producers have more affinity to maintain local non-de scrips and Jersey Crossbreds compared to others.

The Holstein Friesian recorded the longest lactation length followed by Brown Swiss Crossbred, Jersey Crossbreds and local non-descript cows in descending order. In case of lactation yield Holstein. Friesian crossbred recorded the highest, followed by Brown Swiss Crossbred, Jersey Crossbred and local non-de script cows, again in descending order.

KOMUL has provided quite a number of inputs for enhanced production of milk in different societies so that the members' per capita income increased to bring them above poverty line. The implementation of Rural Dairy Development

Scheme is one such; through which a total of 60 dairy cows were distributed to a few number of societies and the societies in turn to individual producers. It may be suggested here that KOMUL may emphasize on the upgradation of existing non-de script animals in the DCS's through Intensive crossbreeding programme than to encourage the member producers towards procurement of dairy animals from outside sources. In respect of breeding programme, the dominance of N.S. over A.I. was quite evident and simultaneously, conception rate was higher in N.S. than A.I. Since the A.I. facility in Anand Pattern Co-operative is a boon for development of dairy cattle towards higher production and upgradation.

7

Constraints of Oyster Mushroom Cultivation in Nagaland

Sharma, A., Jha, K.K.,[1] Kalita, D.C., Nizamuddin[2] & Upadhyay, D.N.[3]*

Introduction

Mushroom has been known to be eaten by man since time immemorial. They were treated as a special kind of food by the Greeks. Romans and the Chinese. There are more than 2000 edible fungi, out of which about 25 species are accepted for human consumption. The five most important cultivated mushrooms are the white button mushroom (*Agaricus spp.*). Black forest mushroom (*Shiitake spp.*), winter mushroom (*Flammulina spp.*), straw mushroom (*Voluariella spp.*) and the oyster mushroom (*Pleurotus spp.)*

Mushroom cultivation is based on recycling of agricultural

* Department of Agricultural Economics, Nagaland University; SASRD, Campus: Medziphema — 797106.

[1] Department of R.D.P., NU, SASRD, Campus: Medziphema - 797106.

[2] Department of A.P.M., NU, SASRD, Campus: Medziphema - 797106.

[3] Department of Plant Pathology, NU, SASRD, Campus: Medziphema - 797106.

residue, which is available in large quantity, specially the paddy straw that is quite abundant in N.E. region. Most of the tribal farmers of this region burn paddy straw thereby causing environmental pollution. Some others dispose straw by allowing it decay in the field. However, excess straw in the field hinders the agricultural operations & presence of decomposing straw can create an unfavorable soil environment for plant growth, therefore this resource can be utilized in the socio-economic development of the tribal farmers of this region by adopting low cost mushroom cultivation.

In our country two species of pleurotus have been domesticated viz.(i) *P. sajor. caju* & (ii) *P. flabellatus.* Out of these species the cultivation of *P. sajor caju* species is most suitable in these regions, as it requires low input technology, which can be easily adopted by the tribal farmers. The cultivation of pleurotus spp. mushroom was initiated as early as 1915 on an experimental basis, but on commercial scale it gained considerable importance recently. It contains above (49.93 per cent) protein, (2.26 per cent) fat, (0.40 per cent) carbohydrate, (0.06 per cent) and vitamins - on dry weight basis.

Method of Cultivations

1. **Growing Season**: - *P. sajor caju* grows very well within a temperature of 22° to 30° C the optimum temperature is around 25°C. This temperature range is quite appropriate both for vegetative & fruiting stage. Therefore the prevailing temperature should be within this range for more than 12 hrs. Based on this factor pleurotus spp. may be grown for about 7-8 months in a year i.e.; March to October in hilly areas, maximum altitude more than 1300 m, about 6 month i.e.; March to May & September to November for areas having altitude of 800 to 1300 m & 3-4 month viz; November to February in areas having altitude less than 800 m.

Thus due to varying altitude in N. E. region, this Mushroom can be cultivated almost round the year with profitability.

2. **For cultivation of this mushroom**: A covered area, preferable a room is required other essential material are wooden trays (1 m x 1/2 m x 0.18 m) or boxes, paddy straw, chaff cutter, spawn, Dal powder, S. S. P., Hand sprayer, insecticide (Malathion

or Cyathion) fungicide (Dithane Z-78 or Captan) Gunny bags, 225 liter drums, newspaper sheets etc.

The wooden tray of given size may be made of locally available cheap wood & can be arranged on self. The trays can be arranged in tiers keeping a distance of 0.25 m between the two successive trays. This arrangement can be helpful in saving space, Paddy straw should not be more than one year old & must hot be exposed to rains and moulds. Before chopping them into 2 to 5 cm, wide most of the leafy portion should be removed.

Mushroom spawn serve as mushroom seeds & it must be pure & of high quality it can be procured from Plant Pathology laboratories or I. C. A. R. Research complexes for N. E. region, located indifferent state on a minimal payment basis.

3. **Method**: Chopped paddy straw should be soaked in water for 4-6 hrs. After this the wetted straw should be subjected to hot water treatment (80^0 C) for about half an hour for sterilizing the straw. Thereafter excess water should be removed from the straw mass & cooled to a temperature of about 25°C. Now the paddy straw should be filled @ 3 Kg dry straw for each tray & immersed in fresh water in drums for over-night (12-18 hrs). Next day the gunny bags are taken out and kept on platform or pucca floor till excess water drain-off. Then materials required for each tray are weighted @ 11 kg of wet straw, 125 gm of dal powder & 125 gm of S. S. P., 1/2 bottle of spawn is sufficient for seedling one tray.

Tray in which spawn is kept are covered with old news papers sheet or wet gunny bags supported on 2 bamboo sticks placed cross-wise over the tray & are arranged in tiers of 4-5 trays in the growing place appropriate temperature (20 to 30^{0}C) & humidity 80 to 85 per cent must be maintained by frequent spraying water on the bed/news papers/gunny bags/sides of the trays/floor etc. Too much watering of the bed should be avoided which otherwise will result into rotting of straw & failure of the crops.

Generally it takes about 10 to 20 days for the vegetative growth of the mushroom & during this period, white cottony treads (mycelium) develop & spread throughout the beds during the mycelium growth, ones the white cottony growth is visible on the entire surface of the bed. The newspaper sheets may be removed & ventilation should be allowed for few hours. However, humidity should not be allowed to drop below 80 per cent, therefore wet gunny bags are hanged around the trays. To keep away the harmful insect & unwanted mould, the trays are sprayed with 0.10 per cent malathion & 2 per cent dithane Z-78 starting from 3 days after seedling, spraying may be continued @ 2-3 spray per week till small pin head are visible in the beds these are the young mushrooms fruit & should not be sprayed with any pesticide to avoid human health hazards. In P. sajor caju it takes about 25 to 30 days for pinhead to appear. The pin heads grow into fully develop mushroom within 3-4 days & become ready for harvesting.

4. Harvest & Yield: Mushroom fruit appeared in flushes normally first flushes quite heavy with larger fruiting bodies & is followed by subsequent flushes at 10-12 days internal, which have lower yield as well as small fruits, generally the farmers should harvest up to 3 flushes from a tray for profitability, after which the used straw is discarded and new sponging is done with new straw. The total harvest from 3 flashes is about 3-4 kg of fresh mushroom per sq. m. of bed area after harvesting of each flush the farmer should take precautions measure to spray the measure with melaitian & diethane Z-78 to maintain healthy conditions. The used and discarded straw is quite rich in Nitrogen. Therefore,

(i) It can be used as compost for kitchen garden or feed to cattle's &

(ii) By mined with other fodders.

5. Economics of Pl. Cultivation:

Table 1: Capital invested, operational & maintenance cost (in Rs.)

S. No.	*Particulars*	*Cost (Rs.)*
1.	For small farmers mushroom house can be constructed with locally available bamboo & other wooden material s with minimum of investment (room of 20 sq. m. is quite sufficient)	1000.00
2.	Operational cost of paddy straw, gram dal powder/rice bran, fungicide, pesticide, spawn, gunny begs, nylon nets, drum, sprayer, bucket, hand-chopper, family labour, misc.	2500.00

Table 2: Cost & pleurotus spp. harvesting of these figures relate to 7-8 crops of Pl. (in a 7 month period)

S. No.	*Particulars*	*Cost & Returns (Rs.)*
1.	Depreciation of fixed capital expenditure except land @ 15 per cent	87.50
2.	Interest on invested capital	75.60
3.	Operational & Maintenance Cost	2500.00
	anticipated yield of the total harvested crop of mushroom in 7th month period about 360 kg	
	Total Revenue @ Rs. 25/Kg.	9000.00
	Expenditure (Investment)	2663.10
	Net Profit	6336.90

6. **Marketing and preservation:** Fruits of Pleurotus spp. can be send fresh to local markets, packed in brown paper bags or paper basket conveniently & mushroom are highly perishable commodity, they should be marketed as early as possible.

For sending the mushroom in distance market the fruits of *Pleurotus spp.* should be dried either in sun or by mechanical dehydrater 45 to 50^0 C fruit of *Pleurotus spp.* generally contain about 90 per cent moisture. Therefore yield of the dried mushroom will be about 1/10 of the fresh (mushroom) weight of the fruits. Such dried fruit may be store for several months in tritely shied polythine bag or container. These fruits regain their shape texture & much of their flavor when shoked in water. Dry fruit crushed into powder can also be sold for its use as flavoring agent. Thus, it can be concluded that are most suited for cultivation by small farmers in N. E. region with minimum investment & high profitability, both in terms of income & self-employment generation.

Constraint

Constraint & future strategy for popularizing of Oyster mushroom cultivation. The main constraint is popularizing of cultivation of oyster mushroom lies with the awareness of the small farmers about the resituate production technology. These farmers generally don't know the expertise of cultivation of the deviate mushroom & the high profit deprieved from this small-scale enterprise with minimum investment & utilization of the local resources.

Therefore the main steps to be taken are to create community awareness & community participation in mushroom cultivation. Apart from it, there is a great need of in parting training in production technology of oyster mushroom to the small farmers at grass-root level.

At present there is a heavy dependent on few laboratories for procurement of spawn, therefore to remove this con strain private organisation should come forward to make the spawn widely available.

The small farmers generally lack proper skill in packing & marketing facilities for this product is also very limited. Thus a good deal of the produce does not fetch remunerative price as per expectation. Therefore with better marketing facilities, improved method of cultivation creating commodity awareness & providing requisite training to the small farmer can bring about successful adoption of oyster mushroom cultivation in N.E. regions.

REFERENCES

1. Agnihotri, V. P. Sarbhoy, A. K. & Kumar, Dinesh: *Perspectives in Mycology and Plant Pathology*. Malhotra Publishing House, New Delhi.
2. Purkayastha, R.P. & Chandra, A.: *Manual of Indian edible mushroom*. Goyal Offset Printer, Delhi.
3. Sharma, A.: 'A study of production & marketing of Potato in Madanpur Block'. A M. Sc. (Ag.) Thesis. Submitted to Agra University. Agra.

8

"Bukhari" an Alternative to Conventional Method of Brooding in Remote and Rural Areas

*R.K. Chaurasia, B. Prakash, and V.B. Sharma**

ABSTRACT

An investigation was carried out in-order to evolve a suitable alternative method of brooding in the remote and hilly areas of rural India. *"Bukhari", a* kind of heating contrivance was scientifically used in the present experiment. A total of 400 chicks, divided into four groups of 100 each, three groups were used for *bukhari* brooding and rest 100 were under conventional brooding method. The chicks were brooded for a period of three weeks under similar managemental conditions. At the end of brooding period, the body weight, weight gain, feed consumption and conversion efficiency were 561±1.80 g and 518.30±4.68 g, 265.20±1.80 and 268.70±3.38g, 1153g and 1054.99g, 2.33 and 2.10 respectively for conventional and *bukhari* brooded groups. However, at the age of six weeks the body weight,

* Department of Animal Production and Management, School of Agricultural Sciences and Rural Development, Nagaland University, Medziphema, Nagaland-797106, India.

weight gain, feed consumption and feed conversion efficiency were 1656.56±5.81g and 16144.79±7.34g, 413.68±2.92g and 382.42±3.10g, 3721g and 3736.25g, 2.33 and 2.72 respectively, for both conventional and *bukhari* brooded groups. The dressing and mortality percentage in both the groups were found to be 74.68±0.24 and 73.92±0.31, 2.00 and 3.34 respectively, showing no significant difference in performance between *bukhari* and conventionally brooded chicks. The study recommends, *bukhari* as a safe and suitable alternative brooding to conventional brooder in remote rural areas having no or limited availability of power/electricity supply.

Key Words: *bukhari*, brooding, broiler strain, growth, feed conversion efficiency

Introduction

In India, the poultry farming has now emerged as the fastest growing professional segment of the agricultural sector. It has become an important constituent of rural and urban economy providing not only significant role in the nutritional needs of the people but has also become a major and economically viable source of employment for weaker sections, small and marginal farmers and landless labours.

In the light of 'household food and nutritional security' the small-scale poultry farming is gaining its socio-economic, nutritional and food securing importance in rural India. The success of present day poultry keeping, rather the industry in large scale, is very much dependent on the basic practice of brooding, be it broiler or layer. In today's socioeconomic scenario of rural India, it is essential that proper brooder is devised for backhanding small scale poultry rearing in inaccessible remotest corners of North East and other packets of India, where the basic amenities are scarce or almost void. Keeping this in view, the present investigation was designed to evolve a new method, which may be used as an alternative method to the conventional brooding in years to come.

Poultry has also emerged as a major source of meat, as it is moderately priced and an alternative to red meat. In 1996, annual production of broiler was 400 million with a growth rate of 20 percent and per capita meat availability was 566 g/

year. (Poultry Industry Year Book, 1997). Brooding of chicks is an important aspect of poultry rearing and proper brooding will result in healthy growers. In rural India, there is shortage of electricity and frequent power failure leading to improper brooding and thereby increasing post-hatch mortality rate resulting in non-profitable poultry farm. To overcome these problems, appropriate technology based on the locally available resources has to be developed, which a farmer can adopt easily and economically. *Bukhari* (Singh, 1981) a kind of heating contrivance was used in the present study to brood the chicks for generating heat by utilizing saw dust and hurricane lantern for lighting the brooding room in lieu of electrical brooder.

The investigation was carried out in order to evolve an alternative method of brooding which can be practiced by the people living in inaccessible hilly terrain having scanty or non availability of power facility, as well as a comparative evaluation was made by using feed consumption, feed conversion efficiency and dressing percentage as indicators in the two feeding systems of brooding i. e., conventional and bukhari. Further, an economic analysis was carried out for estimating cost of production in both the systems.

Materials and Methods

The present study was conducted by a total of 400 day-old-straight-run commercial broiler chicks of Phoenix Cobb strain, with mean body weight of 32.15±0.21 g. Four equal groups of chicks were placed in the brooder houses, three groups being in the *bukhari* brooder and one in conventional brooder. The brooder house was prepared and properly sanitized with disinfectant in both the groups. The litter material was dried in sunshine and placed in the brooder, so as to maintain a thickness of 3-4 inches throughout. The *bukhari* brooder was conceptualized from the traditionally used materials like saw dust as per Singh (1981). For providing light to the *bukhari* brooder house, a hurricane lantern was used throughout the brooding period of three weeks and the temperature was maintained according to the recommendations of Deator et al (1996).

Both the groups were fed through a suitably designed feeder

by using the standard formulated starter ration mash with a CP percentage of 23.24 during the brooding period. The finisher pellet ration with 20.81 CP % was fed during last three weeks of study, till the birds were marketed. The clean potable drinking water was provided *ad libitum* by the automatic waterer. The weak and crippled chicks were culled from the stock during the experimental period. Proper health care measures were strictly followed and a similar feeding and managemental conditions were adopted in both the brooder groups. The brooder house temperature and humidity were maintained as per the standard recommendations (Charles, 1986).

The data pertaining to body weight, weight gain, feed consumption and feed conversion efficiency were collected at weekly intervals from both brooder groups. The feed provided to the chicks were weighed and fed to the different groups. The mortality rate and dressing percentage were recorded at the end of the experiment, from the data collected throughout the experimental period. The digital thermometer and hygrometer were used for recording the temperature and humidity in the microclimate of the brooder houses.

The collected data were subjected to the 't' statistic analysis for unequal samples (Snedecor and Cochran 1967) for testing the significance of difference between the two treatment groups. The rations were analyzed for CP according to A O A C (1984). For the economic study, the method of estimating cost of production as described by Kothandraman and Nahari (1982) was carefully used by introducing some modification to suit the local conditions of the experimental station.

Results and Discussion

The results on the comparative performance of the broiler birds brooded under the two different systems for first three weeks of their life had been presented in Table 1. Any of the parameters did not differ significantly in the two brooding groups. Though the body weight gain, feed consumption and feed conversion efficiency of the chicks under *bukhari as* well as conventional brooder houses were statistically similar, but the *bukhari* brooded group consumed a comparatively higher quantity of feed and showed poor feed conversion efficiency in the third and fourth week of age as shown in Fig. 2.

Mortality rates of 2.66 % and 2.00 % were observed during brooding period in *bukhari* and conventional methods respectively. The higher mortality rate in *bukhari* was attributed to fluctuation in the brooder house temperature. An overall mortality of 3.34 % and 2.00 % was found in *bukhari* and conventionally brooded groups respectively. Dressing percentages of 73.29±0.31 and 74.68±0.24 as observed in bukhari and conventional brooders respectively did not show significant difference.

Economics (cost benefit analysis) of broiler production reared under conventional and *bukhari* brooder were analyzed and presented in Table 1. It was evident that the newly devised *bukhari* brooder excelled over the conventional brooder. Though non- significant, difference of Rs 1.43 per kg of broiler was observed between two brooded groups, the *bukhari* brooded group being less by the amount. However, a slightly higher gross income form conventionally brooded group might be attributed to higher feed conversion efficiency of the birds, resulting in comparatively more broiler production.

Being equally efficient to conventional brooder, *"Bukhari"* a simple contrivance used by the people living in the cooler climate of higher altitude. Being habitual non-vegetarian and having scarcity of electricity supply, small scale broiler farming may be flourished in these areas with this alternative method of brooding for improving socio-economic as well as nutritional status of so called backward hilly tribes.

Table 1: Economics (cost benefit analysis) of broiler production

		Bukhari	*Conventional*
1	Cost of Chicks (day old)	Rs 18.75	Rs 18.75
2	Cost of feeding Cost per Kg/feed*feed conversion efficiency *average weight of the chicks	Rs 41.23	Rs 41.02
3	Cost of brooding Fuel cost	Re 1 per chick	Cost of brooding and rearing with generator is 21.80 per chick
4	Miscellaneous	Rs 2 per chick	Rs 2 per chick
5	Total cost of production of one chick	Rs 62.98	Rs 83.57

6	Gross income	Rs 55*1.614 Kg (Live weight of chicks) Rs 88.77	55*1.656 Rs 91.08
7	Net income	88.77-62.98=**25.79**	91.08-83.57=**7.51**

REFERENCES

AOAC (1984) Official Methods of Analysis. 14th edn. Association of Official Analytical Chemist, Washington, DC.

Charles, D.R (1986). Temperature for broilers. *World Poult. Sci.* **43**(3): 249-255.

Deator, J.W; Branton, S.L.; Simmons, J.D.; Cott, B.D., (1996) Effect of brooding temperature on broiler performance. *Poultry Science* **75**(10) 1217-1220 Cf br 1997 Vol-65 (5) 2519.

Kothandaraman, P. and Narahari, D. (1982). Economics of broiler production in India. *Poul. Guide* 2:45-51.

Poultry Industry Yearbook (1997)

Singh, R.A (1981). *Poultry Production,* Published by Kalayani Publishers, New Delhi, pp. 64.

Snedecor, G.V. and Cochran, W.G. (1967) *Statistical Methods.* 6th edn. Oxford and IBH Publishing Company, New Delhi, India.

9

Comparative Study of Mash vs. Pellet Feeding on the Performance of Broiler Chicken under Cage System

*Nizamuddin and A.K. Singh**

Abstract

An experiment with 300 day-old commercial broiler chicks of Phoenix–Cobb was undertaken to study the performance of broiler chicken on mash and pellet feeding in cage system of rearing upto 42 days of age. The growth rate during the brooding period in the mash feeding was normal. The average body weight and the body weight gained were significantly ($P<0.05$) higher in birds fed on pellet ration than on mash in finisher period. Pellet ration showed better feed conversion ratio at different growth periods than on mash ration. Correlation Coefficient among all the parameters studied was found positive and significant. The maximum dressing percentage was observed in the birds fed with pellet ration. It can be concluded that pellet feeding is more economical for broiler chicken production than mash type of ration even though both may have similar nutrient composition.

* Department of Animal Production and Management, SASRD, NU: Medziphema Campus, Nagaland.

Introduction

Rearing broiler in cages is slowly becoming popular among poultry farmers because of its advantages over other system of rearing.

The broiler production is affected by two major factors. The first one is genetic ability and the other one is the quality feed. The feed alone constitute more than 70 % of the cost of production per kg/ of live birds. Feed can be provided in two different forms, mash and pellet. In feeding mash ration, there is more wastage while in pellet feeding wastage is less. Hence, the present experiment has been conducted to study the comparative broiler chicken performance and the cost of production in two different types of feed viz. mash and pellet under cage system of rearing.

Materials and Methods

For the investigation, 300 a day-old commercial broiler chicks of Phoenix Cobb strain were procured from M/s Universal Hatcheries, Calcutta and reared from 2nd June to 13th July, 1989 at the instructional poultry unit of the Animal farm complex, School of Agricultural Sciences and Rural Development, Nagaland University, Medziphema.

The day-old chicks were reared for the first 21 days in electrically operated battery brooder and measured quantity of standard broiler starter mash was provided. Then the chicks were shifted form brooder to cage compartments and distributed randomly in two groups (150 numbers is group) for further experimentation where they were fed measured quantity of mash and pellet ration separately from 22 to 42 days. The daily feed consumption was recorded.

The chicks were weighed individually at 21, 28, 35 and 42 days of age and average body weights were calculated. The feed conversion ratio (FCR) per week was calculated using the following formula:

FCR = Feed consumption / Gain in body weight.

Ten birds were randomly selected from each group after completing 42 days to evaluate the dressing percentage. After slaughtering the birds were dipped in hot water (55° C) for 60 seconds for scalding and then the feathers were picked up immediately. The shanks and tip of wings were removed. The dressed weight of carcass (without giblets) was recorded and was expressed in terms of percent of pre-slaughter live weight of the birds. Standard statistical methods were used for calculation.

Results and Discussion

Body Weight

The average initial weight of chicks was 31.99 ± 0.66g while at 21 days it was 491.5 ± 4.31g. Mean body weight of the birds at 28, 35 and 42 days are presented in Table 1. At 28 days the highest average body weight (881.5± 14.72g) was recorded in the birds fed on pellet ration whereas the lowest body weight (824.5±3.30g) was noted in the birds fed on mash ration. Similarly, highest average body weight at 35 and 42 days were recorded in the birds fed on pellet ration. The difference in the body weights of the birds at different ages fed on pellet and mash ration was found to be significant. This result is in conformity with the findings of Proud foot and Hulan (1989). Pegin *et.al* (1991) also reported that the body weight of broiler bird is significantly affected by feed texture at different ages.

Body Weight gain:

The average body weight gain of the birds fed on mash and pellet rations at different ages are presented in table 1.Average weight gain during 0 to 21 days was found 459.51 ± 4.32g. Higher body weight gain was recorded in birds fed on pellet ration than on mash ration in all ages, which differs significantly. Similar findings were recorded by Wenk *et.al*. (1979), Proud foot and Hulan (1982) and Kim and Chang (1993) in chickens fed on pellet and mash ration.

Feed Intake

Feed intake of broilers during different periods are presented in Table 1. Feed intake during brooding period (0-21 days) was 894.0 ± 2.76g. During the finisher periods (22-42 days), the feed intake was found to be significantly higher in birds fed on pellet ration than in mash ration. Sengor and Bayne (1987) recorded significantly higher feed intake on the pellet diet by broilers. Higher feed intake on pellet diet over mash diet might be due to selective eating and more palatability.

Feed Conversion Ratio (FCR):

FCR of the broilers are presented in Table 1. During brooding period (0-21 days) FCR was found to be 1.95. During finisher period for 22–28, 29–35 and 36–42 days FCR was 1.78, 2.06 and 2.80, respectively for pellet ration while the corresponding figures were 1.88, 2.16 and 2.95 for mash ration. The difference in FCR was found to be non–significant. Chang *et.al*. (1983) found better feed efficiency value on pellet than on mash ration. Proud foot and Hulan (1989), Deaton(1992) and Kim and Chang(1993) also found better feed conversion for chicken on pellet from 22-42 days.

Dressing Percentage

The average dressing percentage of broiler birds at 42 days of age on mash and pellet rations were found to be 68.46 and 69.39 respectively and the difference was not statistically significant. Pegin *et.al* (1989) also reported non–significant difference on dressing percentage between mash and pellet feeding.

Correlation Coeficient

Correlation Coefficient among different parameters of growth were calculated for the birds fed on mash and pellet ration from 22 to 42 days which are presented in Table 3. Correlation Coefficient between body weight and body weight gain, body weight and feed intake, body weight and FCR were statistically significant at 1% and between body weight and dressing percentage at 5% probability level. Correlation Coefficient between body weight gain and feed intake, body weight gain and dressing percentage was found to be statistically significant at 5% and Body weight gain and FCR at 1% probability level. Correlation Coefficient between feed intake and FCR, feed intake and dressing percent was significant at 5% probability level. Similarly correlation coefficient between FCR and dressing Percentage was significant at 5% probability level.

REFERENCES

1. Chang Sik Park; Soon Ki Kwon and Tae Hyuk Min (1983). Studies on the effect of feeding pelleted diets on energy metabolism and nitrogen retention in growing chickens. Research reports of Agri. Sciences and Tech. 10(2): 206-211. c.f. *Poult.Abst.* 12(3):590.
2. Deaton, J.W. ; Reece, F.N. and McNaughton, J.L. (1978).The effect of temperature during growing period on broiler performance. *Poult. Sci.* 57(4): 1070–1074. c.f. *Poult. Abst* 5(2):347
3. Kin, H.M. and Chung Y.H. (1993). Effect of dietary feed form regimen on broiler chickens performance. R.D.A. *J. of Agri. Sci. Livestock* 35(2): 554–558 c.f. *Nutri. Abst.* 64(7):481
4. Pegin, G. and Supic, B.E. (1989). Effect of pelleted feed on the fattening outcome and meat quality of Broilers. *Poult Abst.* 17(9):2359.
5. Proudfoot, F.G. and Hulan, H.W. (1982). Effect of reduced feeding time using all mash or crumble-pellet dietary regimens on chicken broiler performance including the incidence of acute death syndrome. *Poult. Sci.* 61(4):750-760.
6. Proudfoot, F.G. and Hulan, H.W. (1989). Feed texture effects on the performance of roaster chickens. *Canadian J. of Anim. sci.* 69(3):801-807.
7. Sengor, E. and Bayne, B.E.P. (1987). The effects of feed texture on performance in broilers. *Poult. Abst.* 17(10):2681.
8. Wenk, L. and Es.A.J.H. Van (1979). Feeds as pellets or as meal for growing chickens. *Poult. Abst.* 11(10) : 210-214.

Table 2 : Average dressing Percentage (without giblets) of broiler birds on Mash and Pellet rations

Parameters	*Dressing Percentage*
Mash	68.46±0.76
Pellet	69.39±0.52

Table 1: Average body weight, body weight gain, feed intake and FCR of Broiler Birds at different ages fed on mash and pellet ration

Parameters/ Period	*Body weight(g)*		*Body weight gain(g/week.)*		*Feed intake(g)*		*FCR*	
	Mash	*Pellet*	*Mash*	*Pellet*	*Mash*	*Pellet*	*Mash*	*Pellet*
0-21 days	491.5± 4.31	491.5± 4.31	459.51± 4.32	-	894± 2.76	-	1.95± 0.02	-
22-28 days	824.5± 3.30^{a}	881.5± 14.72^{b}	333± 2.87^{a}	390± 13.94^{b}	629± 4.22^{a}	693± 8.99^{b}	1.88± 0.03	1.78± 0.08
29-35 days	1223.7± 174^{a}	1308.7± 17.28^{b}	399.2± 9.83	427.2± 8.82	864± 2.94^{a}	882± 3.38^{b}	2.16± 0.06	2.06± 0.05
36-42 days	1538± 3.39^{a}	1655.7± 21.4^{b}	314.3± 7.01^{a}	347± 14.6^{b}	927± 2.68^{a}	966± 3.88^{b}	2.95± 0.06	2.80± 0.06

Note: Figures with different superscripts in a row for various parameters differ significantly from each other.

Table 3 : Correlation coefficient amongst different growth parameters of broilers fed on mash and pellet ration(22 – 42 days).

Parameters	*Ration*	*Body wt.*	*Body wt. gain*	*Feed intake*	*FCR*	*Dressing%*
Body wt.	Mash	-	0.58	0.19	-0.19	-0.83
	Pellet	-	0.99**	0.97**	0.99**	0.95*
Body wt. Gain	Mash	-	-	0.51	-0.86	0.90
	Pellet	-	-	0.92*	0.99**	0.95*
Feed Intake	Mash	-	-	-	0.88*	0.11
	Pellet	-	-	-	0.93*	0.91*
FCR	Mash	-	-	-	-	0.55
	Pellet	-	-	-	-	0.95*
Dressing%	Mash	-	-	-	-	-
	Pellet	-	-	-	-	-

* - Significant at 5% probability level.

** - Significant at 1% probability level.

10

Constraints and Prioritization of Strategies of Agricultural Development in Nagaland

*Kalita, D.C., Singh, A.K., Sharma, A. & Nakhro, R.**

ABSTRACT

The present study is an attempt to study the constraints and prioritization of strategies for agricultural development in Nagaland. The study is based on secondary informations that were collected from several government sources and other publications. Only percentages and averages were estimated to serve the purpose. The Low adoption of improved technology such as use of HYV seeds, fertilizers and lack of irrigation facilities, use of traditional cultivation practices more particularly in shifting cultivation, socio-economic constraints, and financial problems are some of the major constraints in the development of agricultural sector in the state of Nagaland. The HYV area under rice is only 1.38 percent coverage, which is far below as compared to regional as well as national level. Fertilizer consumption is very low in Nagaland as compared to other

* Department of Agricultural Economics, Nagaland University, SASRD, Campus, Medziphema—797106.

states of North East India. The number of families dependent on shifting cultivation in the region was highest in Nagaland (1, 16, 046 numbers) amongst the north-eastern states. Contrary to both annual area and minimum area under shifting cultivation one time or other were found to be low in Nagaland. Livestock and fishery sector development is also very poor due the various reasons. Lack of financial facility is also a major problem in the development of agricultural sector. Therefore, the developmental strategies should be taken based on the existing constraints.

Introduction

The northeastern India is a chicken naked region, connected to the mainland with a narrow corridor and supported by international boundaries of Bangladesh and Bhutan. North-east India consists of Assam, Mizoram, Nagaland, Tripura, Arunachal Pradesh, Meghalaya, Manipur and Sikkim covering 255.08 million hectares, which is the 8 percent of the country's total land. Nagaland has a total geographical area of 16,579 sq.kms and out of this, 8,629 thousand hectare is the recorded forest area[1]. Nagaland is highly diverse in terms of agro-systems, sovio-culturals mixtures of the peoples, a blend of multiplicity of ethnicity and geographical variability. The state is also enjoying the abundant of natural resources like flora and fauna. The abundant and rich natural resources are neglected in the past but must put to efficient use now to catalyse the development process. In the absence of concerted efforts, the sate is unable to provide necessary support system to manage these natural resources for the benefit of the people. If the natural resources are not properly developed and managed, the food security in the predominantly agrarian economy will be endangered.

Therefore, appropriate strategies should be taken up to boost up the agricultural development. Before taking any strategies for development, one must identifies the existing constraint that stands in the way of development. Hence in this paper, an attempt is made to identify the major constraints of agricultural development and prioritization of strategies for development.

Methodology

The present study is mainly based on secondary informations, which were collected from several office sources and other publications. The percentages and averages were estimated to meet the objective of the study.

Results and Discussion

Major constraints of agricultural development:

Low adoption of improved technology:

The rate of use of HYV reflects the pace of agricultural development in any state. Table 1 presents the area under HYV in the north-eastern states of India as well as the all India average during the year 1997-98. The area under HYV is mainly collected for the major cereals like rice, wheat, and maize. The area under HYV rice was found to be lowest in Nagaland with only 1.38 percent coverage as compared to other states of the region as well as national level. The adoption rate of the HYV in the region is very low as compared to the national average of 76.92 percent. The main reason of slow growth of HYV area in the state are the non-availability of suitable seeds, predominance of traditional seeds in the hill areas under *jhum* cultivation, short supply of recommended seeds and other defective distribution systems (Saikia, 2001).

Fertilizer is an important input in modern seed-fertilizer-water technology. The productivity of HYV depends upon largely on the application of fertilizers at recommended doses. The farmers on north-eastern region have used very meager amount of fertilizer in terms of nitrogen, phosphorous, and potash compared to national average of fertilizer consumption. On an average, about 16.71 kg of total nutrient per hectare was the per hectare consumption rate in north-eastern region while it was 86.10 kg/ha in the case of national level (Table 2). Further, amongst the north-eastern states, Nagaland used the lowest amount of total nutrient (2.60 kg/ha). The main constraints are defective distributional systems, poor transportation facilities and lack of credit facilities to the farmers (Hazarika *et.al.*, 2001).

Thus the low level of nutrient application has resulted the low productivity of all the major crops in the state.

Irrigation being on of the components of modern technology plays a vital role in the development of agriculture. The region accounts only 2.11 per cent of the country's total area under all crops (Table 3). Depending upon the facilities of assured irrigation, the cropping intensity or the area sown more than once is determined. About 17.86 per cent of total cropped area is under irrigation which far below the national average of 28.86 percent during 1995-96. However, the percentage of irrigated area in the sate of Nagaland is at par with national level (27.19 percent).

Shifting cultivation:

The north-eastern region has the total annual area under shifting cultivation of 3,869 sq km of which Nagaland covers the minimum of 190 sq km (4.91 per cent) (Table 4). The number of families dependent on shifting cultivation in the region was found to be highest in Nagaland (1,16,046 numbers) amongst the north-eastern states. Contrary to both annual area and minimum area under shifting cultivation one time or other were found to be low in Nagaland. The growing pressure on land continuously reducing the fallow period that inturn reduces the productivity because the productivity in *jhum* land has strong bearing on *jhum* cycle. Longer the *jhum* cycle higher is the productivity. It has been estimated that production from shifting cultivation on an average could meet the half of the annual requirement of a cultivator's family. While, the productivity under settled cultivation is comparatively higher than that shifting cultivation. Yield loss is also comparatively lower in settled cultivation (Chauhan, 2001). Besides this, shifting cultivation has other several harmful effects on the ecosystem, soil and forest resources.

Socio-economic constraints:

The state has diverse ethnic groups and social systems bound with customs and traditions like other hilly states of the region. These factors are also stands in the economic activities and economic status which ultimately inhabits the adoption of modern methods (Saikia, 2001).

Constraints of livestock production:

There has been a sharp decline in the area under permanent pasture and grazing land in the region. Nagaland is not exceptional to this. Moreover, there is hardly any plan to grow fodder for the cattle. This causes severe shortage of fodder. The illegal encroachments of village grazing land for cultivation; poor quality and lack of livestock feed are some of the other factors that cause low production of livestock. Goat and sheep are not reared unscientifically but practically no attention is given to these non-bovine animals. These animals are not reared commercially although they have great potential in almost all the north-eastern states (Bhowmick and Kalita, 2001).

Pigs on the other hand, are kept by tribal people but not on commercial basis.

Besides these factors, non-availability of improved breeds, and other breeding facilities in the region as well as in the state are some of the other factors that cause low production of livestock.

Constraints in fishery sector:

The major constraints in fishery sectors are listed below:

1. In most of the water bodies, fast growth of water hyacinth and other aquatic weeds and heavy siltation year after year destroyed the ecology and affected the fish production.
2. The supply of fingerlings was 60 lakh in 2000-2001, which amounted to 0.404 lakh per number of pond fishery, which is one of the major constraints in fish cultivation in the state (Anonymous, 2001).
3. Most of the river and other water bodies are deficient of nutrients, which in turn adversely affect the growth of fish.
4. Fish farming in commercial basis is a capital intensive business. The fish farmer are generally unable to enterprising such a capital intensive business due to their poor economic condition. Lack of fishery finance in respect of timeliness, low interest rate and adequate amount is another factor of low production of fish in the state.

Financial constraints:

Capital is the *sine-qua-non* of any business. The credit deposit ratio in the north-eastern state is only 28.03 per cent (Baruah and Sarma, 2001) which is about half of the national average implies draining out of financial resources from this region. This indicates that the business interest of the bank was met at the cost of the public interest, which needs to be seriously looked into. In Nagaland, the credit deposit ratio of Regional Rural Bank and Scheduled Commercial bank during 1999 was 35.81 and 17.38 per cent respectively (Anonymous, 2001).

The total agricultural advances as percent to aggregate advances by Commercial Bank, Regional Rural Bank and Cooperative Bank varies from a high of 24.50 per cent in Tripura to a low of 10.23 per cent in Assam. Further, commercial bank's advance was around 22 percent in Nagaland while Regional Rural Bank advance was lowest in the state of Nagaland (13.90 per cent) amongst the north-eastern states.

The direct short term credit per hectare area of cropped land in the north-eastern region was less than Rs.100.00 as against a national average of Rs.421.50 per hectare (Baruah and Sarma, 2001). This is a meager amount in the context of modern agricultural technology.

Prioritization of strategies for agricultural development:

Based on the above constraints, the following are the prioritization of strategies.

1. Timely supply of HYV seeds through the efficient distribution systems.
2. Marketing infrastructure to be crated at the primary markets in rural areas for supply of fertilizers i.e. creation of single window input delivery system.
3. Development of Irrigation facilities and promotion of water-harvesting method for assured water supply particularly in the *rabi* season.
4. The deep-rooted shifting cultivation is the main agricultural production system in the hilly areas. It is not possible to stop this production system overnight. Therefore, attempt should be made to update the

traditional production system with modern technology with appropriate technological intervention. The state department of agriculture could help the farmers with suggesting technological intervention. The other field functionaries and NGOs could also play active role in motivating farmers in gradually shift towards settled and scientific cultivation.

Further, shifting cultivation could be raised along with plantation crops a the border to reduce soil loss could provide a basis for multistoried crop canopy with perennial crops like banana, pine apple at the top layer, cereals constituting the middle layer and vegetables and pulses at the lower stratum.

5. Development of local and non-descript stock through artificial insemination programme to be taken up more vigorously. Feed mill should be set up in all the district headquarters for easy availability of animal feeds. Besides, veterinary extension service needs to be strengthened in the state.
6. The existing areas of water bodies, which are in most dilapidated conditions, should be cleaned and reclaimed to create effective area for the fish cultivation and this would require massive investment. Production of fish seed especially to meet the demand of private fish farmers should be taken up in each circle headquarters. The government of Tripura has already been supply the required fingerlings to fish farmers.
7. Fishery extension service should be revamped and strengthened so that technology available can be properly disseminated to fish farmers.

   Taking up of private fishery on commercial line should be encouraged. Given necessary infrastructure, fishery would turn out to be a very profitable business since there is market for the product in the state.
8. The lowest credit deposit ratio of commercial banks having the highest growth in the north-eastern region resulting drain out of huge amount of financial resources to other developed region be checked.

   Lowest proportion of agricultural sector advancing by

lead commercial banks with respect to their aggregate advance in comparison to all financial institution need to be examined carefully.

Credit availability from the institutional agencies must be increased to meet the farmer's production expenditure need to be examined carefully,

Timely, adequacy and supervision of farm credit should be ensured to check large scale overdue particularly in case of cooperative credit.

REFERENCES

Anonymous (1997): Forest survey of India, Dehradun. State Forest Report.

Anonymous (1997): Directorate of Economics and Statistics, Ministry of Agriculture, Government of India.

Anonymous (2000): Basic Statistics for North Eastern Region, NEC, Shillong.

Anonymous (2001): Statistical Handbook of Nagaland, Govt. of Nagaland, Kohima.

Baruah, B.K. & Sarma, A. K. (2001).

Bhowmick, B. C. & Kalita, D. C. (2001).

Chauhan, B. S. (2001): Shifting Cultivation in Perspective. P. 4.

Hazarika, C. Bhowmick, B. C. & Saikia, R. S. (2001): Issues Relating to Agricultural Development and Sustainability in Assam. Report Submitted to NABARD, Mumbai.

Saikia, A. (2001).

1 *Forest Survey of India*, Dehradun, State Forest Report-1997.

Table 1: Area under HYV in North Eastern States and India during 1997-98

State	*Rice*			*Wheat*			*Maize*		
	Total area	*Area under HYV*	*% of HYV area to total area*	*Total area*	*Area under HYV*	*% of HYV area to total area*	*Total area*	*Area under HYV*	*% of HYV area to total area*
Arunachal Pradesh	120	35	29.17	3.80	3.50	92.11	34.50	-	-
Assam	2489.8	1422	57.11	84.70	84.30	99.53	19.20	12.00	62.50
Manipur	157.9	72	45.60	-	-	-	3.60	-	-
Meghalaya	157.9	42	26.60	4.30	4.00	93.02	17.20	15.00	87.21
Mizoram	68.1	5	7.34	-	-	-	8.20	-	-
Nagaland	145	2	1.38	1.80	0.30	16.67	30.00	3.00	10.00
Tripura	257.8	223	86.50	2.00	2.00	100.00	2.00	2.00	100.00
All India	43420.2	33399	76.92	26685.60	23726.00	88.91	6305.30	3764.00	59.69

Source: Directorate of Economics and Statistics, Ministry of agriculture, Govt. of India.

Table 2: Consumption of Plant Nutrient Per Unit of Gross Cropped Area (kg/ha).

State	*1996-97*				*1997-98*			
	N_2	P_2O_5	K_2O	*Total*	N_2	P_2O_5	K_2O	*Total*
Arunachal Pradesh	1.30	0.50	0.40	2.20	1.30	0.50	0.40	2.20
Assam	8.40	1.50	4.70	14.60	10.00	3.90	4.60	18.60
Manipur	42.00	4.60	2.00	48.60	40.70	5.50	2.20	48.30
Meghalaya	9.20	4.40	0.80	14.40	9.30	4.20	0.30	13.90
Mizoram	2.10	0.90	0.50	3.50	1.80	3.90	2.90	8.70
Nagaland	1.90	1.60	0.40	3.80	1.30	1.10	0.30	2.60
Tripura	11.80	4.10	2.90	18.80	13.80	5.00	3.80	22.70
All India	54.80	15.80	5.50	76.00	58.00	20.00	7.30	86.10

Source: Basic Statistics of North Eastern Region, 2000..

Table 3: Gross Sown Area, Irrigated Area and Production of Food Grains in 1995-96 (,000 ha) in North Eastern States

State	*Gross sown area*		*Area sown more than once*	*Irrigated area*		*Net irrigated area*	*Food grains production ('000 tonnes)*
	Food grains	*All crops*		*Food grains*	*All crops*		
Arunachal Pradesh	183	244	59	36 (14.75)	33	36	203.50
Assam	2727	3938	1158	572 (14.52)	538	539	3561.20
Manipur	157	182	42	65 (35.71)	75	75	338.90
Meghalaya	131	247	41	45 (18.22)	45	45	142.90
Mizoram	77	109	—	7 (6.42)	5	7	123.70
Nagaland	193	228	17	62 (27.19)	63	66	238.80
Tripura	244	426	149	35 (8.22)	48	59	477.10
All India	122712	186561	44346	53508 (100.00)	49727	58232	180415

Figures in parentheses indicate percentages to total area under all crops
Source: Directorate of Economics and Statistics, Ministry of agriculture, Govt. of India

Table 4: Shifting Cultivation in North Eastern Region

State	*Annual area under shifting cultivation (sq. kms.)*	*Fallow period (Years)*	*Minimum area under shifting cultivation (sq. kms)*	*Number of families practicing shifting cultivation*
Arunachal Pradesh	700	3-10	2,100	54,000
Assam	696	2-3	1,392	58,000
Manipur	900	4-7	3,600	70,000
Meghalaya	530	5-7	2,650	52,290
Mizoram	630	3-4	1,890	50,000
Nagaland	190	5-8	1,913	1,16,046
Tripura	223	5-9	1,115	43,000
Total in north east	3,869		14,660	4,43,336

Source: Basic Statistics of North Eastern Region, NEC, Shillong, 2000.

11

Crossability Relationships Among Cajanus Species

Jogendra Singh & G.C. Bajpai***

ABSTRACT

Two indeterminate lines, UPAS-120 and PA-134 and one determinate, ICPL-84023 of cultivated *Cajanus cajan* were crossed with *C. acutifalius, Cajanifalius, C. scarabaeoides, C. sericeus, C. platycarpus* and C. *Valubilis* to incorporate resistance to phytophthora blight disease, pod borer, drought tolerance and high protien. Highest percentage was seen with *C. cajanifalius* followed by *C. scarabaeoides, C. sericeus* and *C. acutifalius.* Crosses failed with *C. platycarpus* and *C. valubilis* wild species. Therefore, it is concluded that elite populations may be obtained through interspecific hybridization, which would be helpful in breaking the yield plateau in cultivated *C. cajan* varieties.

Key Words: Pigeon pea, crossability, wild species interspecific hybridization.

* Nagaland University, SASRD, Campus: Medziphema, Nagaland—797106.

** Professor, Department of GPB, G. B. Pant University of Agriculture & Technology, Pantnagar (U. A.)

Introduction

Pigeonpea (*Cajanus cajan* (L) millsp.) is a second major pulse crop of India. It plays a major role in Indian livelihood as each and every part of pigeonpea plant provides economic return to the subsistence farmer. It can be grown under wide range of agroclimatic conditions with enrichment of soil economic use of inputs and utilizing nutrients upto deeper soil nutrients. Despite these strenghts, it was pushed to marginal lands, but recent realization of its value has turned it into cash. Its production was recorded 2.79 million tonnes during 1999-2000. However, it slightly declined to 2.48 million tonnes during 2001-2002 (Venkataramani, 2002). However, the overall productivity in pigeonpea remained more or less stagnant, fluctuating between 637 and 799 kg/ha in the last several decades. Wild relatives of pigeonpea are important genetic wealth because they generally serve as a reserve gene pool for traits viz; disease resistance insect resistance, drought tolerance and high protein that are not available in the cultivated gene pool. Earlier workers believed that wild species of pigeonpea may increase its production through transfer of genes for resistance to many abiotic and biotic stresses from wild to cultivated species (Remanandan, 1981). In present study an attempt has been made to study crossability relationships between wild and cultuvated species of *Cajanus*.

Materials and Methods

The present study was carried out with three cultivated pigeonpea genotypes viz; UPAS-120, PA-134 and six wild species viz; *Cajanus acutifalius, Cajanus cajanifalius, Cajanus scarabaeoides, Cajanus sericeus, Cajanus platycarpus* and *Cajanus valubilis*. The crosses were made at Crop Research Centre, G.B. Pant University of Agriculture and Technology, Patnagar during 2000-2001. Sacrified seed of each wild species were sown in pots in the net house. The cultivated genotypes were used as female parent and wild species as male parent. Young flower buds were emasculated between 8.00 hrs and 11.00 hrs. The pollinations were preferably done just after emasculation. The Percentage success of each cross was calculated as below:

$$\text{Crossability (\%)} = \frac{\text{Number of crossed pods}}{\text{Number of pollinated flowers}} \times 100$$

Results and Discussions

The extent of crossability which depends largely on the strenght of genetic barriers, the similarity in the morphological and anatomical attributes and cytological behavior as reflected from kargomorphology and pairing in meiosis are helpful in understanding the phylogenetic relationship of different species. C. cajanifalius gave the highest percentage of pod setting, when used as male parent.Percentage of pod setting ranged from 0.00 percent (UP As 120, PA 134 and JCPL-84023, when crosses with *C. platy carpus* and *C. vallubilis*) to 8.69 percent (UPAS –120 x *C. cajanifalius*) However, in the present study the crosses were not successful, when C. cajanifalus was used as female parent (Table 1). Successful crosses between *C. cajan* and *C. cajanifalius* have also been reported by Reddy *et al.* (1981), Pundir and Singh (1985) and Pragya *et al.* (1997).

The crosses UPAS-120 x *C. sericeus*, PA-134x *C. sericens* and ICPL-84023x *C. sericeus* resulted in 2.83, 2.14 and 1.88 percent pod setting respectively. There was massive flower shedding in pollinated buds with *C. sericeus* which resulted in poor pod setting. The reason for one way Compatibility in such crosses might be due to exudation composition of stigma of the wild parent which reacted with the substances from the pollen of cultivated types and ultimately resulted in the failure of stimulation of pollen tube growth or crossing barriers at zygotic or post- zygotic levels might be true when wild species were taken as female parents.

The crossability between *C. cajan* x *C. scarabaeoides* ranged from 3.75 percent (UPAS-120x *C. scarabaeoides*) to 6.82 percent (ICPL-84023x *C. scarabaeoides*). Successful crosses *C. sericeus* and *C. scarabaeoides* with *C. cajan* have also been reported by Pundir and Singh (1983), and Pragya *et al.* (1997). Crosses with *C. acutifalius* showed poorest pod set, which ranged from 1.67% (PA-134x *C. acutifolius*) to 2.79 % (UPAS –120x *C. acutifolius*) UPAS –120, PA –134 and ICPL 84023 were crossesed with *C. platycarpus* and *C Volubilis*. In case of UPAS–120x *C. platycarpus*, 1000 pollinations were attempted likewise more than 5000 pollinations were done in all the three lines using as male, but failed to get any crossed pod in these two type of crosses. Present findings are conformity with the results of Pundir and Singh (1985) who observed that *C. platycarpus* could not be crossed with any genotypes of *C. cajan*. Contrary to present findings, a sucessful cross between A. platycarpa x *C. cajan* was reported by Ariyanayagam and Spence (1978) but the results were subsequently identified as selfs.

Alien genes express their full,which may lead to the production of desirable segregants. It is hoped that elite population may be obtained through interspcific hybridization which would be helpful in breaking the yield plateau in cultivated *C. cajan* varieties. Thus, close affinity between these wild and cultivated species can be very well utilized in breeding superior strains of pigeonpea by incorporating some of the useful characters such as resistance to phytophthora blight disease, pod borer pest and drought tolerance and high protein content in cultivated types.

REFERENCES

1. Ariyanayagam, R.P. and Spence, J. A. (1978). A. possible gene source for early day length neutral pigeonpea. *Euphytica*. 27: 505 –509.
2. Deodikar, G.B. and Thakar, G.V. (1956).
3. Pragya, Rajni Raina and Singh, R.M. (1997). Distant hybridization in pigeonpea: crossability and variability. *Madras Agric. J.* 84 (5): 278–280.
4. Pundir, R.P.S. and Singh, R.B. (1983). Cross compatibility among Cajjanus, Atylasia and Rhynchosia species. *International Pigeonpea Newsletter*. 2:12–14.
5. Pundir, R.P.S. and singh,, R.B. (1985). Crossability relationship among Cajanus, Atylosia and Rhynchosia species and detection of crossing barriers. *Euphytica*. 34: 303–308.
6. Reddy, L.J. (1981). Pachtene analyses in *Cajanus cajan, Atylosia lineata* and their hybrids. *Cytologia*. 46: 397 –412
7. Remanandan, P. (1981). The wild genepool of cajanus at ICRISAT, present and Future In: Proceedings of the International workshop on pigeonpeas. 15-19 December, 1980, ICIRSAT, Hyderabad. Pp 29-38.
8. Venkataqramani, G. (2002). Policies need to be farmer frindly. The Hindu survey of Indian Agriculture. 5-7
8. Aman.

12

Efficacy of Biocontrol Agents and Chemical Fertilizers for Control of While Mould of French Bean

N. Tiameren Ao, K.N. Bhagabati**, A.K. Phookan**, B.C. Das** & M.C. Talukdar****

ABSTRACT

Amendment of fertilizers like urea, super phosphate and muriate of potash along with three fungal antagonists, *Aspergillus terreus*, *Gliocladium virens* and *Trichoderma koningii* against *Sclerotinia sclerotiorum* (Lib.) de Bary causing white mould of french bean (*Phaseolus vulgaris* L.) was studied under in vitro condition. Evaluation of the antagonists by dual-culture method revealed that *G.virens* caused maximum mycelial growth inhibition (63.33 %) followed by *T. koningii* (60.29 %) and *A. terreus* (50.00 %).

* Department of Plant Pathology, School of Agricultural Sciences and Rural Development, Nagaland University, Medziphema-797 106, Nagaland, India

** Department of Plant Pathology, Assam Agricultural University, Jorhat - 7985013, Assam, India

*** Department of Soil Science, Assam Agricultural University, Jorhat - 7985013, Assam, India.

Microscopic examination showed coiling around the hyphae, disintegration and coagulation of the hyphal cell wall of *S.sclerotiorum*. Maximum sclerotial inhibition of *S.sclerotiorum vis-à-vis* total number of sclerotia, fresh weight and dry weight occurred when *G. virens* was inoculated in maize-meal sand media (MSM) with NPK @ 14.54 mg urea, 27.90 mg super phosphate and 3.73 mg muriate of potash i.e., @ 60:40:20 NPK kg/ha.

White mould caused by *Sclerotinia sclerotiorum* (Lib.) de Bary is a major constraint of French bean cultivation. The pathogen being polyphagous and soil borne, control through fungicides and host resistance id difficult. Although a few chemical are known to give effective control against the disease (Hunter *et al.*, 1978; Kerr *et al.*, 1992), they are costly besides posing a risk of environmental hazards. It is now recognized that manipulation of existing soil microflora to the disadvantage of the pathogen or by addition of non-resident antagonists offers an excellent alternative in combating the ravages of soil borne diseases. Further, the influence of fungi antagonistic to soil borne plant pathogens following fertilizer application is widely known (Papavizas, 1985; Dinakaran and Marimuthu, 1998). In the present investigation, the efficacy of *Aspergillus terreus*, *Gliocladium virens* and *Trichoderma koningii* along with NPK fertilizers was tested against *Sclerotinia sclerotiorum*.

Materials and Methods

S. sclerotiorum, the causal organism of white mould of French bean, was isolated from diseased tissues of infected plants in the field and further purified and maintained in PDA at 28 ± 1° C. Cultures of *T. koningii* was obtained from the culture collection of the Department of Plant Pathology, Assam Agricultural University, Jorhat while *A. terreus* and *G. virens* cultures were collected from the Institute of Microbial Technology, Chandigarh. Interactions between the antagonists and the pathogens were studied in dual agar culture. Erlenmeyer's flasks of 500 ml capacity containing molten PDA were amended with 7.27 mg urea (NH_2CONH_2), 27.90 mg SSP [$Ca(H_2PO_4)_2$] and 3.73 mg MOP (KCl) per 250 ml of PDA media, i.e., NPK @ 30:40:20 kg/ha. The medium was then thoroughly swirled to ensure uniform distribution before dispensing into petridishes (9.5 cm diam.). *S.sclerotiorum* and the antagonistic fungi were grown separately in petridishes containing PDA for 72 hrs. Two mycelial discs (5 mm diam.) near the periphery. In the centre of each petri dish a disc of *S.sclerotiorum* was placed. Petri dishes inoculated with *S.sclerotiorum* alone served as control. Five replications were kept for each treatment and observation on radial growth of *S. sclerotiorum* was recorded at 24 hr interval. To observe the mode of parasitism, the antagonistic fungi were grown separately with S. *sclerotiorum* in petri dishes containing one per cent water agar and incubated at 28 ± 1° C for 48 hrs.

To test the antagonistic effect of *A.terreus, G.virens,* and *T. koningii* on *S. sclerotiorum,* maize-meal sand media (MSM) prepared by mixing 40 g of maize meal to 960 g clean sand was amended with NPK in Erlenmeyer's flasks containing 250 g of MSM. Following the basal recommendation of 30:40:20 NPK kg/ha, i.e., 7.27 mg urea (NH_2CONH_2), 27.90 mg SSP [Ca $(H_2PO_4)_2$] and 3.73 mg MOP (KCl) per 250 g MSM, zero dose, recommended dose ($N_1P_1K_1$), double the dose of N ($N_2P_1K_1$),, double the dose of P ($N_1P_2K_1$), and double the dose of K ($N_1P_1K_2$), were amended. The flasks were inoculated with three mycelial discs of 5 mm diam. Each of the antagonists and *S. sclerotiorum* from 3 day-old cultures. Treatment inoculated with *S.sclerotiorum* alone served as control. The flasks were incubated at 28 ± 1° C for 30 days. Observations were made on the number of sclerotia produced in each flask and their fresh and dry weights were recorded.

Results and Discussion

In dual culture, *A. terreus, G. virens,* and *T. koningii* showed significant reduction on radial growth of *S. sclerotiorum. G.virens* at 63.33 % was observed to be more aggressive and hence superior to *T. koningii* at 60.29% and *A. terreus* at 50.00% as evidenced by the higher percent inhibition at 72 hr of incubation (Table 1). The per cent inhibition of S. *sclerotiorum* with *G.virens* and *T. koningii* were however, statistically *at par*. Microscopic examination revealed intense coiling around the hyphae of *S. sclerotiorum* by the hyphae of *T. koningii* and *A. terreus* while coagulation and disintegration of the host hyphal cell wall in presence of *G.virens*. The mycoparasitic behaviours followed almost the same patterns as has been reported on *R.solani* by *G. virens* (Aluko and Hering, 1970), on *S. sclerotiorum* by *T. koningii* (Trutmann and Keane, 1990) and *R. solani* by *A. terreus* (Das, 1992). However, in the present investigation characteristic envelopment and coiling around of the host hyphae by *G.virens* was not observed, although their hyphae grew in close proximity to the hyphae of *S.sclerotiorum* before coagulation and disintegration occurred. Henis *et al.*, (1983) observed *T. harzianum* to secrete large amounts of chitinase and â – (1,3)- glucanase while Claydon et al., (1987) reported the production of a pyrone compound, 6-n-pentyl-2H-pyron-2-one by *T. harzianum* which has antibiotic properties. Production of an array of toxic metabolites, antifungal antibiotics, volatile gases and various cell wall degrading enzymes by *Trichoderma* spp., *Aspergillus* spp. and *Gliocladium* spp. that are lytic and detrimental to a number of fungi have also been reported (Aluko and Hering, 1970; Rai and Dhawan, 1978; Papavizas, 1985; Simon *et al.*, 1988; Das, 1992). The high inhibitory activity of the antagonists observed in dual cultures and the frequency of mycoparasitic activities and antibiosis by the antagonists against *S.sclerotiorum* in the present investigation is probably due to the production of these toxic metabolites, antibiotics, volatile gases and cell wall degrading enzymes.

Sclerotial development of *S. sclerotiorum* was significantly arrested with amendment of different doses of NPK in the presence of the antagonists. Maximum sclerotial inhibition was observed when *G.virens* was inoculated in MSM with $N_2P_1K_1$ followed by *G.virens* with $N_1P_2K_1$ and *T. koningii* with $N_2P_1K_1$ respectively (Table 2). The inhibitory effect on sclerotial development was represented by decrease in the number of sclerotia as well as their fresh and dry weights. However, the inhibition among the antagonists and different doses of NPK in respect to the number of sclerotia and their fresh and dry weights were statistically *at par* while interaction between the antagonists and NPK were found to be non-significant. Parasitism and antibiosis were probably the major means by which the fungal antagonists attacked the test fungus and inhibited its sclerotial growth. Increase in population level of soil saprophytes leading to increased antibiosis and competition following fertilizer application have been reported by Kaufman and Willams, (1965), and Papavizas (1985). Krishnamoorthy and Bhaskaran (1993) noticed a significant increase in population of *T.viride* in soil following application of nitrogen and phosphate fertilizers. Similarly, Jayaraj and Ramabadran (1998) reported the enhanced activity of *T. harzianum* in soil due to fertilization with nitrogenous fertilizers. These reports corroborate the present finding, which suggests that NPK have definite influence on the activities of antagonists. *A. terreus, G. virens*, and *T. koningii* appeared to have the ability to readily utilize urea, phosphorus and potash for their energy requirements for growth and proliferation which in turn might have lead to increased antibiosis and competitive saprophytic ability. The substrate MSM probably might have also served as a good food base for the antagonists to grow and proliferate following the application of energy sources.

REFERENCES

Aluko, M.O. and Hering, T.F. (1970). The mechanisms associated with the antagonistic relationship between *Corticium solani and Gliocladium virens*. *Trans. Br. Mycol. Soc.* 55: 173-179.

Claydon, N., Allan, M., Hanson, J.R. and Avent, A.G. (1987). Antifungal alkyl pyrones of *Trichoderma harzianum*. *Trans.Br. mycol.Soc.* 88: 503-513.

Das, B.C. (1992). Antagonism of *Aspergillus terreus* on *Rhizoctonia solani* and its effect on the incidence of sheath blight of rice. Ph.D. Thesis, Assam Agricultural University, Jorhat.

Dinakaran, D. and Marimuthu, T. (1998). Effect of inorganic fertilizers on growth of *Trichoderma viride*. *Plant Dis. Res.* 13: 212-214.

Henis, Y., Adams, P.B.,Lewis,J.A. and Papavizas, G.C. (1983). Penetration of sclerotia of *Sclerotium rolfsii* by *Trichoderma* spp. *Phytopathology* 73: 1043-1046.

Hunter, J.E., Abawi, G.S. and Crosier, D.C. (1978). Effects of timing, coverage and spray oil on control of white mold of snap bean with benomyl. *Plant Dis. Reptr.* 62 : 633-637.

Jayaraj, J. and Ramabadran, R. (1998). Effect of nitrogenous fertilizers on the survival and competitive saprophytic ability of *Trichoderma harzianum* in soil. *J. Mycol. Plant Pathol.* 28: 21-23.

Kaufman, D.D. and Williams, L.E. (1965). Influence of soil reaction and mineral fertilization on number and types of fungi antagonistic to four soil borne plant pathogens. *Phytopathology* 55 : 570-574.

Kerr, E.D., Smith, J.A., Yonis, C.D. and Wilson, R.G. (1992). Fungicide efficacy for bean white mold under different plant population and row spacings. *Ann.Rep. Bean Improv. Coop.*, Fort Collins, Colo. Howard F. Schwartz, Colorado State University (35) pp.52-53.

Krishnamoorthy, A.S. and Bhaskaran, R. (1993). Effect of chemical fertilizers and the antagonist *Trichoderma viride* in the control of damping-off disease of tomato caused by *Pythium indicum*. In : Crop Disease-Innovative Techniques and Management, pp. 205-210, K. Sivapraskasam and K. Seetharaman (eds.) Kalyani Publishers, New Delhi.

Papavizas, G.C. (1985). *Trichoderma* and *Gliocladium*: Biology, Ecology and potential for biocontrol. *An. Rev. Phytopathol.* 23 : 328-330.

Rai, J.N. and Dhawan, S. (1978). Lysis of sclerotia of *Sclerotinia sclerotiorum* and its possible relation with chitinase activity. *Indian J. Mycol. Plant Pathol.* 8 : 103-107.

Simon, A., Dunlop, R.W., Ghisalberti, E.L. and Sivasithamparam, K. (1988). Trichoderma koningii produces a pyrone compound with antibiotic properties. *Soil Biol. Biochem.* 20 : 263-264.

Trutmann, P. and Keane, P.J. (1990). *Trichoderma koningii* as a biological control agent for *Sclerotinia sclerotiorum* in Southern Australia. *Soil Biol. Biochem.* 22 (1) : 43-50.

Table 1. Effect of antagonists on radial growth of *S. sclerotiorum* in dual culture amended with NPK, bioassayed in PDA at 28 ± 1° C for 72 hour of incubation

Treatments	*Radial growth (mm*)*	*Inhibition %*
SS + TK + NPK	35.74 c	60.29 (7.82) a
SS + TK + NPK	45.30 b	50.00 (7.11) b
SS + TK + NPK	33.00 c	63.33 (7.94) a
Control	90.00 a	-
SED±	1.93	0.15
CD 0.05	4.10	0.32

SS, *Sclerotinia sclerotiorum*; TK, *Trichoderma koningii*; AT, *Aspergillus terreus*; GV, *Gliocladium virens*; NPK, Nitrogen, Phosphorus, Potash.

* Average of five replications

Any two mean values separated by DMRT at 5% level showing a common letter are not significantly different.

Figures in the parentheses represent square root transformed values.

Table 2. Effect of antagonists on sclerotial growth of *S.sclerotiorum* in MSM amended with NPK at 28 ± 1°C for 30 days of incubation

Treatments	*Total no. of sclerotia*	*Fresh wt. of sclerotia (g)*	*Dry wt. of sclerotia (g)*
SS (Control)	273.75 (16.57) [a]	10.72 (3.42) [a]	5.82 (2.38) [a]
SS + TK	30.50 (5.53) [bcd]	1.20 (1.43) [bc]	0.58 (1.26) [bcd]
SS + AT	41.00 (6.43) [b]	1.61 (1.61) [b]	0.81 (1.35) [b]
SS +GV	25.25 (5.06) [cde]	0.99 (1.41) [cd]	0.46 (1.21) [b-e]
SS + TK + $N_1P_1K_1$	21.75 (4.71) [c-f]	0.92 (1.38) [cde]	0.45 (1.20) [b-e]
SS + AT + $N_1P_1K_1$	30.25 (5.53) [bcd]	1.21 (1.48) [bc]	0.60 (1.26) [bcd]
SS +GV + $N_1P_1K_1$	18.50 (4.38) [d-g]	0.75 (1.32) [c-f]	0.35 (1.16) [b-e]
SS + TK + $N_2P_1K_1$	8.50 (3.06) [h]	0.33 (1.16) [fg]	0.15 (1.07) [de]
SS + AT + $N_2P_1K_1$	12.25 (3.56) [fgh]	0.49 (1.22) [efg]	0.24 (1.11) [cde]
SS +GV + $N_2P_1K_1$	7.00 (2.79) [h]	0.27 (1.13) [g]	0.11 (1.04) [e]
SS + TK + $N_1P_2K_1$	9.50 (3.17) [gh]	0.37 (1.17) [fg]	0.17 (1.08) [cde]
SS + AT + $N_1P_2K_1$	15.25 (3.95) [bc]	0.61 (1.27) [d-g]	0.30 (1.14) [cde]
SS +GV + $N_1P_2K_1$	7.75 (2.79) [h]	0.30 (1.14) [g]	0.10 (1.05) [c]
SS + TK + $N_1P_1K_2$	20.00 (4.50) [c-f]	0.79 (1.33) [c-f]	0.36 (1.16) [b-e]
SS + AT + $N_1P_1K_2$	32.00 (5.68) [bc]	1.23 (1.49) [bc]	0.64 (1.28) [bc]
SS +GV + $N_1P_1K_2$	15.25 (3.97) [e-h]	0.59 (1.26) [d-g]	0.46 (1.14) [cd]
SED±	0.61	0.09	0.10
CD 0.05	1.22	0.17	0.20

SS, *Sclerotinia sclerotiorum*; TK, *Trichoderma koningii*; AT, *Aspergillus terreus*; GV, *Gliocladium virens*; NPK, Nitrogen, Phosphorus, Potash; $N_1P_1K_1$ @ 30:40:20 NPK kg/ha; N2P1K1 @ 60:40:20 NPK kg/ha; $N_1P_2K_1$ @ 30:80:20 NPK kg/ha.; $N_1P_1K_2$ @ 30:40:40 NPK kg/ha.

Any two mean values separated by DMRT at 5% level showing a common letter are not significantly different.

Figures in the parentheses represent square root transformed values.

13

Water Management for Effective Crop Production in Northeastern Hilly Region

R.C. Nayak and Sewak Ram***

ABSTRACT

The North-Eastern Region is prone to a number of biophysical, institutional and socio-economical problems, resulting into subsistence agriculture with low input–low yield-low risk technology. The technology of the north-eastern region although primarily is agrarian, its full potential is yet to be exploited. Since agriculture and industry have not really taken off in spite of the potential in the form of unexploited resource base available in the region, the pressure of employment is experiencing more now on the service sectors. A land locked region with most of the area under hilly terrains, undulated slopes with high altitudes—all these topographic limitations bring about many constraints in the process of achieving effective crop production in the region. Irrigation, particularly free

* Department of Soil Conservation, Nagaland University, Campus: Medziphema, Nagaland.

** School of Agricultural Sciences and Rural Development, Medziphema - 797106, Nagaland.

flooding or surface method which is the primary and one of the most basic inputs required for any crop production finds it very difficult to be practiced owing to the topographic constraints. Advance irrigation methods such as drip, trickle and sprinkler (the micro-irrigation systems) could be advantageously employed to all hill crops grown in sloppy terrains. However, this advance technology, although favours a high return as well as a high water application efficiency finds in the first place an initially high investment perhaps beyond the socio-economic reach of the farmers in the reason. The paper discuses the various irrigation methods (surface, sub-surface, drip and sprinkler) with their advantages and limitations and prescribes the most suitable techniques / methods applicable to the northeastern region in general and Nagaland in particular.

Key word(s): Dependable rainfall, runoff, farm water management, water application efficiency, surface irrigation, sub-irrigation, check basin, drip/trickle irrigation, sprinkler irrigation, conjunctive use, irrigation scheduling,

1. Introduction

Water is the most important single requirement for the growth of plant. Crop can be raised successfully only if water is available in adequate quantity from either rainfall or surface flow (stream, spring, river, lake, ponds etc.,) or underground. Rainfall in the most parts of the state is confined to only four rainy months of South-west monsoon from June to September. During the remaining months, the water requirements have to be met either from groundwater or surface water resources. The need for applying irrigation water for raising crops during non-rainy periods or when rain failed was felt even in the distance past. Modern research has high lighted the importance of adequate soil moisture during the crucial stages of plant growth. Most irrigation projects in the country are designed for a dependability of 75 per cent, which means that in 25 years in a hundred, there is shortage of water and in 75 years there is some excess over the quantity planned for utilization of the project.

2. Water Resources for Irrigation

According to the National Commission on Agriculture, the

quantity of water utilized on agricultural use until 1973-74 was in the order of 92 per cent. Although the percentage of utilization for purposes other than irrigation was low, this is seen rising gradually with increasing in industrialization and power generation. By 2025 AD, the requirement of fresh water for non-irrigation uses is estimated at 27 percent of the available fresh water and only 73 per cent could be available for irrigation. These demands would increase further beyond that period.

Irrigation as at present practiced in the country is somewhat extravagant in the use of water. It takes on an average 0.65 ha-m of ground water to irrigate a crop of one hectare against 0.90 ha-m if the source is surface water including, of course, conveyance losses. The two together give an average 0.83 ha-m per cropped hectare. On many canal commands, however, the supply of water is inadequate and the crops do not receive the required amount of irrigation. Wherever possible water resources have first to be deployed to remove this deficiency. At the same time, in many irrigation systems the present mode of utilization of water is wasteful. On unlined canals in alluvial tracts, only about two-fifths of water released at the canal head is utilized by crops; the rest is lost in transit (conveyance) and in the field. Not all theses losses can be eliminated but obviously there is scope for saving water. For this, (i) lining of channels (ii) proper levelling or grading of fields (iii) adoption of most suitable mode of application of water to crops (iv) irrigation scheduling (v) proper drainage and above all (vi) conjunctive use of surface and groundwater are important steps. The area which can be irrigated with a given quantity of water also depends on the cropping pattern. It is envisaged that with more scientific and economical use of water in the future, the average water depth for irrigating cropped area will improve to about 0.70m.

3. Farm Water Management

Farm water management in general refers to the management of water resources available either at the head of the farm gate/ outlet from a surface water source or exploiting the groundwater resources or the both (conjunctive use) in the judicious manner so as to obtain optimum production/benefit from the crops under consideration. In order that the available water resources are always in the lower magnitude than the crop requirements, farm water management has always played a key role in successful crop production technology. The criteria that play significantly on the process of a successful farm water management system are:

(i) Lining of channels
(ii) Proper levelling or grading of fields
(iii) Adoption of most suitable mode of application of water to crops
(iv) Irrigation scheduling
(v) Proper drainage and above all
(vi) Conjunctive use of surface and ground water

3.1 *Lining of Canal*

Irrigation water that comes from the reservoir/ponds to the cropped field is conveyed through a net work of canal systems. Canals are generally constructed from soils available in their vicinity. If the soil available for construction of canals is sandy or sandy loam in nature which has got high infiltration/ percolation rate as compared to soils of clay or clay loam type, significant quantity of irrigation water is lost due to conveyance in the canal system. It is estimated that about 30-40 per cent of water released at the canal head is simply lost due to conveyance in canals before reaching in the cropped field. Considering one hectare of land located in a medium/minor irrigation project, the loss of water amounts to range from Rs 30,000 to Rs 40,000. In addition to this, such unlined canals bring about waterlogging situations in the both sides of the canal banks, resulting poor yield of the crops as well as reduction of soil fertility in the region. Of course, if the soils have low permeability and are compacted well in the embankments, canal lining can be omitted but then the problem of seepage remains. Where irrigation water is silt laden, deposition on the canal bed rapidly reduces seepage from an initial high value, but still seepage loss continues and imposes a load on the drainage system.

3.2 *Land Levelling or Grading*

Land grading is essential to irrigation to permit efficient application and more uniform distribution of water, improve drainage and saving of water, labour and other expenses. Land grading is much essential for drainage. Unleveled land causes poor stands in low and high areas, excess water in low areas and inadequate water and crop stress on high areas. This results in over-irrigation of the field, causing waterlogging and possibly salinity problems. For example, if a crop requires 70 mm of irrigation water in a particular water application, a 30 mm high spot may require 40 percent additional water to be applied to the whole field to cover the high spot. As land grading is a costly operation, it should be very carefully planned and executed.

Development of a uniform grade in the direction of irrigation and the removal of slopes at right angle to it should be the aim of a high quality levelling job. Safe limits of longitudinal slope for boarder strip irrigation based on the soil types are presented in Table-1.

Table 1. Recommended Safe Limits of Land Slope for Efficient Irrigation

Type of soil	*Longitudinal slope %*
(i) Heavy (clay)	0.05 to 0.25
(ii) Medium (loamy)	0.20 to 0.40
(iii) Light (sandy)	0.25 to 0.65

To reduce the depth of cut, the bunds should be placed closer for land with steeper slopes. The elevation difference in the width of one strip of land (crosswise between the bund) for border strip irrigation should not be more than 3m. For ridge and furrow irrigation, the cross slope can be steeper but not greater than 2 percent. For basin irrigation, the land must be flat. The other considerations that affect land grading operations are: (i) soil type, (ii) method of irrigation, (iii) climate characteristics, (iv) crops to be grown, and (v) preference of the farmer.

3.3 *Irrigation Method*

3.3.1. Surface Irrigation

Efficient utilisation of irrigation water involves several practices like conveying water from the source to the field with minimum losses, following the right method of irrigation consistence with topography, applying water to the crop at the right time and in proper quantities. As the oldest and most common method of applying water to crop land surface irrigation has evolved into an extensive array. It generally includes the followings.

(i) Wild flooding
(ii) Border irrigation
(iii) Check basin irrigation
(iv) Furrow irrigation

Wild or uncontrolled flooding is the application of water into the field without any bunds to guide the flow. Land is also not leveled. This method is applied when unlimited water supply is available. Pasture lands are sometimes irrigated by this method. Though this method will involve minimum cost in terms of labour and land preparation, the efficiency of water application is low.

Border irrigation is the method of surface flooding wherein the water is applied to the field divided into strips separate by parallel ridges. The width of the border usually varies from 3 to 15 m. Each border is leveled transversely (perpendicular to the direction of flow), but has a natural slope in the longitudinal (flow) direction so that water turned at the upper end of the each strip moves down the slope in the form of a thin sheet. The length of the border varies on the type of soils. Recommended length and slope of border strips are presented in Table-2.

Table-2. Recommended length and slope of border strips

Type of soil	*Basic infiltration rate, mm/h*	*Length, m*	*Slope %*
(i) Sandy and sandy loam soil	12 to 25	60 to 120	0.25 to 0.60
(ii) Medium soil	7 to 12	100 to 180	0.20 to 0.40
(iii) Clay to clay loam soil	Less than 7	150 to 300	0.05 to 0.20

Border method of irrigation is most suitable for close growing crops like wheat, barley and groundnut. There are three types of borders commonly found in practice. They are: (i) Graded border i.e., border with slopes (0.1 to 0.5 %), (ii) Level border i.e., border with no slope, and (iii) contour border i.e., borders with varying widths laid on contours with slopes greater than 2 to 3 percent, particularly suitable to hilly terrains.

Check basin irrigation has been historically the irrigation of small areas having flat level surface and enclosed by dikes to prevent runoff. Water is added to the basin through a gap in the perimeter dike. It is important to cover the basin quickly and shut off when the correct volume has been supplied. Generally, this method is favoured by moderate to slow intake soils, deep rooted and closely spaced crops.

The size of basins in rice fields varies with the size of the irrigation stream available and the size of the land holding. Large irrigation streams and large holdings permit large basins. The infiltration characteristics of the soil also influence the size of the basin. Size of basins will be small in the case of sandy and sandy loam soils with high infiltration rate whereas they will be large in the case of clay soils having low infiltration rates.

In irrigating orchards, square or contour basins may be used as in other crops. When the plants are spaced widely, the ring method of irrigation may be adopted. The rings are circular basins formed around each tree.

Adaptability

(i) Suited to gentle and uniform land slope

(ii) Suitable for row and close growing crops

(iii) Suitable grain and fodder crops in heavy soils where water is absorbed very slowly and is required to stand for relatively long time to ensure adequate irrigation.

(iv) Suitable in very permeable soils which must be covered with water rapidly to prevent excessive deep percolation at the upstream end.

(v) Useful when leaching is required to remove salts from the soil profile.

(vi) It enables the conservation of rainfall and reduction in soil erosion.

Limitations

(a) Ridges interfere with the movement of agricultural implements.

(b) Considerable land is occupied by ridges (bunds) and laterals and hence less yield for unit of land.

(c) Precise land grading and shaping are required.

(d) Labour requirement is more.

(e) Not suitable for the crops which are sensitive to wet soil condition around the stems of plants.

3.3.2. Furrow irrigation

The furrow method of irrigation consists in making the land into ridges and furrows and irrigating the area through the furrows. This method is used to irrigate row crops e.g. sugarcane, cotton, tobacco, potato, vegetables, maize, sorghum etc. Water infiltrates into the soil and spreads laterally to irrigate the areas between the furrows. Furrow irrigation method is the most suitable method if the crops are sensitive to the ponded surface water. The different types of furrows namely are: (i) graded or level furrow, (ii) contour furrow in hilly areas, and (iii) corrugated form of furrow irrigation system in uneven highlands or in steep terrains.

3.3.3. Sub-Irrigation

In this type of irrigation, water is applied below the ground surface by maintaining an artificial water table at some depth depending upon the soil texture and the depth of the plant roots. Water reaches the plant roots through capillary action. Water may be introduced through open ditches or underground pipelines such as tile drains or mole drains. The depth of open ditches or trenches varies from 30 to 100 cm and they are spaced about 15 to 30 m apart. The water application system consists of field supply channels, ditches or trenches suitably spaced to cover the field adequately and drainage ditches for disposal of excess water.

The sub-irrigation method requires special site conditions, as it is necessary to have complete control of the water table through controlled water application and drainage. This method is suited to soil having reasonably uniform texture and permeable enough for water to move both vertically and horizontally within and for some distance below the root zone of crop. Topography must be smooth and nearly level or have very gentle and uniform slope.

3.3.4 Sprinkler Irrigation

The method of applying water above the ground surface somewhat resembling rainfall is known as sprinkler irrigation. The principle of sprinkler irrigation is to provide the right quantity of water (irrigation) at the right time for obtaining optimum crop yield or in other words to maintain the correct soil moisture regime during the crop period. The sprinkler method of irrigation can advantageously be used under one or more of the following circumstances.

a) Land is very uneven and it is uneconomical for leveling (tea growing areas).
b) Soils are too porous, highly erodible or relatively impermeable so that it is difficult to irrigate them by other methods.
c) Stream size or rate of flow available is too inadequate to distribute water efficiently by other surface methods.
d) Frequent light applications are needed

Advantages

- ✓ Costly investment on land development operations such as levelling, bunding etc are totally dispensed with.
- ✓ Teamed with good soil management, it provides the essential soil moisture control required for optimum crop yields.
- ✓ It permits wide range of soil to come under irrigation because of its flexibility to control water application.
- ✓ It helps to conserve both soil and water.
- ✓ It retards the formation of soils either acidic or alkaline
- ✓ It helps the ready absorption of fertilizer.

Limitations

- ➢ High wind distorts and prevents even distribution of water.
- ➢ Ripening soft fruit must be protected from the spray.
- ➢ Evaporation losses when operating under high temperatures become important when the irrigation water has larger amounts of dissolved salts.
- ➢ A stable water supply is needed for the most economical use of the equipment.
- ➢ The water must be clean and free of sand, debris and large amount of dissolved salts.
- ➢ Initial investment and operating costs are much higher when compared to surface irrigation methods.

3.3.5 Drip irrigation

Drip irrigation (also referred to as trickle irrigation) is a method that makes small, measured amounts of water available to the root areas of trees, vines or plants at regular intervals in optimum quantities. Released drop by drop from properly spaced emitters, the water enters the soil with ease and moves by capillary beneath the surface to wet the root zone area.

Advantages

The drip irrigation system has the following advantages:

- ❑ Saves time: The drip irrigation system takes care of the time-consuming operation of irrigation and orchard/ plantation. Hence, labour can be shifted to other, equally productive tasks.
- ❑ Saves water and fertilizer: By directing water straight to plant root zones in amounts matched to their needs, over watering and waste from runoff are minimized. If less water is used, less injected fertilizer is required.
- ❑ Leads to increase growth rates, greater yields: Under drip irrigation, optimum soil moisture can be maintained, thus reducing the stress on plants caused by too much or too little irrigation. With every plant receiving the same and balanced amount of water and nutrients, growth is more uniform and much faster.

- Reduces disease and leaf spotting : By watering the soil directly and not the foliage, the incidence of disease often associated with constant leaf wetting from overhead irrigation, is minimized and leaf spotting caused by evaporated salts is eliminated.
- Saves energy: The drip irrigation system brings down pumping/energy costs to as low as 30-40 percent of other systems viz. Sprinkler of flood methods. This is because of its comparatively low discharge at low pressures.
- Ease cultivation and discourages weeds: Since emitters place the water where it is needed, weed growth in the un-irrigated interspaces is minimized so that inter-spaces remain firm and dry, facilitating cultivation, crop-picking and other operations.
- Has high salt tolerance : Experiments worldwide as well as in India have shown that drip irrigation with saline water can be successful since, with optimum soil moisture being maintained, salts are leached outward of the drip wetted bulb, towards its periphery.
- Works on gravity, wind or solar systems: Another advantage of the low flow, low pressure demands of drip system in remote areas, where power is at a premium—a storage tank with a 3 to 4 m head is all that is required and the low rate of flow is ideally suited to output of windmills or solar stills.

3.4 Irrigation Scheduling

Farm irrigation scheduling can be accomplished successfully by a variety of different techniques. Several techniques for determining the timing and amounts of irrigation have been used in the country. Among these are:

(i) Soil moisture budgets based on climatic data, soils, etc.

(ii) Resistance blocks, tensiometers and other moisture sensors. These are placed at various levels in the soil profile and at several strategic stations. Moisture is kept above a given threshold level.

(iii) Determination of irrigation timing and amounts by feel and visual methods.

(iv) Combination of soil moisture budgeting from climate, crop and soil data and monitoring of soil moisture gravimetrically or otherwise.

(v) Stage of growth applications: Water applied at various critical growth stages with depleted moisture applied at each irrigation.

(vi) Irrigation according to fixed intervals as would occur in some irrigation projects.

Knowledge of soil, crop, climate and system parameters which have been presented can be integrated into useful relationships for irrigation scheduling. Irrigation intervals, net application and gross application depths, volume of water required for irrigation and irrigation duration verses flow rate are some of the essential parameters which can be derived.

3.5 Drainage

Presence of excess water either on the surface of the soil or in the root zone beneath the surface of the soil demands its removal by properly designed and built surface drainage system or subsurface drainage system through natural or artificial channels, technically called drains, which are either open or closed.

Benefits of drainage

- Adequate drainage improves soil structure and increases the productivity of soils.
- It totally prevents waterlogging of the lands.
- Waterlogged saline and alkaline lands can be reclaimed.
- Proper drainage lowers the water table in an area and thereby (a) provides more available plant food by increasing depth of root zone of the soil (b) increases soil aeration (c) favours growth of soil bacteria and (d) assures high soil temperature.
- Prevents the accumulation of excess soluble salts on the surface of irrigated land and in the root zone of the soil, by leaching.
- Flooding and consequent loss of seeds and fertilizes are eliminated and flood menace is minimized.

- ➢ Brings under cultivation ponds and marshy lands by reclamation.
- ➢ Adequate drainage leads to early ploughing and planting.
- ➢ Improves salinity conditions and helps malaria control.

3.6 *Conjunctive Use*

Simultaneous or alternative use of surface and ground water resources for purpose of irrigation is referred to as *conjunctive use*. As for the farmers, such of those who invest in wells for the utilisation of ground water have recognised their importance either as an independent or as a supplemental source of irrigation worth investing, in order that they can maximize benefits through investments. The relative importance of various modes – surface water (canal and tanks) and groundwater (dug well and tube wells) depends upon the physiography, geology and climate of the region. However, it is necessary to make use of scarce resources in the best possible manner, economically and efficiently, wherever and in whatever form they are available. That is primarily the objective of conjunctive use of one or the other form of water either simultaneously or alternatively according to its availability, to facilitate growing of irrigated crops.

Advantages of conjunctive use

- ✓ It meets the water requirement of the crops.
- ✓ It controls the waterlogging and salinisation.
- ✓ It controls the problems of salinity ingress in coastal areas.
- ✓ It controls over-pumping of ground water reservoir.
- ✓ It can use saline water mixed with fresh water for irrigation.
- ✓ It helps in augmentation of water resources.
- ✓ It increases the intensity of land use.

3.7 *Conclusion*

Since most of the land surfaces excepting some plain river valley areas of Assam state are hilly and undulated topography in nature, introduction of any kind of surface irrigation method for raising crops would prove unscientific and worrisome as much of the fertile surface soil would be lost in the runoff irrigation. As the unscientific 'jhum' cultivation has already taken a heavy toll of the soil resources of the region, introduction of any further surface irrigation method would strongly defend the 'jhum' practice. Taking into account these aspects, it is recommended not to introduce such practices of irrigation as to stand in the way of further soil degradation in the area, particularly at farm levels. Sprinkler irrigation and drip/trickle irrigation are found to be the appropriate method of application of water to the crops in the region. Excepting in rice growing areas (on relatively flat slopes, valley bottoms and level bench terraces in the hills) where these methods are not economic, these new methods may be practiced anywhere irrespective of the kind of the crops grown. As pointed out earlier, the initial investment for installation of the machineries in the farm is high, Govt and NGOs and the line Departments/Agencies should come up to lend their hands, particularly extending some kind subsidies/rebates to the interested farmers/beneficiaries, for procurement and installation of the instruments.

14

Variability and Character Association in Various Rice Ecotypes

Chaturvedi, H.P.* and D.M. Maurya**

ABSTRACT

Analysis of variance revealed significant variation among genotypes in respect of all the characters under study except emergence of radicle and plumule. Twenty-six genotypes of rice belonging to seven ecotypic situations were evaluated for variability and character association. Wide range of variation was recorded for all the traits. The highest PCV and GCV were recorded for test weight, days to 50% flowering and dormancy indicating the presence of ample variation for these traits in the present material. High estimates of heritability and genetic advance were obtained for days to 50% flowering, tillers number at 60th day, dormancy, seedling length at 20th day, shoot length at 20th day and number of leaves at 20th day. Correlation and path coefficient analysis revealed that number of leaves at 20th day, length of seed, root length at 20th day and breadth of seed exerted positive direct effect and exhibited significant positive

* Department of Genetics & Plant Breeding, NDUAT, Kumarganj, Faizabad, U.P.

** Department of Genetics & Plant Breeding, NU-SASRD, Medziphema-797106.

correlation with test weight indicating a true relationship among the traits.

The plant breeder's success in devising suitable and effective breeding program for incorporating useful gene(s) in a single genotype depends to a large extent on nature and magnitude of genetic variability existing in a given species. Greater the variability in the initial material better would be the chances of evolving desirable type (Vavilov, 1951). The characters of economic importance are generally quantitative in nature and exhibit a considerable degree of interaction with the environment. Therefore it becomes necessary to compute variability present in the population. To utilize various quantitative traits in breeding program, inter-relationship between the characters are of immense value (Lerner, 1958). Therefore, through the present investigation an attempt has been made to study the correlation and path coefficient analysis, which are helpful in selecting the desirable traits.

Materials & Methods

Twenty-six genotypes of rice belonging to seven different ecological conditions formed the experimental materials. Those are Upland rice(Bagari, Mutmuri, Ranikajal, Sathi), Lowland rice(T-26, T-100, T-22A, Cross-116), Deep water rice (Jalmagan, Tundia, Sainger, Kariawa), Flooded rice (Chakiya-59, Madhukar, FRG-10, Bellar), Scented rice (Kalanamak, Tilakchandan, Badshahpadsand, Bhantaphool), Saline- Alkaline Resistant (SRA-41, Dosal, Pokali, CSR-3), Boro-Paddy (Borogazipur, Boromirzapur). The experiment was conducted in pots as well as in field. The experimental material was grown in randomized complete block design following three replications at the Instructional Farm of Narendra Deva University of Agriculture & Technology, Kumarganj, Faizabad, U.P. All the recommended agronomic practices were followed for raising a good crop. The observations on 20 characters were recorded on 5 plants sampled randomly in each replication in the field.

Heritability (broad sense) was estimated according to Allard (1960). Phenotypic and genotypic coefficients of variation were estimated as per Burton (1951). Genetic advance as percent of mean was estimated according to Johnson et al. (1955). Genotypic and phenotypic correlation coefficients for all possible comparisons were computed as per formulae suggested by Miller et al. (1958). The partitioning of genotypic correlation coefficient of traits into direct and indirect effects was carried out using the procedure suggested by Dewey and Lu (1959).

Result and Discussion

Analysis of variance revealed significant variation among genotypes in respect of all the characters under study except emergence of radicle and plumule. The estimates of phenotypic coefficient of variation (PCV) were higher than those of genotypic coefficient of variation (GCV) for all the traits except emergence of radicle and plumule indicating environmental factors influencing the characters (Table-1). The results were in agreement of earlier reports of Singh et al. (1986) and Sundaram et al. (1988). The highest PCV and GCV were recorded for test weight, days to 50% flowering and dormancy indicating the presence of ample variation for these traits in the present material. Variation in test weight and days to 50% flowering offers great potential in selecting high yielding rice cultivars. Reliability of selection depends not only on heritability but it should also be accompanied by high genetic advance as well (Johnson et al. 1955).

In this study, high estimates of heritability and genetic advance were obtained for days to 50% flowering, tillers number at 60th day and dormancy, seedling length at 20th day, shoot length at 20th day and number of leaves at 20th day. Thus selection for these traits is likely to accumulate more additive genes leading to further improvement of their performance and these traits may be used as selection criteria in breeding programs. Chauhan et al. (1993) and Barbora & Hazarika (1998) reported similar observations for days to 50% flowering.

The genotypic and phenotypic correlation coefficients between different characters are presented in Table-2. In general, magnitude of genotypic correlations tended to be higher than phenotypic correlations. This suggested a strong genetic association between the traits and the phenotypic expression suppressed due to environmental influence. Enyi (1965) and Rangel et al. (1980) recorded similar observations. The present study also indicated that both genotypic and phenotypic correlations were in the same direction (except between root length at 20th day and seedling length at 20th day), suggesting less effect of environment in changing the association pattern among the character pairs.

Path coefficient analysis (Table-3) was done to resolve the direct and indirect effects of different characters on test weight at genotypic level. Awan and Cheema (1986) also reported similar work. The path analysis revealed that shoot length at 20th day had the highest positive direct effect on test weight (8.03) followed by number of tillers at maturity (1.71), lysine content (0.98), number of leaves at 20th day (0.60), days to 50% flowering (0.59), length of seed (0.47), root length at 20th day (0.44) and breadth of seed (0.37). No. of leaves at 20th day, length of seed, root length at 20th day and breadth of seed exerted positive direct effect and exhibited significant positive correlation with test weight indicating a true relationship among the traits. The residual effects estimated were low (-0.133) indicating that the traits under study are sufficient to account for variability.

This study suggests that direct selection for No. of leaves at 20th day, length of seed, root length at 20th day and breadth of seed would likely be effective in increasing test weight. The information gathered may be used in planning rice-breeding programs in Nagaland.

Acknowledgement

Financial assistance received from Narendra Deva University of Agriculture & Technology, Faizabad, U.P. in form of merit scholarship to first author is thankfully acknowledged.

REFERENCES

Allard, R.W. 1960. *Principles of Plant Breeding*. John Wiley and Sons Inc. New York.

Awan, M.A. and Cheema, A.A. 1986. Relationship among test weight, plant height and height components in rice. *Pakistan J. of Agril. Research* 7(1):17-20.

Barbora, T.K. and Hazarika, G.N. 1998. Study of genetic variability, heritability and genetic advances for panicle characters in rice. *Oryza* 35, 19-21.

Burton, G.W. 1951. Quantitative inheritance in pearl millet (Pennisetum glaucum). *Agron J* 43, 409-417.

Chauhan, J.S.; Chauhan, V.S. and Varir, M. 1993. Genetic variation and character association in rainfed upland rice. *Oryza* 30, 116-119.

Dewey, D.R. and Lu, K.H. 1959. Correlation and path coefficient analysis of components of crested wheat grass seed production. *Agron J* 51, 515-518.

Enyi, B.A.C. 1965. Relationship between root and panicle characters in rice. *Advancing Front. Sci.* 10, 25-30.

Johnson, H.W.; Robinson,H.G. and Comstock, R.E. 1955. Estimates of genetic and environmental variability in Soybean. *Agron J* 47, 314-318.

Lerner, I.M. (1958). The genotype in Mendelian populations. *Proc 9th Int Cong Genet* 124-128.

Miller, D.A.; Williams, J.C.; Robinson, H.F. and Comstock, K.B. 1958. Estimates of genotypic and environmental variances and co-variances in upland cotton and their implication in selection. *Agron J* 50, 126-131.

Rangel, P.H.N.; Galvao, J.D.; Silva, J.C. and Cardose, A.A. (1980). Phenotypic, genotypic and environmental correlation in rice. *Revista Ceres* 27, 180-195.

Singh, R.S.; Chauhan, S.P. and Maurya, D.M. 1986. Genetic variability in 98 upland rice cultivars of India. *Int Rice Res Newsl* 11, 9-10.

Sundaram, T.W. Manuel, W. and Palanisami, S. 1988. Genetic variability and correlation coefficient in early rice (Oryza sativa L.). *Indian J Agric Sci* 58, 629-630.

Vavilov, N.I. (1951). Origin, variation immunity and breeding of cultivated plants. *Chro. Bot.* 13, 364.

Table 1. Estimates of variance components and genetic parameters for different characters

S N	Characters	G	E	P	GCV	PCV	Hbs	GA% mean
1	Germination %age	9.54	1.21	10.75	3.41	3.62	88.74	6.53
2	Emergence of radicle	$9.92^{.04}$	0.00	$9.92^{.04}$	1.05	1.05	100	2.00
3	Emergence of plumule	0.18	0.00	0.18	10.16	10.16	100	20.33
4	Coleoptile length	0.93	1.29	2.22	9.84	15.22	41.89	12.54
5	Shoot length at 20th day	9.70	0.16	9.86	12.78	12.88	98.37	25.72
6	Root length at 20th day	0.83	0.12	0.95	9.13	9.77	87.36	17.26
7	No. of leaves at 20th day	0.31	0.03	0.34	12.59	13.15	91.17	24.16
8	Seedling length at 20th day	9.65	0.12	9.77	12.74	12.82	98.77	25.76
9	Tillers No. at 45th day	0.07	0.13	0.20	8.41	14.40	35.00	9.84
10	Days to 50% flowering	623.35	2.54	625.89	24.54	24.59	99.59	50.11
11	Tillers No. at 60th day	0.77	0.21	0.98	10.58	11.95	78.57	43.61
12	Length of reproductive phase	3.51	2.30	5.81	6.51	8.37	59.59	10.13
13	Tillers No. at maturity	1.18	0.55	1.73	10.00	12.13	68.20	16.83
14	Test weight	32.25	0.95	33.20	25.40	25.77	97.13	11.50
15	Length of seed	0.50	0.02	0.52	8.89	9.04	96.15	17.72
16	Breadth of seed	0.07	0.01	0.08	12.10	12.50	87.50	21.39
17	Dormancy	32.60	2.07	34.67	15.94	16.44	94.02	31.74
18	Protein content	0.20	0.02	0.22	6.29	6.60	90.90	11.61
19	Lysine content	$4.94^{.03}$	$6.00^{.03}$	0.01	2.15	3.24	49.40	3.05
20	Tryptophane content	$4.47^{.03}$	$7.91^{.03}$	0.01	5.31	9.01	44.7	7.19

Table 3. Direct and indirect effect of different characters on test weight at genotypic level

Characters	1	2	3	4	5	6	7	8	9	10	11	12	13	14	15	16	17	18	19
1	**0.47**	0.20	0.03	0.09	0.01	0.08	1.73	0.18	-1.79	0.01	-0.17	0.06	-0.02	0.15	-0.01	0.19	-0.52	0.03	0.69**
2	0.26	**0.37**	0.00	0.09	0.06	0.22	4.33	0.35	-4.64	0.00	0.34	-0.47	0.02	0.004	0.07	-0.19	-0.17	0.01	0.64**
3	0.08	0.00	**0.16**	0.03	0.01	0.10	0.89	0.08	-0.94	0.01	-0.16	-0.04	0.09	-0.21	0.14	0.18	-0.30	0.02	0.14
4	-0.17	-0.13	-0.02	**-0.26**	-0.01	-0.08	-0.20	-0.03	0.15	-0.02	-0.20	0.38	0.17	0.14	0.03	0.11	0.14	0.00	-0.01
5	0.05	0.19	0.007	0.03	**0.12**	0.09	2.95	0.14	-3.11	0.01	-0.35	0.07	0.09	-0.02	0.02	-0.17	0.32	-0.01	0.42*
6	0.08	0.19	0.04	0.05	0.02	**0.44**	3.80	0.32	-4.06	0.01	0.55	-0.57	-0.08	-0.10	0.02	-0.02	-0.19	0.01	0.49**
7	0.10	0.20	0.02	0.007	0.05	0.21	**8.03**	0.50	-8.68	-0.01	0.09	-0.04	0.02	0.03	0.07	-0.11	-0.14	0.01	0.34
8	0.14	0.21	0.02	0.01	0.03	0.23	6.70	**0.60**	-7.21	0.00	0.16	-0.14	-0.12	-0.04	0.05	-0.15	-0.08	0.01	0.43*
9	0.10	0.20	0.02	0.005	0.04	0.21	8.03	0.50	**-8.68**	-0.01	0.10	-0.04	0.02	0.03	0.07	-0.11	-0.14	0.01	0.34
10	-0.07	-0.03	0.03	0.06	0.02	0.07	-1.60	-0.02	1.75	**0.07**	-0.95	0.55	-0.26	-0.12	-0.08	0.09	0.28	-0.02	-0.23
11	0.04	-0.06	0.01	-0.03	0.02	-0.12	-0.37	-0.05	0.42	0.03	**-2.06**	1.64	0.16	0.16	0.03	0.14	-0.19	0.02	-0.19
12	0.02	-0.10	0.00	-0.06	0.005	-0.15	-0.20	-0.05	0.22	0.02	-1.98	**1.71**	0.18	0.12	0.03	0.16	-0.22	0.03	-0.28
13	-0.02	0.02	0.03	-0.07	0.02	-0.06	0.24	-0.13	-0.29	-0.03	-0.56	0.52	**0.59**	-0.33	0.20	0.09	-0.19	0.01	0.03
14	-0.07	0.00	0.03	0.04	0.003	0.05	-0.27	0.03	0.28	0.009	0.34	-0.20	0.20	**-0.98**	0.11	0.00	0.13	-0.01	-0.34
15	-0.02	0.08	0.07	-0.02	0.008	0.02	1.65	0.09	-1.79	-0.02	-0.17	0.14	0.37	-0.34	**0.32**	-0.02	-0.44	0.03	-0.03
16	-0.16	0.13	-0.06	0.05	0.04	0.02	1.56	0.16	-1.70	-0.01	0.54	-0.51	-0.90	-0.01	0.01	**-0.54**	0.50	-0.03	-0.11
17	-0.25	-0.07	-0.05	-0.04	0.04	-0.09	-1.17	-0.05	1.26	0.02	0.40	-0.39	-0.12	-0.13	-0.14	-0.28	**0.98**	-0.08	-0.13
18	-0.26	-0.08	-0.04	-0.02	0.03	-0.07	-1.47	-0.11	1.55	0.02	0.68	-0.80	-0.13	-0.17	-0.18	-0.29	1.24	**-0.06**	-0.15

Residual effect = -0.133

- and ** = Significant at P<0.05 and 0.01 levels, respectively
- Values in bold are direct effects

Table 2. Genotypic and phenotypic correlation coefficients between different characters

Characters	2	3	4	5	6	7	8	9	10	11	12	13	14	15	16	17	18	19	20
1G	0.69**	0.64**	0.14	-0.01	0.00	0.42*	0.49**	0.34	0.42*	0.34	-0.23	-0.19	-0.28	0.03	-0.34	-0.03	-0.11	-0.13	-0.15
P	0.60**	0.62**	0.14	-0.01	0.00	0.28	0.46*	0.34	0.41*	0.33	-0.13	-0.17	-0.23	0.03	-0.27	-0.03	-0.10	-0.09	-0.09
2	G	0.54**	0.17	-0.35	0.00	0.10	0.17	0.22	0.30	0.21	-0.14	0.08	0.03	-0.03	-0.15	-0.04	-0.35	-0.22	0.30
	P	0.52**	0.17	-0.35	0.00	0.07	0.16	0.21	0.27	0.20	-0.04	-0.08	0.02	-0.03	-0.13	-0.04	-0.33	-0.36	-0.35
3		G	-0.01	-0.35	0.00	0.53**	0.51**	0.54**	0.58**	0.54**	-0.08	-0.16	-0.27	0.04	-0.01	0.23	0.35	-0.18	-0.21
		P	-0.01	-0.34	0.00	0.35	0.45*	0.51**	0.53**	0.51**	-0.02	-0.15	-0.23	0.04	-0.02	0.21	0.33	-0.05	-0.07
4			G	-0.11	0.00	0.04	0.23	0.11	0.13	0.11	0.15	0.08	-0.02	0.16	0.21	0.43*	-0.34	-0.30	-0.26
			P	-0.11	0.00	-0.01	0.21	0.10	0.13	0.10	0.10	0.09	0.01	0.15	0.14	0.41*	-0.31	-0.21	-0.09
5				G	0.00	-0.11	-0.18	-0.03	-0.05	-0.02	-0.24	0.10	0.22	0.29	-0.14	0.07	-0.20	0.14	0.07
				P	0.00	-0.07	-0.17	-0.03	-0.05	-0.02	-0.14	-0.09	0.18	0.29	-0.11	0.08	-0.19	0.09	0.04
6					G	0.00	0.00	0.00	0.00	0.00	0.00	0.00	0.00	0.00	0.00	0.00	0.00	0.00	0.00
					P	0.00	0.00	0.00	0.00	0.00	0.00	0.00	0.00	0.00	0.00	0.00	0.00	0.00	0.00
7						G	0.19	0.37	0.23	0.36	0.14	0.17	0.04	0.15	0.02	0.07	0.31	0.33	0.24
						P	0.06	0.23	0.11	0.13	0.13	0.01	-0.02	0.09	-0.01	0.07	0.16	0.19	0.11
8							G	0.47*	0.53**	0.42*	0.15	-0.27	-0.33	-0.14	0.10	0.05	0.04	-0.20	-0.17
							P	0.43*	0.46**	0.43*	0.06	-0.24	-0.27	-0.13	0.08	0.04	0.04	-0.16	-0.11
9								G	0.83**	1.00**	-0.20	-0.05	-0.03	0.03	-0.03	0.21	0.19	-0.08	-0.18
								P	0.79**	0.99**	-0.12	-0.05	-0.03	-0.03	-0.02	0.20	0.18	-0.13	-0.12
10									G	0.83**	-0.03	-0.08	-0.08	-0.21	0.04	0.16	0.27	-0.08	-0.18
									P	0.79**	-0.03	-0.09	-0.09	-0.19	0.00	0.14	0.25	-0.04	-0.07
11										G	-0.20	-0.05	-0.03	0.03	-0.03	0.21	0.20	-0.15	-C.18
										P	-0.12	-0.05	-0.03	0.03	-0.01	0.20	0.18	-0.12	-0.11
12											G	0.46*	0.32	-0.44*	0.12	-0.25	-0.17	0.28	0.27
											P	0.27	0.11	-0.25	-0.02	-0.17	-0.04	0.19	0.12
13												G	0.96**	0.27	-0.17	0.08	-0.26	-0.19	-0.33
												P	0.85**	0.23	-0.05	0.05	-0.22	-0.15	-0.15
14													G	0.31	-0.12	0.08	-0.30	-0.23	-0.47*
													P	0.24	0.01	0.05	-0.28	-0.17	-0.20
15														G	0.33	0.62**	-0.16	-0.19	-0.22
														P	0.22	0.60**	-0.15	-0.13	-0.13
16															G	0.34	0.03	0.13	0.18
															P	0.24	0.02	0.07	0.10
17																G	0.04	-0.45*	-057**
																P	0.02	-0.30	-0.28
18																	G	0.51**	0.53*
																	P	0.46*	0.36
19																		G	0.87**
																		P	0.67**

*and ** = Significant at $P<0.05$ and 0.01 levels, respectively;

1. Test weight 2. Length of seed 3. Breadth of seed 4. Germination percentage 5. Emergence of plumule 6. Emergence of radicle 7. Coleoptile length 8. Root length at 20th day 9. Shoot length at 20th day 10. No. of leaves at 20th day 11. Length of seedlings at 20th day 12. No. of tillers at 45th day 13. No. of tillers at 60th day 14. No. of tillers at maturity 15. Days to 50% flowering 16. length of reproductive phase 17. Dormancy 18. Protein content 19. Lysine content 20 Tryptophane content.

15

Relevance of Indigenous Farming System in Solving Food Security Problem: A Case Study of Phek District

*A.K. Tripathi, K.K. Datta, D.K. Sonowal & A.K. Khan**

Agricultural production system in Nagaland is mostly rainfed, mono cropped and subsistence level; the tribal farmers adopt local methods to utilize their land and water resources in an optimum manner in order to meet the local demand and needs. The state is substantially rich in indigenous techniques and system developed by tribal farmers, using their ingenuity and skills.

Basically there practices are characterized by specific solving approach in farming situation with the available resources based of the farmers. Indigenous knowledge's and practices, which are based on peoples, accumulated experiences in dealing with ITK practices situation and problem in various aspects of life such as knowledge and practices are special to a particular culture.

ITK is a valuable national resources its system are dynamic never static and are continued influenced by internal creativity

* ICAR Research Complex for NEH Region, Umroi Road, Umiam, Barapani-793103, Meghalaya.

and experimentation. A growing number of case studies conducted in recent years shown that ITK system can play an important facilitating role in establishing a dialogue between rural populations and development workers. Recent studies of CGIAR system, recognize the active role of rural people in problem definition and in the search for their solution through local level experimentation and innovation, viewing the importance of ITK, in this paper efforts have been made to analyze the relevance of ITK in relation to agricultural production and also solving food security problem.

Indigenous Farming System

Zabo: an indigenous farming system practice in Phek district, which had tried to combine land and water in such a manner that it may take care of forest, agriculture and animal husbandry simultaneously. Figure 1.

Meaning: Zabo Farming practiced by Chakhesang farmers of Kikurama village; locally this system is called as "Ruza" or Ponds. The practiced of cultivation is called" Zabo" Means cultivation with impounding of water".

The main factor, which affects the success story, is mainly guided by the demand driven forces as its location is coming under rain shadow zone. Since the place is located on very high ridge and comes under rain shadow the drinking water both for human and domestic animals. Due to the constant pudding by animal like cow, buffalo, pig etc in the storage ponds the bed become compact and seepage proof. The harvesting water in the ponds was available round the year for drinking purposes and afterwards they started utilizing the stored water for irrigating the crops.

Site Characterization

Chakhesang tribe inhabits Kikurma village and farming is their main occupation. 1190 households inhabit the village with a total population of 6336 comprising 3136 male and 1130 female (Village profile of Nagaland 2001)

The soil is silty clay loam of grayish brown co lour and sticky. The soil of village is moderately acidic in nature (pH.6.27) and medium in fertility. Directorate of Agril. Nagaland 1979)

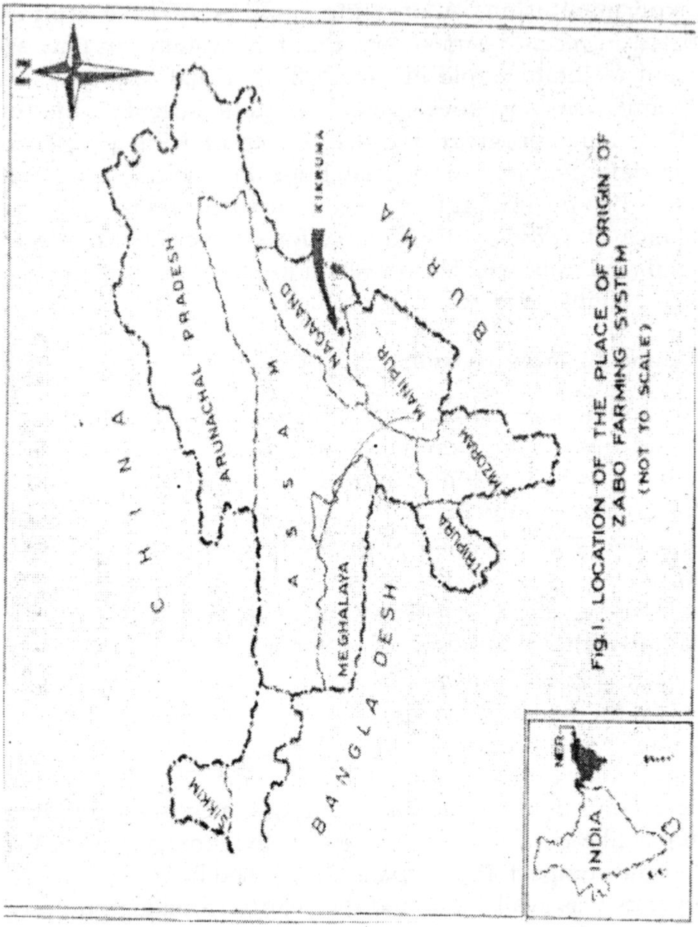

Fig.1. LOCATION OF THE PLACE OF ORIGIN OF ZABO FARMING SYSTEM (NOT TO SCALE)

The village comes under rain shadow of Pfustero town where is the average rainfall is 1613 mm. The whole Kikurma village is on flat ridge bounded on south by Sedzu river and on the north by the Khuzha river. Taping of water from theses river to irrigate the cultivated area on ridges is not possible as the ridge is higher the river levels by several hundred meters. Due to steep slope the construction of terrace or irrigation channel across the slope is difficult.

During the study period it is observed that farmers of Kikurma village realized the importance of natural resource conservation and management and started stopping Jhum cultivation. During 1981 total area under Jhum cultivation was 857.93 ha which is now reduced by fifty percent (400 ha).

There are three type of farming system practiced by the farmers and selection of crop are done on the basis of micro situation Paddy is main crop grown in such a Jhum, rainfed upland terrace cultivation,. And terrace rice cultivation (terrace cultivation). Maize is grown under rainfed upland condition the area under under TRC increase manifold from 36.42 ha to 500 ha during 1991-2001. Modest increased in forest area (4086.80 to 4800 ha) was also observed which was result of decline of area in Jhum cultivation.

Potato tomato and cabbage is important vegetable crop grown in wide farming situation. The fruits crops, which are grown, are passion fruits, peach pear and plums. Farmers are also maintaining pine forest and other forest surrounded to village to provide that timber as well as biomass for fertility buildup. The piggery and poultry are the important components, which provide subsidiary income as well as livelihoods for the farmers.

As mentioned earlier main factor, which is responsible for evolving the indigenous farming system called Zabo, was water scanty and food security. Since both important aspects was taken care by the system without any help of external forces and this has now become a tradition for the people of Kikurma village.

Components of Farming System

Land management system: The farming system comprises of protected forestland on hilltop, well planned water harvesting tank at the middle and cattle yard and paddy fields towards foothills. In case, a suitable location for water storage is not available, the run-off water from the upper catchments is taken directly to paddy field, which acts water storage for paddy crops. Special technique for seepage control in the plots is followed, which includes thorough pudding and use of paddy husk on shoulder bunds. The concept of the farming is common on individually owned land of about 2.5 ha area. The various components of Zabo system are described as follows: Figure 2.

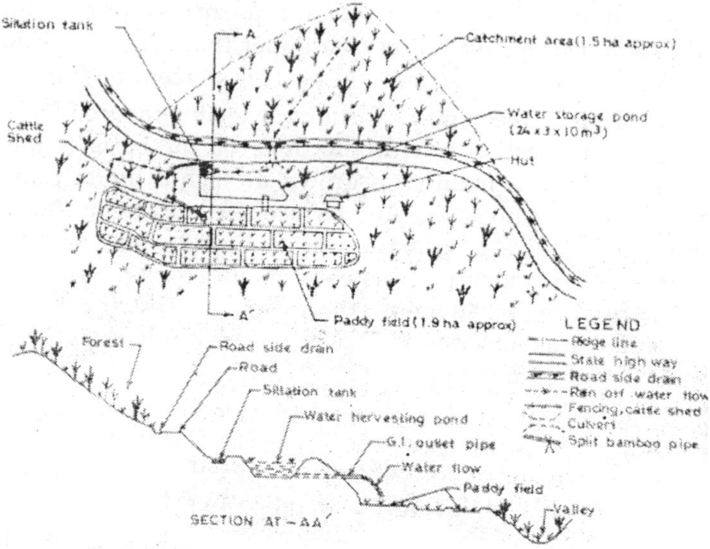

Fig. 2 : LAND MANAGEMENT SYSTEM UNDER ZABO FARMING SYSTEM

1. ***Forestland***: The catchments area (about 1.5 ha or more) is kept under natural vegetation on upstream side of the pond to serve as water sources for the pond during monsoon. Normally cutting or burning of trees does not distribute this area. However, cattle, pigs, poultry birds etc. are occasionally let loose in the forest areas. Slope of the catchments area is generally 100 percent or more.
2. ***Water harvesting system***: Adjacent to the catchments area (middle hill slope), water-harvesting ponds are dugout towards down streamside with formation of earthen embankment. The size of the pond is usually kept as 24X10X2m. Slit retention tanks are constructed at several points, before the run off water enters into the pond. The water harvesting system occupies about 0.2 ha area. Slit retention tanks are cleared annually as a part of maintenance of the water harvesting system. At the time of construction of the pond, considerable efforts are made towards a ramming for compacting the inner surface area so as to avoid water loses through seepage

3. ***Cattle shed:*** It is a common practice of every farm to maintain an enclosure fenced with ordinary woods and branches or bamboo for open cattle yard, which is managed by a group of farmers by stocking cattle on rotation basis, preferably a little below the water harvesting pond.

   Buffaloes are the common animals available with the farmer, and 20-30 numbers are kept in one yard for 10-15 days. Washing of the cattle is done with run off water, which undergoes afterwards to the paddy fields for manuring. When there is an overflowing of water it finds way through a diversion passing through the cattle yard and washes down the manures to the field below. Split bamboo channels are used to carry such dungs and urines from the cattle yard to the central point of the field from where it spreads in the entire field.

4. ***Agriculture land***: Paddy fields are located at a lower elevation than the water-harvesting pond. The area of the paddy fields varies between 0.2 to 0.5 ha. Use of green manures like (Albizia Lebbeck) and Mekhonu tree leaves, application of cowding and diversion of run-off through open cattle yard are the usual methods of manuring of paddy crops. Farmers also use Azolla growing naturally for enhancing the soil fertility wherever permanent impounding water sources are available. Paddy fields are thoroughly rammed at the time of puddling following various methods, viz. treading by human and cattle in groups, ramming by wooden sticks etc. to create a hard pan so as to avoid percolation losses. Seepage losses through shoulder bunds are checked with the use of paddy husk on the upstream side. Buffaloes are the main source of farm power.

Only one paddy crop (Var. Tanyekemugah) is grown. This is a local tall variety of 180 days duration. The seed rate is 60 kg/ha; transplanting time is June; spacing used 12X12 cm; and two irrigations from the storage pond (as supplement) maintaining 10 cm water depth in terraces are applied. The yield of paddy is about 16-20 q/ha. Most of the farmers practise paddy cum fish culture technique and derive about 50-60 kg of fish per hectare as an additional output.

Terrace Construction Technique

The terrace construction practiced by the villagers is more laborious but scientific. Cutting and burning the jungle clear area proposed for terracing. The width of terrace depends upon the slope, keeping the height of the risers to 1 to 2 m on an average. Scraping the topsoil upwards so that the sub soil layer is exposed for a firm foundation draws contour lines. After removing the thin top soil layer the sub soil below the proposed riser where sub-soil is kept exposed is dug and heaped up fir compaction with wooden clubs vertically and horizontally to form the riser and the side bund. After the riser is properly made the space left behind\above is filled up with stones and shales removed in digging, and leveling of the terrace is done by half cut and half fill method by pressing and compacting the filled soil with feet and sticks taking care that the top soil is not buried. After the terrace is completely leveled and

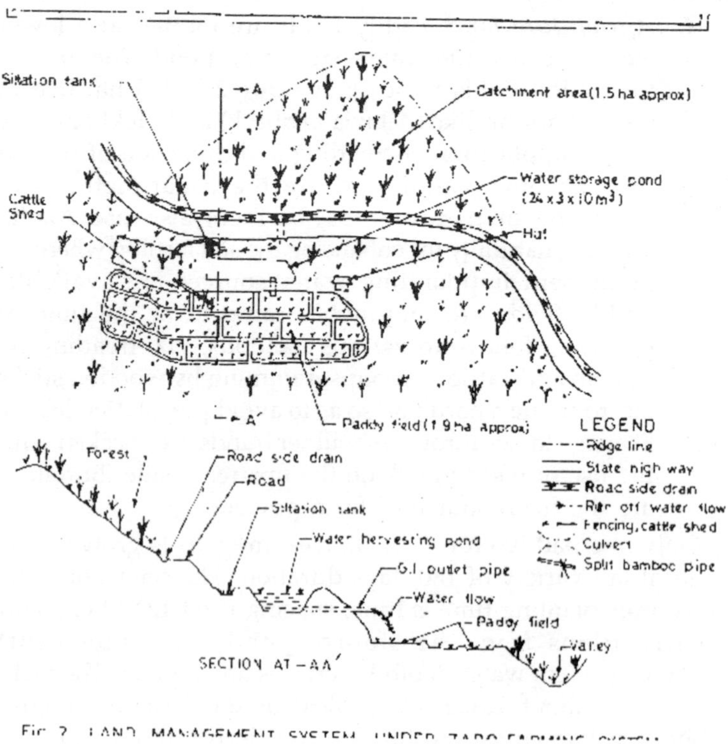

Fig. 2 LAND MANAGEMENT SYSTEM UNDER TARO FARMING SYSTEM

complete, the topsoil earlier removed and kept aside is spread evenly over the surface of the terrace. As soon as these come in contact with water they disintegrate and form a fine clay layer with blocks the pore spaces and stops seepage and percolation.

The terraces are constructed from bottom upwards so that the topsoil from the upper proposed terraces is removed and thrown to fill the terrace just completed below. To the newly constructed terraces, leaves and twigs of Alders, Albizzia sp and other trees and trashes are added and allowed to decompose and fertilize the soil. Initially beans, Naga dal, pumpkins, potatoes etc. are grown to recondition the soil for cultivation.

Crop productivity in System: The average productivity of rice in Zabo- System is higher than traditional jhum paddy yield. The yield ranges between 16-20q/ha against jhum paddy yield, which is ranged between 12.50 to 15.00q/. Productivity of paddy cum fish culture range between 60-80kg/ha the productivity of potato, tomato and cabbage and tomato range between 120-170q/ha.

Economics of the system: Zabo system comprising of 14.5X8X2.5 meter square pond and 0.4 ha paddy field is estimated to cost about 700-800 mandays, which is equivalent to Rs 70000-80000. The cost of terrace may vary mainly depending upon slope and land situation. The average income per year from same piece of land, from paddy, fish, tomatoes, and potatoes altogether ranges from Rs 8000- 10000. The investment made on whole system may be recovered returned in 8-9 years time span

Conclusion

The above study indicate that this system have greater potential, since it posses all criteria of sustainable agriculture and intend to meet the immediate challenge of food security and household security. Since this system has enough scope for increasing productivity by introducing suitable HYV of crops particularly on rice. Potato, tomato and cabbage. There is urgent need to popularize this system in another part of Nagaland in similar situation.

16

Constraints Faced by Lowland Paddy Cultivators in Dimapur District of Nagaland

*Jha, K.K.**

Introduction

Agriculture is the predominant occupations in Nagaland where about 73% of the population depends on Agriculture. Rice is the staple food in this state and occupies about 70% of the total cultivated area and constitutes about 75% of the total good grain production. It is grown under varying conditions and situations viz, rain-fed uplands/jhumlands, rainfed low land and wetland terrace. Rice grows best on clay loam to clay soil, but it can adapt to a wide range of soil conditions and thrives best under high humidity and temperature. It has been observed that soil having P^H between 5 to 8.5, soil conductivity below 4 mmhas/cm and exchangeable sodium percentage lesser than 15 may suit the crop to grow and produce well. As per the statistical record of directorate of Agriculture, Kohima, the average yield of rice was 14.86 quintals per hectare. In Nagaland, rice not

* Department of Rural Devt. & Planning, Nagaland.

only occupies the highest area but highest production as well among all the cereal crops grown, besides having traditional value to the people.

Majority of the cultivable land under Dimapur district comprise of plane land which abounds in paddy cultivation. Most of the cultivations are being done on a shared basis with the local land owners employing migrant labourers from outside the state. Relatively traditional method of farming is practiced, use of HYV seed and fertilizer is minimal, thereby achieving only a moderate level of yield per hectare making the farmers confined to subsistence farming. Irrigation potentials exists but are not being harnessed in a scientific manner. Therefore a research study was undertaken in Dimapur district to asses the constraints faced by the paddy cultivators which has kept them away from adoption of improved technologies and achieve higher productivity in context of production of rice.

Methodology

The study was conducted in all the four R.D. blocks of Dimapur district viz; Medziphema, Dhansiripar, Kuhuboto and Niuland. Selecting a total of 100 paddy cultivators as the respondents from six villages following a proportionate random sampling procedure. The selected villages were, Chumukedima A and Tenyiphe II under Medziphema R.D. block, Neikhekhu and Kuhoxu under Niuland R.D. block, Old showba under Kuhuboto R.D. block and Dhansiripar village under Dhansiripar R.D. block. A list of all the head of the farm families growing low land paddy in all the six selected villages was prepared and out of this about 20 percent of them were selected based on proportionate random smapling procedure so as to make a sample size of 100 respondents, personal interview was conducted to assess the constraints faced by them in paddy cultivation and the constraints were ranked based on frequency and percentage distribution.

Results and Discussions

Table 1 and figure (1) reveals the constraints faced by the respondents in paddy cultivation.

Table 1. Constraints faced by the farmers in paddy cultivation

n= 100

Sl.No.	Nature of Problems	Frequency	Percentage	Rank
1.	Soil fertility	88	88	V
2.	Incidence of disease and pest attack	98	98	I
3.	Lack of irrigation facilities	91	91	II
4.	Soil and water conservation	89	89	IV
5.	Inadequate knowledge about improved package of practices	91	91	II
6.	Low economic status	62	62	XI
7.	Traditional belief	30	30	X
8.	Inadequate availability of input materials in time	75	75	VI
9.	Inadequate training exposure	90	90	III
10.	Lack/Inadequate credit facilities	84	84	V
11.	Poor extension contact	67	67	VII
12.	Lack of proper marketing facilities	64	64	VIII
13.	Low rate of sale of the farm produce	78	78	VII
14.	Low demand of farm produce in local areas	60	60	XII
15.	Inadequate transport facilities.	62	62	IX

As per the above table it is evident that the most important constrain faced by the paddy cultivators was the incidence of disease and pest attack as reported by 98 percent of them. This was observed to be critical problem because farmers lacked adequate knowledge about handling plant protection equipments as well plant protection measures to control the disease and pest attack. This was in accordance with the findings of Vasanth Kumar (1998).

The next prominent constraint was observed to be lack of irrigation facilities and inadequate knowledge about improved package of practices as reported by 91 percent of the respondents. These respondents were found to be heavily dependent on monsoon which most oftenly disturbed the smooth flow of agricultural operation. These farmers were also found to have inadequate knowledge about improved package of practices. They were found to be confined mostly with the traditional practices only.

Inadequate training exposure was experienced as constraint by 90 percent of the paddy cultivators. This was mainly because that training programmes related to paddy cultivation was not being frequently conducted by the State Agriculture Department. Even if some training programmes were conducted sufficient number of trainees were not selected. Therefore most of the farmers were devoid of the appropriate knowledge and skills related to the specific package of practices in paddy cultivation.

89 percent of the respondents faced problem in relation to soil and water conservation. This was due to the fact that most of the farmers didn't maintain proper drainage system in the field. This resulted in soil moisture depletion as well as nutrient loss adversely affecting the productivity. This was in accordance with the findings of Hatcho (1997).

Lack or inadequate availability of the credit facilities was observed to be the constraint as reported by 85 percent of the farmers. This problem was found to be quite peculiar since most of the farmers were not aware of the different facilities or agencies from which agricultural loan could be procured at minimum rate of interest.

75 percent of the respondents reported that lack or inadequate availability of input material posed a great problem before them in context of paddy cultivation. This was due to the fact that quantity of input materials supplied by the block agencies didn't meet the requirements of the farmers. Moreover, there was lack of good quality materials available in the market. In this situation, farmers were not able to use the standard input materials for their farm operations.

Poor extension contact was viewed as a constraint as reported by 67 percent of the respondents. This was mainly due to the irregular visit of the VLW's & Agril. Inspectors thereby resulting in a situation of communication gap in terms of transfer of improved technology.

Lack of proper marketing facilities was reported to be the constraint as by 64 per cent of the paddy cultivators. This was due to the fact that some of the villages didn't have proper road conditions to buy or sell their harvested produce. This was in accordance with the findings of Thyagrajan and Vasantha (1998).

62 percent of the respondents were observed to face problem in relation to inadequate transport facilities. This was mainly

because most of the villages didn't have proper agricultural link road or main road connected to their village.

Traditional belief was reported as a constraint by 30 percent of the respondents which dettered them in adopting improved package of practices. Having traditional belief deep rooted in their psyche, they found it difficult to switch over to modern and improved package of practices.

Conclusion

Rice being the staple crop and the favourable agro-climatic and topographic factors available in Dimapur district plays an influential role in keeping the farmers engaged mostly in paddy cultivation. The major constraints faced by the farmers were observed to be incidence of disease and pest attack. Lack of irrigation facilities and inadequate training exposure. The other important constraints were soil and water conservation, lack or inadequate availability of the credit facilities, lack or inadequate availability of the input materials, poor extension contact followed by proper marketing facilities and inadequate transport facilities. The least important constraint was found to be the traditional belief.

In particular, these specific problems could be overcome by imparting proper training to the farmers at a periodic interval at the appropriate time to make them aware about improved technology. Extension support should be strengthened and a strong linkage between technology development and dissemination could be promoted. Since plenty of water resource like, streams, rivers are available therefore suitable irrigation projects could be undertaken by the Department of Agriculture to help the farmers. Village Councils should take proper initiative to facilitate proper agricultural link road and main road for better and cheaper road transport facilities. State government, specially the Department of Agriculture should undertake proper measures so that quality inputs are made available to the farmers at appropriate time in adequate quantity and last but not the least proper marketing should be developed and made known to the farmers which may ultimately help them to take strategic decisions in respect of their farm planning.

REFERENCES

Allport, G. W (1935). Attitude in Murchism (Eds.). *A Handbook of Social Psychology*, Warester Mass; Clark Univ. Press. 25–311.

Anonymous (1991). *Agricultural Census Report of Nagaland (90-91)*: 1 – 6.

Hatcho, N. (1997). Irrigation water management through information management. Memories of the faculty of Agriculture of Kinke University. (30): 73-91.

Thyagovrajan, S. and Vasantha Kumar, J. (1998). Constraints of high yield in rice at farm level. *Indian Jl. of Ext. Ed.* 34 93 & 40: 85–87.

17

Relevance of Jhum Cultivation in Nagaland

*Jha, K.K.**

Agriculture is the source of perpetual creation on which human civilization depends and thrives as well. People have used the land resource both for agricultural as well as non-agricultural purposes. With the progress of civilization, and increasing population, there has been immense pressure on the limited land resource in terms of sustaining agricultural production to faced our people. Nagaland a prominent, progressive and jubilient state of NE region of India is blessed with a varied agro-climatic regimes with altitude levels varaying from 200m to 3800m. It has a total geographical area of 16,579 sq.km. out of which about 44% of the land is suitable for cultivation. Agriculture is the main land use and the people are primarily occupied in this profession making the state economy heavily dependent upon it. The major land use pattern in this state is slash and burn cultivation known as "Jhum". With the limited introduction of modern scientific agricultural technology in the early part of 1960s, the impact have been observed to be feeble. This is due to the fact that most of the so called modern

* Department of Rural Devt. & Planning, Nagaland.

technologies comprising of complicated external inputs are not found to be suitable for prevailing high altitudes and predominant rainfed conditions in Nagaland.

The practise of jhum cultivation is deep root in the psychological framework of the farmers in Nagaland. This is being practiced since time immemorial and having evolved through the years has strong emotional attachment with the customs and beliefs of the practicing farmers. Jhum cultivation which is so tightly interwover into the culture and traditions of the Naga farmers, constitute about more than 90% of the total cultivable land in Nagaland and more forest areas are being cleared for cultivation every year. Therefore, to have research study was undertaken in Dimapur and Kohima district of Nagaland with the following objectives:

1. To know the present trend of jhum cultivation.
2. To know the attitude of the farmers towards jhum cultivation.
3. To judge the relevance of jhum cultivation.

Methodology

A research study was undertaken in Dimapur and Kohima district of Nagaland. One R.D. nlock viz; Medziphema and Jakhama was selected purposively under the respective districts. Proportionate random sampling procedure was followed for selection of respondents which comprised of a total of 250 farmers from both the districts who were engaged in jhum cultivation. The data was collected with the help of a pretested schedule by means of personal interview of the respondents.

Findings

1. Present trend of the jhum cultivation

Under jhum cultivation jungle is felled, the vegetation is slashed, burned, tilled and sown. The individual parcels out his field into a number of plots and cultivates a plot for one or two years. After this the land is left fallow for some years to regain its fertility. The average period of fallow was found to be 08 years. In the following year the farmers shift to the next plot, cultivate it for the same period, kept it fallow for the required number of years as stated above and when the rotation is complete, the first plot is taken up again.

Mixed cropping was found to be practised by majority (91%) of the farmers in the jhum fields with rice as the main crop although in some cases, (9%) maize and millet were found to be practiced as the staple crop. A broad range of 20 to 40 crop species was observed in a single jhum field. In addition to the staple crop, supplementary crops like maize, millet, job's tears, beans, root crops, legumes, vegetables, oilseeds etc are widely practiced in the jhum field so as to minimize the risk of crop failure and in particular make the farmer self sufficient in terms of his requirement of food crop.

Jhum cultivation was found to be highly influenced and attached with the tradition, and culture of the farmers, with the active participation of the village council. Village council plays an active role in deciding the calendar of events involved in the jhum cultivation. The village council plays an important requlatory role in other activities of the jhum like assigning important role to the group of the farmers on the basis of age, for clearing and maintenance of the link road from the village to the jhum fields, construction of cattle fences, setting the jhum and an fire, weeding, harvesting and post harvest operations.

2. *Attitude of the farmers towards jhum cultivation*

Attitude of the farmers towards jhum cultivation was measured by adopting the attitude index developed by Punyu & Jha (2002) with slight modification. The findings are presented in table 1.

Table 1. Relationship of the selected independent variables with the dependent variable—attitude of the farmers towards jhum cultivation

Sl.No.	*Independent variables*	*Correlation (r) value*	*'t' value*
1	Age	+ 0.025 NS	0.393
2	Education	-0.275*	4.502
3	Farm size	-0.157 NS	2.50
4	Size of family	-0.360**	6.07
5	Annual income	+0.005 NS	0.78
6	Mass media exposure	-0.267*	4.36
7	Risk orientation	-0.132 NS	2.093
8	Scientific orientation	-0.324**	5.390

NS – Non significant
** - Significant at 1% £
* - Significant at 5% £

Table 1 reveals that the independent variables viz; Age, Farm size, Annual income and Risk orientation were non-significant. Therefore, there is no association between these selected independent variables and the attitude of the farmers towards jhum cultivation.

Further, the variables like education, size of family, mass media exposure and scientific orientation were found to have significant association with the dependent variable attitude of the farmers towards jhum cultivation.

Education was found to have negative and significant relationship with the farmer's attitude. This implies that higher is the level of education of the farmers lower degree of favourable attitude is exhibited by the farmers towards practise of jhum cultivation. This may be due to the fact that higher education might have promoted greater awareness about the adverse consequences of the jhum cultivation thereby developing a negative outlook towards jhum cultivation.

Size of family had negative and highly significant relationship with the attitude of the farmers towards jhum cultivation. This envisage that greater is the size of the family, lower is the favourable attitude of the farmers towards jhum cultivation. This may due to the fact that greater family size might have created undue pressure on the farmer to depend upon the diversified nature of cropping system to meet the needs of his family.

Mass media exposure was also found to have negative and significant association with the attitude of the farmers. Thus, it may be inferred that higher the mass media exposure, lower is the attitude of the farmers towards jhum cultivation. This may be due to the fact that relative exposure of the mass media sources might have inculcated awareness among the farmers about the adverse consequences of jhum cultivation as well as have motivated them to adopt alternative eco-friendly and use system.

Scientific orientation was found to have negative and highly significant association with the attitude of the farmers towards jhum cultivation. This infers that with increase in scientific orientation, there is a decrease in the attudinal level of the farmers towards practise of jhum cultivation.

Thus the variables viz, education, size of family, mass media exposure and scientific orientation play an important role in educating the farmers, to adopt alternative to jhum cultivation.

3. *Relevance of jhum cultivation*

The findings of the present study envisage that the farmers in Nagaland are heavily dependent on jhum cultivation. At present the average jhum cycle has reduced to about 8 years which is inordinately short for nutrient recovery. Longer cycle of 10 years is the minimum requirement (Tiwari & Jha 1993) whereas a jhum cycle of 15-20 years may be considered suitable in terms of sustainability (Kevichusa 1999). According to Chauhan 1990 in jhum cultivation, organic matter of the surface soil gets oxidized which may cause decrease in soil organis matter and the loss of crop yield, plant nutrient and land degradation contributes about 48.2, 39.6 and 12.2 percent respectively towards the on-site cost of soil degradation. Among the plant nutrient, nitrogen loss was reported to be maximum (29.2%) followed by phosphorus (7.8%), potassium (1.6%) and sulphate (1.0%).

According to Kevichusa 1999, in jhum cultivation, the massive top soil erosion is observed from March to May when the first monsoon rain occur and the crops has not grown enough to cover and protect the top soil. As per an estimate of ICAR, up to 40 metric tons of top soil per hectare per year is eroded in a Naga jhum field. Though the there is no proper account of contribution of pollutants to the atmosphere by burning the vegetation in jhum cultivation but it is estimated to be substantial.

Conclusion

Based upon the findings of this study it is evident that majority of the farmers in Nagaland are heavily dependent on jhum cultivation which has indepth influence on the psychological make up, being strongly inter oven with their tradition and customs. Growing population pressure and ensuing high demand for food, has resulted in decreased jhum cycle thereby creating environmental hazards like soil erosion, loss of soil fertility and productivity. Eventhough, this practise is having adverse effect on productivity sustainability and ecological security jhum cultivation assures a measure of food security for most of the people in Nagaland. The prevalence of varied agro-climatic conditions, and undulating topography offers a greater degree of limitations for the application of modern technologies. Moreover, the state government doesn't have a very sound policy of food distribution system and therefore, in absence of such system, jhum cultivation to the Naga farmers is an asset of insurance that required food is available to them when other systems have failed.

. However, the need of hour is to make the farmers aware of the long term adverse consequences of the prevailing practices of jhum. The important variables such as education, size of family, mass media exposure and scientific orientation were found to be important, therefore, these variables may potentially be utilized for creating awareness and motivating them to adopt promising alternate land use system such Agro-horti-silvo-pastoral system as recommended by ICAR research complex for NEH region Barapani. This system was evaluated on 1.03 ha area with 42% average slope and soil depth below 1.5 m. Top one-third area being utilized for forestry and pasture, middle one-third for horticulture and lower one-third terraced land for agriculture. Rice, maize, soybean, mustard, groundnut, radish and ginger and guinea grass were found to be most promising; maize, ginger, groundnut, radish and mustard gave yield of about 4.0, 3.4, 1.1, 43.4 and 0.26 tonnes/ha respectively from this system.

Orange, guava, pineapple were found to be promising horticultural crops whereas *Alnus nepalensis* (alder), *Symingtonia populnea,.ficus auriculata* and thysanolaena maxima were found to be promising silvo-pastoral components, that thrived well in the micro watershed. Guinea grass, pine-apple and rice bean were found suitable as inter crops in the middle portion of the watershed. A unit of 10 goats and 10 pigs could be reared on the silvo-pastoral component and crop by products. There was no soil loss from the system and this system was adjudged to fulfil the requirements of food, fodder, fuel and timber of the marginal farmers living in remote areas. Moreover it was visualized as economically viable and ecologically sustainable. The cost benefit ratio of the system was 1: 1.48.

The farmers of Nagaland can't be stopped to practise jhum immediately. Rather the alternate land use system may further be refined to suit the specific needs of the different agro-climatic regions of Nagaland and gradually the farmers may be motivated and adequately convinced to adopt it for increased productivity, sustainability and ultimate prosperity.

REFERENCES

Anonymous (1999). Annual Report, ICAR, New Delhi:146.

Anonymous (2003). Annual Report, Deptt. of Agriculture, Govt. of Nagaland: 1.

Chauhan, B.S. (1990). Onsite degradation due to shifting cultivation in North Eastern Region. *Jl. of Social Sciences and Humanities*. 8(3):5-8.

Jha, L.K. and Sarma, P.K.S. (1993). *Agroforestry—Indian Perspective*. Ashish Publishing House, New Delhi: 71-76.

Kevichusa, R. (1999). Building upon traditional agriculture in Nagaland:1-7.

Punyu, K. and Jha, K.K. (2002). Training needs of terrace paddy cultivators in Kohima district of Nagaland. Unpublished M.Sc.(Ag.) thesis, Deptt. of Rural Development & Planning, NU:SASRD, Medziphema, Nagaland:39-40.

18

Technology for Improving Agricultural Productivity in Nagaland

*Dr. Supong Keitzar**

Prologue

Dr. M.S. Swaminathan once said, "Gentleman, all of us should keep in mind that if agriculture goes wrong nothing can go right and if agriculture goes right every country or state can move forward with hope and success." This is a prophetic saying. Agriculture must be brought into forefront in order to achieve sustainability in all spheres of developmental activities. Agriculture is the live-stream to sustain life on this planet Earth. The History of Agriculture began with the History of Man. Man cannot live without food. Therefore, every man must have his share of daily food in order to live. It is agriculture which provides food for everybody. This means agriculture must not go wrong.

Nagas have a great heritage of simple, honest and hard working people. They were agriculturists and experts in their own ways. Today, with the change of time and space, the society and the people, and also the life style changes with the passage

* Director, Directorate of Agriculture, Nagaland, Kohima – 797001.

of time. Therefore, we require a new conscientious shift to cope with time and space. This is the reason that we need a new policy considering all the local needs such as tradition, culture, custom and norm keeping in view the fragile environment and ecosystems.

Agricultural production should not aim at the destruction of forest, ecology and environment but aim at preserving and improving the ecological spheres. The National Commission on Agriculture has prescribed for at least 60 % forest cover in the hill areas in order to maintain the ecological balance so necessary for the stability of agriculture and other life support system in the hills. Our main objectives and prime needs should consequently be focused on regenerating the land and remodeling "Agro-eco-systems".

There is no denying the fact that our state despite being basically agrarian with large potential in natural resources, no significant success has yet been achieved in agriculture. Although modern scientific agriculture in Nagaland was initiated as early as 1960's with the introduction of HYV the impact has not been very appreciable as most high external input technologies are not suitable for high altitudes and rainfed conditions. As a consequence may be, our economy is still dilapidated. No doubt efforts are on with a focus on sustaining and improving agriculture in the state but one may ponder whether our agricultural development strategy is rolling on the right track or not. In the context of the today's fast changing era, prior to taking steps on revitalizing our agriculture, we should ensure that our agricultural development policies and plannings are not wrong.

Outlook on Agriculture

Nagaland is basically a land of Agriculture with more than eighty per cent of the population earning their livelihood from agricultural production. The contribution of agricultural sector in the state is highly significant. Rice is the staple food. It occupies about 70 % of the total area and constitutes about 75 % of the total food grain production in the State. However, like most of the world's tribal populations, production system in the state is largely subsistent and traditional. Literally, farming in Naga perspective may be defined as a profession but not a business. The tendency of the farmers for improvement and increasing production to earn more by adopting necessary technology is still unpredictable. This is mainly due to their resistance to give up the present system of agriculture which is intrinsically related to social, religious, and traditional values. Another reason is due to illiteracy of the farming communities which renders the complexities of the technology too hard to understand for them.

The present outlook towards cultivation as a mere subsistence undertaking should therefore be changed to farming as a business venture. This change in attitude and outlook contributes towards higher production by way of imbibing new technologies towards production system. To bring about a change in their outlook, a sound and effective extension service capable of commanding the confidence of the cultivators should be built up.

Shifting Cultivation

Shifting cultivation is referred to as slash and burn agriculture and locally known as "jhum" cultivation. Because of poor statistics, it is difficult to report correct figures on the area of jhum in the state. An anonymous report however, states that out of the state's total area of 16,579 sq km at least 7000 sq km of land is subjected to this kind of cultivation. With the rapid growth of population the area under jhum cultivation is inexorably increasing. It is estimated that in the last decade additional 1000 sq km land may have been brought under jhum. With the present trend in the population growth, further increase of land under jhum is expected. This will further reduce in jhum cycle (intervening fallow phase period in between successive cropping on the same site) and average yields of different crops will reduce drastically. The ecosystems are speedily losing their resilience characteristics rendering the land unproductive from the agricultural point of view.

One remarkable feature of jhum is that almost all the varieties of cereals and vegetables are grown in one jhum field which is impossible under irrigated field. This is, probably one of the reasons as to why the farmers still cling to this method of food production, besides, *jhum* cultivation is a way of life for the Nagas, yet the viability of this system of cultivation, once sustainable under low population density is today being threatened with unprecedented population growth in the state. It is imperative therefore to find an alternative system in which crop yield should be substantial and as diverse. The approach to this problem should however, be persuasive and gradual.

Shifting cultivation though not scientifically planned, is a forest dependant culture and therefore, this can be termed as "agro-forestry". The alder jhum system practiced by the Angamis of Khonoma village in Kohima district is one such example. The system, which integrates the use of Alder tree (*Alnus nepalensis*), is well established, and is perfected into a fine art. The tree is a fast growing species and is known to fix free nitrogen, about 150 kg/ha and also adds biomass in the form of leaf litters, which improves the soil fertility status of jhum fields within short jhum cycle. The tree also coppices profusely, normally 5-7 selected coppices are retained during the fallow period. A wide diversity of crops is produced in this system. An alder jhum is generally cropped for two years and then allowed to fallow for two years. To evolve such carefully planned "agro-forestry" system in harmony with the nature has become all the more crucial.

Agro-Silvi-Horticulture

The Research Complex of the Indian Council of Agricultural Research (ICAR) for the North Eastern Hill areas at Shillong has suggested a model land use plan for the entire region as an alternative to shifting cultivation. This is a three tier system where the top one third of the hill slope to be under forest, middle one third to be horticulture and the bottom one third to be under bench terrace cultivation. Forestry and Horticulture provides protective cover to the steep land, and the lower one third benefits from upslope. This model, however, requires wider demonstration and field trails for testing its adaptability.

Watershed Management

National watershed development programme for rainfed agriculture (NWDPRA) was introduced in 1986-87 with the objective of increasing overall productivity of crops of a given area depending upon the land and rainfall pattern. Under this programme provision has been made for work component which includes land and moisture management works for increasing the moisture availability for sustained and increased cropping intensity. It also includes alternate land use system for developing dryland Horticulture, farm forestry and silvi-pasture. All these programmes are to be undertaken on a watershed basis.

It is now recognized by many experts that watershed management approach is by far the most appropriate for rain water conservation for achieving sustained production and also to replace shifting cultivation gradually. The most important feature of this programme is the people's participation, a programme where every person is involved. Watershed is a multipurpose approach for sustainable production keeping "environment" in view as the most important component. Co-development is thus one of the main objectives of watershed management. Every farmer knows more than any expert, the benefits of soil and water conservation and the method of augmenting soil moisture and nutrients in his fields. Watershed is nothing but what the hill farmer knows about the conservation in harmony with nature. The only difference is that the watershed programme is implemented in carefully planned manner involving all sorts of people from top to bottom. It is an integrated system of production. The farmer would definitely participate in such a programme filled with a feeling of gratitude rather than rejection.

The decreasing productivity of land particularly under rainfed conditions has forced many farmers to reduce his dependence on agriculture leading to diversion of their time and energies to non-farm activities without which they find it difficult to survive in the present day world. Many youths even among the rural population are disillusioned and have started migrating enmass to urban areas expecting greater things and some remunerative jobs only to be landed in an illusive world in which many become a victim of drug culture. Generation of appropriate technologies and sustainability is therefore not an option but an imperative.

Epilogue

The North-Eastern Region is a potential region for development in terms of natural resources. Out of 10 hot spots of biodiversity in the world, two are in India; the Western Ghats and North-Eastern Region. This asset needs to be protected. To safeguard our natural wealth, any technological introduction should be in a holistic approach of conservation. Development should be based on ecological, economic, and social and cultural considerations. Imported technology from outside the region may sometimes be unavoidable however; in such circumstances sustainability should always be ensured. This warrants a shift and reorientation from the conventional approaches like;

- Chemical inputs to integrated management and organic inputs
- Scientist-oriented academic research to problem-solving on-farm participatory research
- Maximum production targets to optimum sustainable and eco-friendly production
- Cropping system to farming system approach.

19

Effect of Simulated Erosion and Nitrogen Levels on the Uptake of N, P and K and Yield of Upland Rice

*Manoj Dutta, Zakir Hussain and B.S. Chauhan**

ABSTRACT

Effect of simulated erosion and nitrogen levels on the uptake of N, P and K and yield of upland rice was studied in a field experiment designed in split plot format. Soil removal depths of 0, 5, 10 and 15 cm were assigned as main plot treatments and nitrogen levels of 0, 60, 120 and 180 kg ha^{-1} were allocated in sub plots. The uptake of N, P and K decreased significantly with increased rates of simulated erosion. Lowest uptake of N, P and K was recorded where 15 cm of soil was removed. Addition of different levels of nitrogen resulted in a significant increase in the uptake of all the nutrients. The highest uptake of N, P and K was observed with the application of 180 kg N ha^{-1}. On an average, removal of 1 cm of soil caused a decreased of 3.03, 2.95 and 3.50 per cent in the uptake of N, P and K,

* Department of Soil Conservation, Nagaland University, Campus: Medziphema, School of Agricultural Sciences and Rural Development, Medziphema - 797 106, India.

respectively. Increased rates of simulated erosion caused a significant decrease in grain yield while addition of N on eroded soil caused a significant increase in grain yield. The highest dry matter and straw yield was recorded in uneroded soil (control) with 180 kg N ha^{-1}, where as the highest grain yield was obtained in uneroded soil with 60 kg N ha^{-1}. Simulated erosion rates of 5, 10 and 15 cm caused a yield reduction of 22.16, 25.03 and 32.48 per cent, respectively. On an average addition of 60, 120 and 180 kg N ha^{-1} could compensate 27.58, 30.14 and 23.26 per cent towards the yield loss due to erosion, respectively.

Introduction

Top soil is the most productive part of solum. Accelerated erosion is probably the most serious form of land degradation as it removes the most fertile surface layer. The loss of surface soil often causes a reduction in the production potential of land Erosion brings about considerable change in soil properties. Soil erosion affects the chemical properties of soils mainly through the loss of organic matter, minerals and exposure of sub-soil material with low fertility and high acidity. However, negative effects can be eliminated by means of appropriate agro-technology e.g. higher levels of fertilization, especially fertilizer nitrogen as it is required by the plant in huge amounts. The purpose of this study was to evaluate the effect of surface soil removal and nitrogen levels on the uptake of nitrogen, phosphorus and potassium and yield of upland rice.

Materials and Methods

A field experiment was conducted on the experimental farm of School of Agricultural Sciences and Rural Development, Nagaland University, Medziphema, Nagaland during kharif season of the year 1997 with rice crop (var-Teke) cultivated as upland. The soil of experimental field was sandy loam and well drained. Physico-chemical properties of surface and desurfaced soils are presented in Table 1. The experiment was laid out according to a split plot format. The treatments were replicated thrice. Four soil removal depths of 0, 5, 10 and 15 cm were used as main plot. Nitrogen levels of 0, 60, 120 and180 kg ha^{-1} were used as sub plot. Nitrogen was applied as urea in three equal split doses and a basal dose of 50 kg P_2O_5 ha^{-1} as single super phosphate and 40 kg K_2O ha^{-1} as muriate of potash was applied at the time of final land preparation.

Before sowing of the crop, soil samples were collected from each plot and processed for various laboratory analyses. Soil samples were analysed for mechanical composition using international pipette method (Piper, 1966). Bulk density and water holding capacity was determined by the method as described by Kanwar and Chopra (1966). P^H was determined by the method outlined by Jackson (1964). Available N in the soil was determined following the method of Subbiah and Asija (1956). Available P was extracted by Brays Method No.1 (Bray and Kurtz, 1945) and determined colorimetrically (Dickman and Bray, 1940). The available K was extracted by neutral normal ammonium acetate (Jackson, 1964) and measured flame photometrically (Jackson, 1964). Plant samples were collected at maturity. The grain yield/m^2 was obtained after harvesting 1 sq. meter undisturbed area separately. The grains were separated from the panicles and oven dried at 55 ± 5^{0}C to constant weight. The weight of seeds was recorded. This data was used to compute the grain yield in q ha^{-1}. The N content in plant components was estimated colorimetrically using Nessler's Reagent (Jackson, 1964) in H_2SO_4 and H_2O_2 digested plant materials. Phosphorus and potassium content in plant components was determined in triacid digested plant material (Jackson, 1964). Phosphorus and potassium was estimated colorimetrically and flame photometrically, respectively. The dry matter yield and nutrient content in plant at maturity was used to compute the uptake of N, P and K (kg ha^{-1}). The difference between observed yield and expected yield in eroded soil when expressed as per cent of uneroded soil for any dose on N was taken as per cent compensation of yield due to addition of that dose of N.

Results and Discussion

Nitrogen uptake:

The data pertaining to N uptake of rice is presented in Table 2. The data showed that increasing rates of simulated erosion decreased the N uptake significantly at all the levels as compared to control. Maximum N uptake (191.22 kg ha^{-1}) was recorded in control and minimum (116.48 kg ha^{-1}) where 15 cm of soil was removed. Simulated erosion rates of 5, 10 and 15 cm caused a decrease of 20.80, 30.97and 39.08 per cent in N uptake, respectively. It is evident from the data that N uptake increased with increasing level of N application. The effect of N on the uptake of N by the plant was significant at all levels. Maximum uptake (204.08 kg ha^{-1}) was recorded with highest dose of N (180 kg ha^{-1}) and minimum (78.83 kg ha^{-1}) in uneroded (control). Addition of 60, 120 and 180 kg N ha^{-1} caused an increase of 58.49, 92.07 and 125.25 kg ha^{-1} in N uptake, respectively. N is an essential constituent of plant (Russell, 1973) and under condition of high availability of N such high uptake can be expected and have been reported by Sinha (1968).

Phosphorus uptake

The data (Table 3) showed that increasing rates of simulated erosion decreased the P uptake significantly. Maximum uptake (32.26 kg ha^{-1}) was observed in control. Removal of 10 cm of soil could not cause any significant decrease as compared to 5 cm soil removal. Similarly, removal of 15 cm soil did not cause any significant effect as compared to 10 cm soil removal. Erosion rates of 5, 10 and 15 cm on an average, caused a decrease of 21.57, 27.37 and 39.58 per cent P uptake, respectively. The decrease in P uptake by plant appears to be related to the erosion induced low level of P in the soil. Similar results were obtained by Reuss and Campbell (1961).

It is observed from the data (Table 3) that P uptake increased significantly with increasing levels of N application. Highest P uptake (31.12 kg ha^{-1}) was recorded with application of 180 kg N ha^{-1} and lowest (14.18 kg ha^{-1}) in control. Treatment with 120 kg N ha^{-1} resulted to a significant increase in P uptake as compared to 60 kg N ha^{-1}. Application of 180 kg N ha^{-1} did not show significant effect as compared to 120 kg N ha^{-1}. Addition of 60, 120 and 180 kg N ha^{-1} caused an increase of 10.58, 16.24 and 16.94 kg ha^{-1} P uptake, respectively. The significant increase in the P uptake as influenced by N may be due to the ability of N to increase the cation exchange capacity of roots and causing maximum proliferation of a root mass in a specified area and thereby resulting relatively more efficient absorption of P. Similar results were reported by Kanwar (1976).

Potassium uptake

A perusal of the data (Table 4) showed that highest K uptake (200.76 kg ha^{-1}) was observed in control and lowest (108.26 kg ha^{-1}) where 15 cm of soil was removed. Simulated erosion rates of 5 cm caused a significant decrease in the K uptake by plant as compared to control but removal of 10 cm and 15 cm of soil did not result in a significant decrease in the uptake of K as compared to 5 cm. Simulated erosion rates of 5, 10 and 15 cm caused a decrease of 26.25, 32.73 and 46.07 per cent K uptake at maturity stage, respectively. The decrease in K uptake might be due to low available K in eroded soil.

The data further revealed that increased dose of N caused a significant increase in the uptake of K. Application of 120 kg N ha^{-1} did not cause any significant increase as compared to 60 kg N ha^{-1}. Treatment with 180 kg N ha^{-1} caused a significant effect as compared to 60 kg and 120 kg N ha^{-1}, respectively. Application of 60, 120 and 180 kg N ha^{-1} caused an increase of 52.81, 74.43 and 102.58 kg ha^{-1} in K uptake, respectively. The increase in K uptake may be due to the increased dry matter production on addition of N. Nitrogen simulates the growth of plant which influence the utilization of K and other nutrients considerably resulting higher nutrient uptake (Russell, 1973).

Dry matter yield

The data on dry matter yield at maturity stage of the rice is presented in Table 5. A perusal of data showed that the highest dry matter accumulation (192.36 q ha^{-1}) occurred in control and the lowest (135.72 q ha^{-1}) where 15 cm of soil was removed. Simulated erosion rates of 5, 10 and 15 cm caused a decrease of 15.87, 22.36 and 29.44 per cent in dry matter yield, respectively. Maximum dry matter yield (186.50 q ha^{-1}) observed with 180 kg N ha^{-1} and minimum (115.31 q ha^{-1}) in control. Effect of N on dry matter yield of rice was significant at all levels over control. The application of 60, 120 and 180 kg N ha^{-1} could only compensate 22.69, 22.83 and 23.44 per cent towards the erosion induced loss in dry matter production, respectively.

Straw yield

The data pertaining to straw yield (Table 6) indicated that the straw yield of rice decreased with increasing levels of simulated erosion. Maximum straw yield (150.6 q ha^{-1}) was recorded in control and the minimum (107.52 q ha^{-1}) where soil was removed up to 15 cm. The simulated erosion rates of 5, 10 and 15 cm caused a decrease of 14.12, 21.60 and 28.61 per cent of straw yield, respectively. Similar result was also reported by Khybri *et al.* (1980) and Lal (1987). The decrease in straw yield due to removal of surface soil might be because of the loss of top soil containing organic matter and essential plant nutrients which besides affecting nutrient availability to plants also affect other soil properties favourable for plant growth. The data further, revealed that increased levels of N caused an increase in straw yield. The maximum straw yield (152.54 q ha^{-1}) was recorded with 180 kg N ha^{-1} which was significantly superior over control (89.36 q ha^{-1}). The addition of N caused a significant increase in straw yield at all levels as compared to control. On an average, addition of 60, 120 and 180 kg N ha^{-1} could compensate 21.04, 18.58 and 22.91 per cent towards the straw yield loss due to erosion.

Grain yield

The data on the effect of erosion on grain yield (Table 7) clearly established that grain yield decreased with increasing rates of erosion. The maximum grain yield (41.75 q ha^{-1}) was obtained in control which decreased gradually with increase in simulated erosion rate and the minimum grain yield (28.19 q ha^{-1}) was obtained where soil was removed up to 15 cm. The data further, showed that the reduction in grain yield was maximum in absence of N. In control (0 kg N ha^{-1}), yield loss of 32.21, 46.80 and 62.24 per cent was recorded on the removal of 5, 10 and 15 cm of soil, respectively. On an average, yield loss was computed to be 22.16, 25.03 and 32.48 per cent (9.25, 10.45 and 13.56 q ha^{-1}, respectively) on removal of 5, 10 and 15 cm of soil, respectively.

The data (Table 7) on the effect of N on grain yield further revealed that highest grain yield (37.24 q ha^{-1}) was recorded with 60 kg N ha^{-1}. Addition of 60, 120 and 180 kg N ha^{-1} on an average, could compensate 27.58, 30.16 and 23.28 per cent towards the yield loss due to erosion, respectively. The data clearly indicated that N alone could not compensate for the entire yield loss due to simulated erosion. The data established that up to a limited extent fertilizer N could compensate for the yield loss due to erosion. The decrease in grain yield due to erosion seems to be related to changes in fertility levels and physical properties of soil. These findings are in agreement with those reported by earlier research workers (Khybri *et al.*, 1980; Lal, 1987). Comparison of data for N, P and K uptake established that the P uptake was affected most at all the levels of simulated erosion.

REFERENCES

Bray, R. H. and L. T. Kurtz. (1945). Determination of total, organic and available forms of phosphorus in soil. *Soil Sci.* 59: 39-45.

Dickman, S.R. and R.H. Bray. (1940) Colorimetric determination of phosphate. *Indus. and Engg. Chem. Anal. Ed.* 12: 665-668.

Jackson, M.L. (1964). *Soil Chemical Analysis*. Prentice Hall, Englewood, Cliffs, New Jersey, USA.

Kanwar, J.S. (1976). *Soil Fertility, Theory and Practical*. Published by ICAR, New Delhi.

Kanwar, J. S. and S.L. Chopra. (1966). *Practical Agricultural Chemistry*. S. Chand and Co. Ned Delhi.

Khybri, M.L., S.N. Prasad and Sewa Ram. (1980). Effect of top soil removal on the growth and yield of rainfed maize. *Indian J. Soil Conserv.* 8: 164-170.

Lal, R. (1987). Response of maize (*Zea mays* L.) and cassava (*Manihot esculenta*) to removal of surface soil from an Alfisol in Nigeria. *Int. J. Trop. Agri.* 2: 77-92.

Piper, C. S. (1966). *Soil and Plant Analysis*. Hans Publishers, Bombay.

Reuss, J.O. and R.E. Campbell. (1961). Restoring Productivity of leveled land. *Soil Sci. Soc. Am. Proc.* pp. 302-305.

Russell, E.W. (1973). *Soil Condition and Plant Growth.* 10th Ed. Longman, London.

Sinha, M.N. (1968). Relative availability of maize plant to absorb P placed at different soil zones. *Indian J. Agron.* 13: 234-236.

Subbiah, B.V. and G. L. Asija. (1956). A rapid procedure for determination of available nitrogen in soils. *Curr. Sci.* 25: 259-260.

Table 1. Physico-chemical characteristics of surface and desurfaced soils (0-15 cm).

Characteristics	*Surface soil*	*Desurfaced soil – Soil depth removed (cm)*		
	Control	*0-5*	*0-10*	*0-15*
Sand (%)	52.85	46.56	43.21	40.60
Silt (%)	17.42	22.27	23.50	21.55
Clay (%)	26.33	28.07	30.59	35.25
Bulk density ($g.cm^{-3}$)	1.35	1.37	1.40	1.43
pH	4.92	4.85	4.68	4.50
Organic C (%)	1.97	1.79	1.56	1.49
Water holding capacity (%)	45.60	44.70	43.33	42.58
Available N (kg ha^{-1})	542.53	528.10	580.03	473.54
Available P (kg ha^{-1})	20.91	11.30	10.70	9.90
Available K (kg ha^{-1})	351.81	306.27	266.38	253.39

Table 2. Effect of simulated erosion and N levels on the uptake of N (kg ha^{-1}) by upland rice

Simulated erosion rates (cm of soil removed)	*Levels of N (kg ha^{-1})*				
	0	*60*	*120*	*180*	*Mean*
0	128.05	167.65	218.95	250.20	191.22
5	71.88	140.96	174.31	218.60	151.44
10	61.29	126.16	150.79	189.71	131.99
15	54.11	114.52	139.51	157.80	116.48
Mean	78.83	137.32	170.90	204.08	147.78

SE (E) = 9.29 CD at 5 % = 22.72
SE (N) =10.76 CD at 5 % = 22.21
E X N = NS

Table 3. Effect of simulated erosion and N levels on the uptake of P (kg ha^{-1}) by upland rice

Simulated erosion rates (cm of soil removed)	*Levels of N (kg ha^{-1})*				
	0	*60*	*120*	*180*	*Mean*
0	23.90	30.80	35.04	39.30	32.26
5	14.40	23.95	32.16	30.70	25.30
10	11.15	23.52	31.18	27.87	23.43
15	7.29	20.77	23.31	26.61	19.49
Mean	14.18	24.76	30.42	31.12	25.12

SE (E) = 2.17
SE (N) = 2.17
E X N = NS CD at 5 % = 5.32
CD at 5 % = 4.48

Table 4. Effect of simulated erosion and N levels on the uptake of K (kg ha^{-1}) by upland rice

Simulated erosion rates (cm of soil removed)	*Levels of N (kg ha^{-1})* 0	60	120	180	*Mean*
0	142.43	197.59	220.83	242.17	200.76
5	83.04	138.33	173.51	197.33	148.05
10	75.58	127.97	142.64	193.96	135.04
15	61.21	109.65	123.04	139.13	108.26
Mean	90.57	143.38	165.00	193.15	148.03

SE (E) = 17.79
SE (N) = 11.58
E X N = NS CD at 5 % = 43.54
CD at 5 % = 23.90

Table 5. Dry matter yield (q ha^{-1}) in eroded soils treated with different N levels

Simulated erosion rates (cm of soil removed)	*Levels of N (kg ha^{-1})* 0	60	120	180	*Mean*
0	165.12	187.41	203.39	213.52	192.36
5	108.79	161.51	180.30	193.76	161.84
10	99.97	154.80	160.69	181.95	149.35
15	87.35	147.32	150.84	157.37	135.72
Mean	115.31	162.76	174.55	186.65	159.82

SE (E) = 13.01
SE (N) = 12.21
E X N = NS
CD at 5 % = 31.84
CD at 5 % = 25.19

Table 6. Straw yield (q ha^{-1}) in eroded soils treated with different N levels

Simulated erosion rates (cm of soil removed)	*Levels of N (kg ha^{-1})* 0	60	120	180	*Mean*
0	124.96	143.79	161.69	171.99	150.61
5	81.55	126.94	146.60	162.28	129.34
10	78.74	117.12	125.19	151.28	118.08
15	72.19	114.19	119.11	124.61	107.52
Mean	89.36	125.51	138.15	152.54	126.39

SE (E) = NS SE (N) = 11.18
E X N = NS CD at 5 % = 23.08

Table 7. Grain yield (q ha^{-1}) in eroded soils treated with different N levels

Simulated erosion rates (cm of soil removed)	Levels of N (kg ha^{-1})				
	0	*60*	*120*	*180*	*Mean*
0	40.17	43.62	41.70	41.53	41.75
5	27.23	34.57	36.70	31.48	32.50
10	21.37	37.68	35.50	30.67	31.30
15	15.17	33.10	31.73	32.77	28.19
Mean	25.99	37.24	36.41	34.11	33.44

SE (E) = 2.26
SE (N) = 2.49
E X N = NS CD at 5 % = 5.52
CD at 5 % = 5.13

20

Constraints of Crop Production in Nagaland

M.K. Singh*

ABSTRACT

Nagaland has very rich heritage of biodiversity, unique socioeconomic conditions and diverse agro climatic conditions. In spite of rich resources base, productivity of many crops is low as compared to national average. This can be primarily be attributed to inherent co-nutrients as well as faulty agrarian practices. The major inherent constraints of crop production are soil erosion resulting in loss of organic matter and nutrient runoff, extremely acidic soil, unpredictable rainfall, lack of assured irrigation and undulated topography. The faulty agrarian practices include rainfed monocropping, improper rainwater utilization (except few practices like *zabo* system and *panikheti*), age old traditional method of shifting cultivation non characterization of agro climatic conditions, non availability of package of practices for the exploitation of full genetic potential, poor communication and lack of mechanization.

* Department of Agronomy, Nagaland University, School of Agricultural Sciences and Rural Development Medziphema – 797106.

Crop production on a long term basis can only be sustainable in the resources are utilized judiciously. There is and urgent need of multidisciplinary intensive research based on watershed approach in various agro climatic conditions for sustainable crop production.

Introduction

Nagaland located in the north-eastern region of India, with a population of 1.9 million, covers an area of 16.57 lakh hectare. The climate ranges from sub-tropical to sub-temperate and the altitude ranges from 200m to 3,800m above mean sea level. Agriculture is the main occupation of more than 80 per cent population. The major crop production system in the state is *jhum* cultivation and terrace cultivation. *Jhum* is a way of life for a large section of Naga society, however, this crop production system is becoming more intensive and less sustainable due to increase in the population. In spite of all incentives and support by the government and other agencies, the agriculture is predominantly traditional and subsistence in nature. There has not been much influence of green revolution in the state as in other parts of the country. The food deficit in the state is 24,441 metric tones on the basis of average per capita requirement of 175 kg/capita/year during 2000–2001 (Anonymous, 2002). The average productivity of rice, wheat and other cereals is low in comparison to national average except pulses (Table 1). The low productivity of crops can primarily be attributed to inherent constraints as well as faulty agrarian practices.

Table 1. Area, production and productivity of rice, wheat, pulses and total food grains in Nagaland (2000–2001)

Food crops	*Area (ha)*	*Production (metric tonnes)*	*Average state productivity (kg/ha)*	*Average national productivity (kg/ha)*
Rice	1,50,400	2,30,560	1,532	1,913
Wheat	4,500	10,500	2,333	2,743
Total cereals	2,02,674	3,20,610	1,493	1,857
Total pulses	25,500	20,960	821	533
Total food grains	2,28,174	3,23,570	1,418	1,636

Inherent Constraints

(a) Soil erosion by water

Soil erosion by water is influenced greatly by precipitation (its intensity and amount), the slope of land (its degree and length), the type of soil and the native of ground Coeur and lead use. Soil erosion is the major cause of loss of organic matter and nutrient ran off. Jungle cutting burning, cleaning and dibbling of seeds account for nearly 3.7 tonnes/ha of soil materials to slide/rot down to foot hills (Singh, 1978). Soil erosion from hill slopes (60–70%) under first year, second year and third year (abandoned *jhum*) was reported to be 146.6, 170.2 and 30.2 tonnes/ha/year, respectively (Singh and Singh, 1978) Estimates reveal that nearly 181 million tonnes of soil is lost annually as a result of shifting cultivation.

(b) Soil acidity

The pH of Nagaland soils varies between 4.0–6.5. High soil acidity accompanied with high rainfall affect the availability of macro and micro nutrients, the soluble bases are leached out of the root zone. The native and applied phosphorus becomes unavailable due to presence of high amount of iron and aluminum. Excessive availability of Fe, Mn and Cu, and unavailability of Mo and B exert adverse effect on crop growth. This also leads to nutrient imbalance in the soil affecting the optimum growth and development of crops.

Soil acidity also exert adverse impact on growth and multiplication of soil micro-organism. The beneficial activities of *Azotobacter* and nodule forming bacteria of legumes are adversely affected as the acidity increases. The satisfactory granulation of soils also becomes difficult to achieve.

(c) Dependence on monsoon rainfall

Water has perhaps the greatest influence on the growth and yield of a crop. It is needed in much larger quantity than that of any other substance that contributes to growth and yield. The annual average rainfall in Nagaland is very high (2500mm) which is unpredictable, and often leads to moisture stress at critical growth stages of crops due to prevalence of dry spells, and may occur in any of the *monsoon* months. Out of 16.57 lakh hectare of geographical area, irrigated area in the state is only 62 thousand hectares (Sharma, 1998). The major area of the state will continue to be rainfed due to hilly terrain.

(d) Physiography

The phisiography of Nagaland limits the cultivation of many field crops. Due to hilly terrain it is difficult to take up major imigation project as it would need heavy financial involvement. The undulated topography leads to decrease in the human efficiency and also limits the introduction of heavy machineries viz., tractor and its associated implements.

Faulty Agrarian Practices

(a) Rainfed monocropping

In spite of relatively high and prolonged duration of rainfall, the cropping intensity in the state is very low (111%). After all the incentives, the production and productivity of crops has not gained momentum due to monocropping. There is ample scope of increasing cropping intensity through intercropping and multiple cropping. Incorporation of horticultural crop in agricultural production system will increase the system productivity in time and space dimension.

(b) Improper rainwater harvesting

Water harvesting encompasses all the techniques methods or innovations which induce collection and storage of water from various sources for its beneficial use. There are few instances of indigenous methods of rainwater management like *Zabo* system and *Panikheti*. These methods adopted traditionally by tribal farmer's of the state, due to their ingennity, skill and experience are simple, make use of locally available resources, required less investment and are most suitable for hilly terrains. These methods have combination of soil and water conservation techniques and doesn't involve deforestation and, therefore, are eco-friendly and helps in resource conservation. (Sharma, 1998) However, majority of areas are still rainfed and doesn't have proper rain water harvesting techniques available at their end. Combination of traditional wisdom in water management and feasible modern techniques for hilly areas could go a long way in improving irrigation system in the state.

(c) Prevalence of shifting cultivation

The tribal Nagas live in about 1200 villages located on the hills. In the days when this system of food production emerged, it worked well and there was a balance between population and soil fertility as a result cycle larger fellow cycle of 20 – 30 years. The cycle in present time has reduced to 3 to 6 years (Table 1). The system at present has become not only unproductive but hazardous to environment. (Prasad and Singh, 1990).

Table 2. Number of villages and *jhum* cycle range in some districts/subdivision of Nagaland

Sample/District/Subdivision	*Village*	Jhum *cycle(yrs)*	*No. of villages*
Kohima	Peducha	4	24
Dimapur	Seithekima	5	50
Satakha	Satakha new	6	77
Jalukie	Pedi	7	135
Jalukie	Inkeo (new)	8	195
Longleng	Nian	9	130
Dimapur	Ura	0	149
Tening	Najauma	10	201

(Anonymous, 2002).

(d) Non characterization of agro climatic conditions

Farmers in Nagaland are raising crops depending on the altitude viz., cold region (1,800m–1,500m) - cole crops, regular *jhum* (1,500–1,200m) - *jhum* crops, intermediate range (1,200m –600m) - warm season crops. These agro ecosystem are not scientifically characterized. Each crop require certain agroecological conditions for their growth and development. The full characterization of agroecological regions will guide the selection of crop and varieties for the particular condition. Characterization of districts on the basis of altitude range is given in (Table No. 3).

Table 3. Altitude range and corresponding district in Nagaland

Altitude range (m)	*District/Subdivision*
0 - 500 m	Dimapur, Baghty, Medziphema,
500 - 1000 m	Mon, Kiphire, Changtongya, Mangkolemba
1000 - 1500 m	Kohima, Mokokchung, Tuensang, Wokha, Peren, Tseminyu, Sangsangnyu, Wakching
1500 - 2000m	New Phek, Zunheboto, Kikruma, Shamator, Noklack, Longkhim
2000 m - 2500m	Tokiye, Pfutsero

(Anonymuos, 2001)

(e) Non availability of package of practices:

Each crop requires certain management practices viz., time of sowing, spacing, varieties, nutrient and water management, plant protection measures. The management practices are not available for crops and varieties under different situations. The poor communication leads to unavailability of agricultural inputs at the right timeliness is very important in agricultural production system, delay in sowing of seeds even for one day results in drastic reduction in yield. Farmer's in the state still depends on family labour and traditional method of cultivation which leads to non adoption of improved method of cultivation and mechanization. The total fertilizer consumption in state is very low (4 kg/ha) in comparison to national average (86.71 kg/ha), but there is imbalance between N, P and K: (10.46 : : 7.89 : 1) . In most of the agriculturally advanced state like Punjab and Haryana the fertilizer consumption is high.

Crop Production on Watershed Basis

The concept of watershed management involves optimum use of natural resources of land and water with in a natural physiographic or hydrological unit, which in turn, is governed by factors like geological base, topography, soil characteristics, present land use, socioeconomic and ecological conditions. An optimum interaction among these factors can be observed with a watershed and can be employed specially for proper utilization of land and water resources to increase production of food, fiber, fodder and fuel, and to prevent degradation of land or wastage of water. This would also include reclamation of cultivable wasteland within a watershed for settlement of tribal cultivator from thickly populated or denuded and less productive areas (Kaul, 1981).

Using a geographical information system (GIS) in a watershed will enable placement of any kind of data on a digital map and then visualized, compared, measured and analyzed. GIS combines layers and layers of information about a place and puts them on a single map, so a problem can be viewed in a number of ways and unique solution could be found.

GIS provides the analytical capabilities for a successful precision agriculture system. GIS lets farmers perform site – specific spatial analyses of agronomic data. The study of geographic features and the relationship between than can be applied to all agriculture sectors. By understanding better how features within the landscape interact, decision makers can optimize efficiency and improve economic returns (Anonymous, 2003).

Conclusions

(1) No single pattern can be evolved as a common solution for the entire state for tackling the problem. In every location, a specific approach would have to be devised based on climate, physiographic and traditional occupation of families involved.

(2) Settling of the *jhumias* on irrigated terraces has been most successful means of weaning them from *jhuming*, at the same time use of slopes for horticultural or cash crop plantation, particularly in easily accessible areas should be popularized.

(3) *Jhum* control is a multidisciplinary problem and calls for well integrated and co-ordinated approach involving various disciplines like agronomy, horticulture animal husbandry, forestry, soil and water conservation engineering, rural sociology etc. The stake holders are to be involved in planning and implementation of the watershed programmes through participatory approach.

REFERENCES

Anonymous. 2002. Fertilizer statistics 2001–2002 the fertilizer association of India, New Delhi.

Anonymous. 2002. Nagaland village profile Government of Nagaland Department of Agriculture, Nagaland.

Anonymous, 2002. Statistical hand book of Nagaland, Directorate of economics and statistics, Government of Nagaland, Kohima, pp. 51–64.

Anonymous 2003. Gobar times supplement society for environmental communication Sept. 15 Down to earth supplement, pp. 71–75.

Kaul, G.L. 1981. Shifting cultivation magnitude of the problem and lessons learnt, *Journal of the North Eastern Council* 4 (1) : 19 – 21.

Prasad, R.N. and A. Singh. 1990. Technology for wasteland development, ed. I. P. Abrol and V.V. Dhurva Narayan, ICAR, New Delhi 214 – 222 pp.

Sharma, U.C. 1998. Water management by the tribes of North Eastern Region the traditional wisdom and future strategies, *Fertilizer News,* 43 (2) : 43–49.

Singh, A. 1978. Shifting cultivation and soil erosion problems in North Eastern Hill Region XVI Annual convention of ISAE, IIT Khargapur.

Singh, A. and Singh, M.D. 1978. Effect of various stages of shifting cultivation on soil erosion from steep hill slopes, *Indian Forester,* 106 (2) : 115-121.

21

Constraints Faced by the Mushroom Growers of Dimapur District of Nagaland

Tzudir, Bendangmenla, Sharma, A., Kalita, D.C.. & Sharma, Y. K.***

ABSTRACT

India is a country of about 1.1 billion human population and about 450 million livestock; 75 per cent of human population lives in about 6,50,000 villages and is mainly engaged in agricultural and allied activities. Government of India is giving a lot of emphasis on agro-based industries due to advantage of rural employment generation and gainful utilization of natural and farm resources. Large quantities of renewable lignocellulosic residues are generated every year as a result of extensive agriculture practices. Their direct use as food is non-existent. Mushrooms have the ability to transform nutritionally useless waste into highly acceptable nutritious food. The humanity is passing through a difficult competitive area of its civilization.

* Department of Agricultural Economics, Nagaland University, SASRD, Medziphema: Campus. Nagaland.

** Department of Agricultural Chemistry & Soil Science, Nagaland University, SASRD, Medziphema. Nagaland.

At present, mushrooms are being cultivated in more than 100 countries. Globally, the production of mushroom is increasing at a rate of 7 per cent the world over. It has been projected that if the present growth is sustained, the country's mushroom production may cross 1 lakh tones mark by the turn of the century, 3 lakhs tones by 2010 and 6 lakhs tones by 2020.

Since paddy is cultivated by most of the farmers, abundant paddy straw is produced annually. These agro-wastes can be easily used for the production of oyster mushroom. Cultivation technology of oyster mushroom is easier to take up due to involvement of low initial investment and cost of production. Its cultivation and maintenance is also easy. Thus, the rural entrepreneurs can enjoy high return as compared to other agricultural allied enterprises. The present study was conducted in Dimapur district of Nagaland. The primary data were collected with the help of specially designed pre tested schedules through personal interview of the sample growers pertaining to the agriculture year 2005-2006. Simple Random Sampling technique was used to draw the desired sample size of the study. The study reveals that on an average, 47.74 per cent of the produce was marketed in the local market, while 52.25 per cent was utilised for home consumption. The different types of problems encountered by the mushroom growers viz; availability of spawn, lack of good quality spawn, marketing problem, lack of finance, lack of training and lack of knowledge etc.

Introduction

India is a country of about 1.1 billion human population (Year, 2005) and about 450 million livestock; 75 per cent of human population lives in about 6,50,000 villages and is mainly engaged in agricultural and allied activities. Government of India is giving a lot of emphasis on agro-based industries due to advantage of rural employment generation and gainful utilization of natural and farm resources. Large quantities of renewable lignocellulosic residues are generated every year as a result of extensive agriculture practices. Their direct use as food is non-existent. Mushrooms have the ability to transform nutritionally useless waste into highly acceptable nutritious food. The humanity is passing through a difficult competitive area of its civilization.

Forever increasing population, the demands are multiplying. India has made tremendous progress in production and productivity of several food grains. But still there is food shortage and deficiency of nutrients. In the last one-decade, there is almost stabilization and or stagnation in agricultural production. It is high time to divert resources and energy to develop alternative source of employment and quality food production. Undoubtedly, mushroom farming looks not only promising but also enterprising and adaptable. The varied climatic conditions in different parts of the country help in growing mushroom without artificial temperature and humidity control.

Mushrooms have been utilized as an article of food since ancient times. Mushroom is the fleshy, spore-bearing edible part of fungus. They are unlike green plants as they lack chlorophyll and therefore, depend on the performed food for their nutrition. It consists essentially of two portions; the portion above the substratum is the white thread-like structure known as mycelium. The portion above the substratum is a fruiting body; consist of a cap or an umbrella-like structure and stalk. There are over 10,000 kinds of fleshy mushrooms out of which some are edible while other is poisonous. About 100 species of mushroom are consumed widely while about 50 species are internationally traded (Tewari, 2003). The commonly cultivated mushrooms in India and also in the North-Eastern part of the country are *Agaricus spp.*(European white button mushroom), *Volvariella spp.*(paddy straw mushroom) and *Pleurotus spp.* (Oyster or Japanese mushroom).

At present, mushrooms are being cultivated in more than 100 countries. Globally, the production of mushroom is increasing at a rate of 7 per cent the world over. It was 50 lakhs tones in 1997 and it is expected that the world production of mushroom would increase to 70 lakhs tones per annum by the year 2010 and to 110 lakhs tones by the year 2021. India has virtually witnessed a revolution in mushroom production during the last few decades, from 100 tones in 1970, 25,000 tones in 1995, 40,000 tones in 1997 and 45,000 tones in 2000. In India, mushroom production is increasing at a rate of 30 to 40 per cent. It has been projected that if the present growth is sustained, the country's mushroom production may cross 1 lakh tones mark by the turn of the century, 3 lakhs tones by 2010 and 6 lakhs tones by 2020 (Dhar, 1997).

In North Eastern states there are hardly any white button mushroom farms in production presently. But there are scores of oyster and paddy straw mushroom farms in the area and the production of all types of mushroom in the region is about 1000 tones. Though the common people in this area like mushrooms, their consumption is confined to mushrooms harvested from nature (wild mushrooms).

Mushroom cultivation has a special relevance to India because straw and plant residues are abundantly available with our farmers and our environment is conducive to the cultivation of mushrooms. Hence the future of this industry is bright. The awareness for the mushrooms among the general consuming public has been created. Since rice is the main food and paddy cultivation is done in large scale by the farmers of the North-East, large quantity of paddy straw is available for making compost and as a source of basic raw material for mushroom cultivation. Cultivation of mushroom will be of great benefit to the village farmers who have straw. They can raise mushroom crops and earn substantial profit for their socio-economic development. They can also use the used compost after mushroom cultivation as manure in their backyard kitchen gardens. Mushroom cultivation requires less space as they can be grown both indoors and outdoors. Under it can be grown in basements, verandah, abandoned poultry farms, mud huts with windows, wooden/bamboo framed thatch house etc. However, modern mushroom houses have insulated walls and roof equipments for controlling temperature and relative humidity. Educated unemployed may take up cultivation as self-employed programme whereas low paid employees and landless labourers may take up as their additional source of earning.

Although commercial cultivation is done in controlled conditions particularly temperature and humidity, experiments have shown that it can be cultivated successfully in variable natural conditions on small scale. European white button mushroom can give one crop in plains and 2-3 crops in hills. White oyster mushroom can be grown through out the year except in winter months on the hills.

Mushrooms are used as food as fresh, dried, or canned. A variety of products like mushroom ketchup, soup, pickle, powder, dehydrated mushroom etc. can be prepared. It forms valuable fodder for pigs, poultry and for fishes. The spent straw or compost is also good manure. Mushrooms are a good source of proteins, minerals, vitamins etc. Mushrooms are low in sugar content and as such used as selective food for diabetics. P: Na ratio is very high in mushroom, which is desirable for patients of hypertension. Thus mushrooms provide high protein and low calorie diet. Anti-tumor effects have been reported by the extracts of *Lentinus edodes, Pleurotus ostreatus, Agaricus bisporus, Auricularia auricula* etc. Compounds extracted from *Agaricus bisporus, Lentinus edodes, Coprinus comatus* have been reported to have antifungal and antibacterial properties. Fresh mushrooms can be sold as vegetables in the market. Mushrooms preserved in the form of pickles, drying and canning have got internal market in metro cities. Canned mushrooms have got a good export market also. The various uses, nutritional and medicinal advantages provided by mushrooms along with its capacity of income and employment generation prompt the scientist to strongly advocate the cultivation of mushrooms. This could be the step towards solving the problems of employment, income generation and malnutrition among rural population.

The congenial climatic conditions and abundance of raw materials for mushroom cultivation, places Nagaland in an advantageous position for production of mushroom on commercial scale. In Nagaland, four species can be cultivated round the year depending upon their climatic requirements. From October to March, oyster mushroom; from April to September paddy straw and milky white mushroom and from November to February, button mushroom can be easily grown in Nagaland. From the experience, till date, it has been seen that oyster mushroom has proved to be the most popular among the people.

Since paddy is cultivated by most of the farmers, abundant paddy straw is produced annually. These agro-wastes can be easily used for the production of oyster mushroom. Cultivation technology of oyster mushroom is easier to take up due to involvement of low initial investment and cost of production. Its cultivation and maintenance is also easy. Thus, the rural entrepreneurs can enjoy high return as compared to other agricultural allied enterprises. The study reveals that overall average, 47.74 per cent of the produce was marketed in the local market, while 52.25 per cent was utilised for home consumption.

Research Methodology

The present study was conducted in Dimapur district of Nagaland. The primary data were collected with the help of specially designed pre tested schedules through personal interview of the sample growers pertaining to the year 2005-2006. Simple Random Sampling technique was used to draw the desired sample size of the study. Two blocks viz; Medziphema block and Kuhoboto block were selected for the present study. A list of SHG's engaged in mushroom production was prepared in consultation with DAO's office, Dimapur and Mushroom Development Centre, Green Park, Dimapur. Also private growers were contacted. The sample mushroom growers thus selected were classified into three size groups viz; (i). Group I: 9 to 12 bags, (ii). Group II: 13 to 16 bags & (iii). Group III: 17 to 92 bags respectively.

Table 1: Disposal pattern of mushroom across various size groups of sample growers in Dimapur district

S.N.	*Size group*	*Home consumption*	*Local market*	*Average total production (in kg.)*
1.	Group - I	13.33 (100.00)	—	13.33 (100.00)
2.	Group - II	11.90 (68.19)	5.55 (31.80)	17.45 (100.00)
3.	Group - III	11.01 (35.74)	19.79 (64.25)	30.80 (100.00)
	Total	11.60 (52.25)	10.60 (47.74)	22.20 (100.00)

(Figures within parentheses indicate percentage of the total production)

Result and Discussion

Table 1 reveals that the quantities of mushrooms that are marketed in local market as well as for home consumption. It is observed that on an average, 47.74 per cent of the produce was marketed in the local market, while 52.25 per cent was utilised for home consumption. In group I, there was no sale of mushroom in the local market. In group II, 31.80 per cent of the produce was marketed in the local market and in group III, 64.25 per cent was sold in the local market. Also their is a direct relationship between the size group and quantum of mushroom sold in the local market. The quantity sold in the local market decreased as the size increased.

Since the marketing of mushroom is not well established in Dimapur district, the mushrooms are sold by the producer themselves in the local market. There was absence of market middleman in the study area. Majority of the growers were having small number of mushroom bags and so the quantity of mushroom produced was confined mostly for home consumption.

Table 2: Percentage of sample mushroom growers according to the problems encountered by them in Dimapur district

S. N.	*Types of problems*	*Group I*	*Group II*	*Group III*	*Total*	*Rank*
1.	Non-availability of spawn	77.77	78.57	58.82	82.50	I
2.	Lack of good quality spawn	44.44	64.28	58.82	57.50	IV
3.	Disease and insect pest attack	55.55	35.71	41.17	42.50	VI
4.	High price of spawn	33.33	14.28	29.41	25.00	VIII
5.	Marketing problem	—	64.28	64.70	50.00	V
6.	Lack of finance	22.22	35.71	52.94	40.00	VII
7.	Lack of training	77.77	85.71	76.47	80.00	II
8.	Lack of knowledge	55.55	78.57	64.70	67.50	III

The table 2 reveals that the mushroom production being a profitable enterprise is associated with many constraints. Constraints under each group along with their frequency percentage are presented in Table. The different types of problems encountered by the growers were availability of spawn, lack of good quality spawn, marketing problem, lack of finance, lack of training and lack of knowledge. Among these problems, non-availability of spawn in time ranked first with 82.50 per cent. It was reported by a maximum of 58.82 per cent in group III and a minimum of 77.77 per cent in group I. So far, Mushroom Development Centre, Green Park, Dimapur is the only place where majority of the growers procure the spawn.

Although, there are various sources of spawn in Dimapur district viz., School of Agricultural Sciences and Rural Development (SASRD), Medziphema, ICAR, Jharnapani, the growers were unaware of these sources. This may be due to lack of proper extension services in the villages.

Lack of training and lack of knowledge ranked 2nd and 3rd among the problems faced by the grower with 80.00 per cent and 67.50 per cent. The growers in the study area felt that more frequent training should be given especially how to grow different types of mushroom both during summer and winter and how to produce spawn on their own. Many of the sample mushroom growers were unaware about the nutritional value of mushroom. The village people are unaware of the fact that the protein content of mushroom is similar to that of meat or fish, which leads to less consumption of mushroom. Although mushroom is becoming a popular food item even now a major portion of the people especially in village consider mushroom as poisonous.

Lack of good quality spawn ranked 4th with 57.50 per cent of the respondent reporting that they received contaminated spawn packet because of which the yield was poor. Marketing problem ranked 5th with 50.00 per cent. Marketing problems identified were lack of regular market and absence of buyers. In group I, the sample growers produced mushroom only for home consumption ad the number of mushroom bags were less in number. The quantities of mushroom yield were not enough to be sold in the market.

Disease and insect pest attack ranked 6th with 42.50 per cent. Even though mushrooms and mushroom bags were infested, majority of the growers did nothing due to lack of knowledge about these infestation. It was highest in group III with 41.17 per cent.

Lack of finance ranked 7th with 40.00 per cent. The common financial problems encountered by the sample mushroom growers were difficulty in getting credit and lack of government initiatives for funding of loans and granting of subsidies. Majority of the growers are deprived of these financial facilities except few.

High price of spawn ranked 8th with 25 per cent of

respondent reporting this problem. Majority of the growers from the village area reported the problem. It must also be due to the fact that although spawn is produced in limited number, the number of interested mushroom grower is more.

Suggestions for Policy Implications

Based on the study the following suggestions can be made

1. Government as well as Non Government Organisations should conduct necessary training and other arrangements for spawn production, so that the growers can produce their own spawn themselves.
2. Awareness programmes should be taken up regarding nutritional and medicinal value of mushroom with a view to boost mushroom cultivation.
3. Necessary training to mushroom growers as well as to interested growers should be given at regular interval on judicious use of resources in mushroom cultivation.
4. Government should take initiative to enhance mushroom cultivation in the state by extending loan as well as subsidies to the growers/entrepreneurs.
5. Government should take appropriate measures to create market.. Apart from Government initiatives, growers themselves can establish cooperative societies for sale of mushroom.

REFERENCES

1. Anonymous. (2005). *A Year handbook of India today.* P. 2.
2. Dhar, B.L. (1997). *Mushroom Industry in India – a view.* Mushroom Society of India, NRCM, Chambaghat, Solan - 173213, p. 369.
3. Tewari, R.P. (2003). World of mushroom, their role in nature and society. Compedium of Lectures. Summer institute on recent development in the cultivation technology of edible mushroom. NCMRT (ICAR), Chambaghat, Solan-173213 (India).

22

Soil Conservation and Its Fertility Management Systems Practice of Sloping Land in Northeast India

*Sapu Changkija**

Introduction

- Mountain farming system is a unique with many problems
- Mountain farmers working continuously looking for a better scope to its sustenance.
- Hi-tech system of farming technology - not suited in mountain - not accepted by the tribal farmers because of drastic departure from the traditional land use practices and socio-cultural system - technology they have been advocating are extremely rigid and totally different from what is currently in practice.
- Any alternative strategy will have to build upon the traditional system in context to the tribal mountain farmers.

* Dept. of Genetics and Plant Breeding, Nagaland University.

Northeast region India

- Numerous ethnic groups of tribal population.
- Geography: difficult terrain; comparatively backward.
- Endowed with rich natural resources; represents transition zone between the Indian Indo-Malayan, Indo-Chinese; meeting place of Himalayan with that of peninsular India; Region acts as a bio-geographic gateway for plant migration.
- Zone is one of the richest of biological diversity in the world.
- Practice various types of indigenous cultivation systems
- Limitation of modern agricultural machinery in hilly terrain.
- Choice and investment restriction of financial resources due to Small land holdings to get higher yields.

Indigenous farming systems are also good from the point of view of resource conversation and maintenance of ecology balance.

Indigenous knowledge on soil conservation and its fertility management practices in mountain farming systems.

- IK is a valuable resource for development activities.
- IK is product of over centuries experience acquired in a spectrum of information, skills and technology in various fields often with trial and error methods which are transmitted through generation to generation.
- Soil management is a dynamic process and the problems changes continually.
- Over a period of several hundred years farmers themselves have tested, implemented, evaluated, modified and developed practice in the system of agriculture, soil conservation and fertility management and etc.

In many instances, IK is blended with exogenous knowledge in mountain farming systems.

Indigenous practice	Indigenous practices blended with exogenous knowledge	Practice by the ethnic group
1. Carry biomass form the forest and mulch or burn it on field	Enhance soil fertility and promote the growing crops and trees on farms for biomass production	Khasi and Jaintia hills in Meghalaya, Kohima dist in Nagaland and in Mizoram state.
2. Burn plant residues on the farm and distribute the ashes	Reduce burning on farm; incorporate at least half of the unburned residues into the soil.	All over NE India.
3. Build walls from dry branches shrubs and bamboo	Combine wall with contour ditch uphill from wall. Strengthen wall with live hedgerows	All over NE India.
4. Integrate trees into fields	Improve planting patterns of existing practice	All over NE India.
5. Build rock terraces	Strengthen terraces and control soil erosion	Nagaland and Mizoram
6. Build log or bamboo terraces	Strengthen terraces, control soil erosion and fertilize the soil by its decomposition	Nagaland, Arunachal Pradesh, Tripura and Mizoram
7. Build terraces from the unburned twigs and biomass	Strengthen the terrace, control soil erosion and fertilize the soil by its decomposition.	Nagaland, Arunachal Pradesh, Mizoram and Meghalaya.
8. Weeds/green biomass kept in the surface of rocks and top of the tree stumps without contact to the soil.	Recycling of biomass back to the soil—for its fertility.	Nagaland, Meghalaya, & Arunachal Pradesh.
9. Banana plant collect from the forest and splits made into contour and shade to seedlings.	Maintain the soil moisture and temperature.	Nagaland, Mizoram, Arunachal Pradesh, and Manipur
10. Building bamboo channels	Efficient irrigation.	All over NE India.

Integrated Soil Conservation and Fertility Management Technology

(a) Soil conservation practices in the region:

Contour tillage, contour ridging/planting, mulching, hedgerows, Cover crops, minimum tillage, intercropping, crop rotation (practices relatively simple and by which means increase crop yields as well as protect the soil); bench terrace, soil barriers, soil traps, selected plants sp. Plantation for holding the soil (protect the soil erosion).

(b) Soil Fertility improvement practices

Farmyard manure (FYM), use of green manure, crop rotation, use of legumes, use of forest litters, residual materials of households, use of ashes, in-situ manuring, lime application, shifting cultivation, home/kitchen garden and etc.

The risks of simple technologies are relatively low, and the effort of adoption is much less than that of building terraces and hillside ditches and etc.

Contour cultivation is one of the simplest and efficient methods in reducing run-off and soil erosion, but less than 30% of the slope lands in this region are under this practice. Many farmers prefer labor saving practices along the slope in the farms.

Some indigenous farming systems in soil conservation and its fertility management practices in the region:

Following are the indigenous sustainable farming system practiced in this region by the farmers on mountains can be mention as follows:- Shifting (Jhum) cultivation based on Alder (Alnus Nepalensis) tree, Bench terrace cultivation, Zabu farming system, Kitchen garden or home garden system, So-omni/Yokya farming system, jhum farming system practice by Konyak tribe in Nagaland and Water dribbling farming system practiced by Jaïntias in Meghalaya.

An appropriate technology for soil and water conservation and fertility management:

Sloping Agriculture Land Technology (SALT) developed in Philippines, has applied with in indigenous farming system, using the local materials with the indigenous cropping patterns along with the local hedgerows species. This farming technology is achieving a successful result throughout Hindu Kush Himalayan mountains as well as in the Northeast region India.

Conclusion

Today soil erosion is almost universally recognized as a serious thread of man's well being, to his very existence. The formation of gully, sheet erosion, landslides and slips are the major process of soil erosion in the mountains. Loss of soil productivity is much more important than the loss of soil itself. Therefore, soil conservation and management must be integral part of a general agriculture development strategy that focuses on improved production practices. Generally, conservation measures designed to control soil loss precede soil improvement practices. However, the two are interrelated and must be considered in combination, even if one practice would actually follow the other in sequence.

In mountain farming systems, plant yields are reduced more by a shortage or excess of soil moisture than they are by soil loss. Therefore, there should be also emphasis on water management. Soil conservation efforts will be more successful when applied through long-term programs rather than through short-term approaches. The lack of technical solution is rarely the major obstacle to accelerating agriculture development. A soil fertility management strategy must be based on a holistic outlook and in integrate many seemingly unrelated components that directly or indirectly influence soil fertility management.

23

Performance of Maize (*Zea mays* L.) Under Various Nutrient Management Practices on Terraced Land

Sewak Ram, B. S. Chauhan and Manoj Dutta*

ABSTRACT

The performance of maize (*Zea mays* L.) under various nutrient management practices on terraced land was evaluated in a field experiment using eleven treatment combinations involving farm yard manure (FYM), N, P and K (NPK) fertilizers, lime, Surface soil, Alder (*Alnus nepalensis*) litter incorporated and burned. After seven years of cultivation and nutrient management maximum stover, grain and dry matter yield was recorded in FYM+NPK+Lime treatment. NPK+Lime, FYM+NPK and FYM+$^1/_2$NPK produced appreciably higher grain yield as compared to addition of NPK alone. Different nutrient management practices could not significantly alter the N, P and K content of the plant. The N, P and K content of grain on an average was 1.23, 7.40 and 3.6 times higher than stover. The plant utilized highest

* Department of Soil Conservation, Nagaland University, Campus: Medziphema, School of Agricultural Sciences and Rural Development, Medziphema- 797106, India.

amount of N, P and K from FYM+NPK+Lime and lowest from Surface soil treatment. Maximum N, P and K uptake by maize crop yielding 7842.6 kg ha^{-1} grain in FYM+NPK+Lime treatment was found to be 126.2, 18.0 and 158.3 kg ha^{-1}, respectively. The N, P and K in grain on an average accounted for 71.7. 93.1, 88.2% of the total N, P and K uptake by crop, respectively. Among the non-fertilizer treatments, maize in Surface soil+FYM produced highest grain yield (1982.3 kg ha $^{-1}$) which was however, only 25.3% of the best yield recorded in FYM+NPK+Lime. The crop in Surface soil+FYM utilized only 31.1% N, 30.7% P and 26.2% K of that utilized by maize in FYM+NPK+Lime treatment. On an average, uptake of 1 kg of N, P and K by crop yielded 58.2, 395.8 and 49.6 kg ha^{-1} grain, respectively. The treatments based on their response towards grain yield could be grouped into three categories. First category includes FYM+NPK+Lime, which produced significantly higher than NPK. The second category consists of NPK+Lime, FYM+NPK and FYM+ $^1/_2$ NPK, which produced appreciably higher than NPK. The third category includes FYM, Forest litter incorporated, Forest litter burned, Surface soil + FYM, Surface soil and Control which either produced significantly less than NPK or nothing.

Introduction

Mechanical soil conservation technique like bench terracing is the most reliable conservation measure frequently employed to protect cultivated slopes. It permits sustainable economic yield to be maintained on long term basis under more intensive use than otherwise be possible. Bench terracing is used to manipulate surface topography of hill slopes to convert them to suit agriculture. Terracing encourages permanent farming, besides conserving fertilizers, moisture and soil. Bench terracing usually exposes infertile and biologically inert sub-soil of less desirable properties for crop growth than those of the topsoil and therefore the production potential of terraced land is rather low at initial stage. Development of soil fertility of terraced land for sustained production however, is a time taking process. To increase immediate as well as long-term productivity of the terraced land, sound fertility management practices are obviously needed.

These practices should ensure a steady build up of soil fertility and other physico-chemical properties desirable for plant growth.

The deficiency of most plant nutrients in sub-soil can be corrected through the addition of fertilizers, manures and other amendments either alone or in combinations. These materials however, increase the cost of production. Organic residues like straw, compost and farm yard manure (FYM) have been successfully used to improve soil tilth and increase the proportion of water stable crumbs in soil. Most of the phosphate and probably all the potassium FYM contains are as effective as fertilizer phosphate and potassium, but only one-quarter of the nitrogen is as effective as fertilizer nitrogen (Russell, 1973). The present investigation was therefore carried out to study the effect of continuous cropping and various nutrient management practices on maize (*Zea mays* L.) yield and N, P and K uptake by the plant on terraced land in Nagaland.

Materials and Methods

A field experiment was established in 1991 on newly constructed bench terraces at the experimental farm of the School of Agricultural Sciences and Rural Development, Medziphema, Nagaland to assess long-term effects of various nutrient management practices on the maize yield and N, P and K uptake on terraced land. The changes in physico-chemical characteristics of 0-15 cm plough layer of the experimental site before and after terracing is presented in Table 1. The FYM was applied @10 t $ha^{-1}yr^{-1}$. The sources of N, P, K fertilizers were urea, single supper phosphate and muriate of potash and were applied each year @ 120 kg N, 60 kg P_2O_5 and 50 kg K_2O ha^{-1}, respectively. Lime as calcium carbonate was added every alternate year beginning 1991 @ 4000 kg ha^{-1}. The leaves of Alder tree (*Alnus nepalensis*) were collected from forest and after drying applied @ 5.0 t $ha^{-1}yr^{-1}$. Surface soil equivalent to 2.5 cm surface soil depth was applied once at the time of construction of bench terraces. The entire dose of phosphorus and potassium and $^1/_3$ dose of nitrogen were applied at the time of final land preparation. Remaining $^2/_3$ nitrogen was applied in two equal splits at 30 days after sowing (DAS) and 60 DAS. Alder litter, FYM and lime were applied one month before final land preparation and mixed well. The Alder litter was burnt on soil surface and the ash mixed well in the soil. Since then, all the plots continued to receive the same treatment every year till 7th year (1997) of cultivation. During this period maize (*Zea mays* L.) (Vijay composite variety) was cultivated every year. Other details of experiment have been reported elsewhere (Chauhan and Game, 2002).

At the time of harvest of 7th year crop, plant samples from each plot were collected at maturity and grain and stover yield was measured separately. Plant samples were analysed for N, P and K content to evaluate the N, P and K uptake by maize plant. The nitrogen content of the plant was determined colorimetrically using Nesseler's Reagent in sulphuric acid (H_2SO_4) and hydrogen peroxide (H_2O_2) digested plant materials (Jackson, 1964). Phosphorus and potassium content in the plant was determined in triacid digested plant materials (Jackson, 1964). Phosphorus was estimated colorimetrically and potassium content was estimated flame photometrically (Jackson, 1964). The nutrient content in plant was used to compute the uptake of N, P and K (kg ha^{-1}).

Results and Discussion

Effect of various nutrient management practices on grain, stover and dry matter yield

The data pertaining to the effect of various nutrient management practices on grain yield (Table 2) clearly showed that the grain yield increased in all the treatments except Alder litter burned when compared with Surface soil which produced lowest yield (715.7 kg ha^{-1}). In Control however, no yield was recorded due to non-survival of plants beyond 60 DAS. Maximum grain yield (7842.6 kg ha^{-1}) was recorded in FYM+NPK+Lime that was significantly higher as compared to other treatments. The grain yield in FYM+NPK and FYM+ $^1/_2$NPK did not differ significantly. These treatments however, produced significantly lower yield as compared to NPK+Lime. The yield in NPK and FYM+ $^1/_2$NPK was significantly higher than that observed in FYM. The yield in Surface soil+FYM, FYM and Forest litter incorporated treatments did not differ significantly. Also, the grain yield in Surface soil and Forest litter burned treatments did not differ significantly. The data (Table 2) established that the addition of NPK fertilizers in combination with FYM or lime or both produced higher grain yield than when applied alone. Among the combinations, NPK+FYM+Lime produced maximum grain yield followed by NPK+Lime. Similar results were obtained by other workers (Donahue *et al.*, 1987; Chauhan and Game, 2002). Further, the application of NPK alone produced lower yield than that obtained with NPK+Lime, FYM+NPK and FYM+$^1/_2$ NPK. These findings are similar to those observed by Bhatia and Shukla (1978) and Sharma (1983).

The data pertaining to the stover yield (Table 2) clearly showed that stover yield increased in general in all the treatments as compared to Surface soil treatment. The maximum stover yield (2858.3 kg ha^{-1}) was recorded in FYM+NPK+Lime followed by NPK (2522.0 kg ha^{-1}). However, the difference in the stover yield of these treatments was not significant. The effect of FYM+NPK on stover yield (2158.5 kg ha^{-1}) was not significant when compared with NPK (2522.0 kg ha^{-1}), Surface soil+FYM (1804.3 kg ha^{-1}) and FYM+$^1/_2$NPK (1760.8 kg ha^{-1}). No significant differences in stover yield among Forest litter incorporated (1630.3 kg ha^{-1}), NPK+Lime (1571.5 kg ha^{-1}), FYM (1235.0 kg ha^{-1}) and Forest litter burned (1190.3 kg ha^{-1}) were observed. The lowest stover yield was recorded in Surface soil (1057.9 kg ha^{-1}) treatment. The stover yield in NPK+Lime, FYM, Forest litter burned and Surface soil treatments differ significantly. The data established that the addition of NPK fertilizers in combination with FYM or lime or both produced higher yield than when applied alone. Addition of nitrogenous fertilizers obviously is expected to enhance vegetative growth. Among the combinations, FYM+NPK+Lime produced maximum stover yield followed by NPK. Similar findings were observed by other investigators (Pande *et al.*, 1970; Russell, 1973; Roy and Singh, 1986; Chauhan and Game, 2002). Application of Surface soil+FYM caused significant increase in stover yield as compared to Surface soil. This result was in conformity with other investigators (Suri and Goswami, 1984).

The data pertaining to dry matter yield is presented in Table 2. Various nutrient management practices on dry matter yield showed that all the treatments except Forest litter burned (2146.6 kg ha^{-1}) caused a significant increase in dry matter yield over

Surface soil (1772.7 kg ha^{-1}) treatment, which produced lowest yield. In Control however, no yield was recorded due to non-survival of plants beyond 60 DAS. Maximum dry matter yield (10700.9 kg ha^{-1}) was recorded in FYM + NPK +Lime treatment which was significantly higher as compared to other treatments. The difference in dry matter yield obtained in NPK +Lime (8419.7 kg ha^{-1}) and FYM+NPK (7601.4 kg ha^{-1}) was not significant. The dry matter yield in NPK (7120.0 kg ha^{-1}) treatment was not significantly different when compared with FYM+$^1/_2$NPK (6840.1 kg ha^{-1}). Further, no significant difference in dry matter yield was observed among Surface soil + FYM (3786.7 kg ha^{-1}), Forest litter incorporation (3220.0 kg ha^{-1}) and FYM (2989.3 kg ha^{-1}) treatments. The data pertaining to the effect of various nutrient management practices on dry matter yield led to conclude that the application of FYM and NPK alone was less efficient as compared to when applied in combinations (FYM+NPK+Lime, FYM+NPK and NPK+Lime). This may be partly due to the availability of all essential nutrients and partly due to other soil conditions for plant growth in these treatments. These findings were in conformity with the findings of other investigators (Maurya and Ghosh, 1972; Cooke, 1977; Singh *et al.*, 1983; Bonsu, 1985; Chauhan and Game, 2002). Barrows and Kilmer (1963) also concluded that fertilizers have been found to be more effective on soils having adequate organic matter content than on soils with depleted organic matter content.

Effect of various nutrient management practices on N, P and K content and uptake by plant

N, P and K content:

The data pertaining to the effect of various nutrient management practices on N, P and K content in plant (Table 3, 4 and 5) showed that there was no significant effect of treatments on N, P and K content of stover, grain and dry matter of plant. The N, P and K content in stover, grain and dry matter in Control could not be estimated because of non-survival of plant beyond 60 DAS. The maximum N and P content in stover were recorded in FYM+NPK (11.23 and 0.40 g kg^{-1}, respectively) treatment. The minimum N and P content were recorded in Surface soil (8.9 g kg^{-1}) and Surface soil+FYM (0.27 g kg^{-1}). The maximum K content in stover was recorded in FYM+NPK+Lime (6.0 g kg^{-1}) treatment and minimum was recorded in FYM and Surface soil+FYM (4.0 g kg^{-1}). The maximum N content in grain was recorded in Forest litter incorporated (13.46 g kg^{-1}) treatment and minimum N content in grain was recorded in Surface soil (10.8 g kg^{-1}). The maximum P content in grain was recorded in Forest litter burned (3.0 g kg^{-1}) treatment and minimum P content in grain was recorded in NPK and NPK+Lime (2.30 g kg^{-1}). The maximum K content in grain was recorded in NPK (21.0 g kg^{-1}) treatment and minimum in Forest litter burned (15.80 g kg^{-1}) treatment. The maximum N content in plant was recorded in Forest litter incorporated (14.4 g kg^{-1}) and minimum N content in plant was recorded in Surface soil (9.9 g kg^{-1}). The maximum P content in plant was recorded in Forest litter burned (1.70 g kg^{-1}) and minimum P content in plant was recorded in FYM+NPK+Lime (1.20 g kg^{-1}). The maximum K content in plant was recorded in NPK (13.0 g kg^{-1}) and minimum K content in plant was recorded in FYM and Surface soil (10.60 g kg^{-1}). The data clearly revealed that the N, P and K content in grain was higher as compared to the stover in all treatments. On an average, N, P and K content of grain was 1.23, 7.4 and 3.03 times higher than that of stover, respectively.

N, P and K uptake:

The data pertaining to the effect of various nutrient management practices on N, P and K uptake by the plant (Table 3, 4 and 5) clearly showed that the maximum N, P and K uptake by plant (126.20, 18.00 and 158.30 kg ha^{-1}, respectively) was recorded in NPK+FYM+Lime which was significantly higher as compared to all other treatments. The lowest uptake of N, P and K by plant (16.7, 2.4 and 16.9 kg ha^{-1}, respectively) was recorded in Surface soil treatment. Similarly, the N, P and K in grain and stover were also highest in FYM+NPK+Lime and lowest in Surface soil treatment. In Control however, no N, P and K uptake was recorded due to non-survival of plant beyond 60 DAS. The N, P and K uptake in FYM+NPK+Lime was 44.1, 58.4 and 42.0% higher as compared to NPK, respectively.

The N uptake by plant in FYM+NPK, NPK+Lime, NPK and FYM+$^1/_2$ NPK treatments (92.3, 91.6, 87.6 and 83.3 kg ha^{-1}, respectively) did not differ significantly. The N uptake in Forest litter burned (21.1 kg ha^{-1}), Forest litter incorporated (38.9 kg ha^{-1}), Surface soil + FYM (39.2 kg ha^{-1}), and FYM (36.0 kg ha^{-1}) treatments did not differ significantly when compared with the lowest N uptake (16.7 kg ha^{-1}) recorded in Surface soil treatment. The N uptake by crop varied from 16.7 to 126.2 kg ha^{-1} with an average of 63.3 kg ha^{-1}. The N in grain varied from 7.4 to 99.2 kg ha^{-1} with an average of 45.2 kg ha^{-1}. The N in stover varied from 9.2 to 27.1 kg ha^{-1} with an average of 17.9 kg ha^{-1}. The N in grain accounted for 44.3 to 84.0% of the total N uptake with an average of 66.4%. The N in stover was less than that present in grain in all the treatments. It accounted for 16.0 to 49.8% of the total N uptake of the crop with an average of 33.6%. The data established that on an average grain and stover accounted for $^2/_3$ and $^1/_3$ of total N uptake, respectively. This may be due to the fact that grain is the storehouse of food richer in protein and minerals. The maximum N uptake by plant was recorded in FYM+NPK+ Lime followed by FYM+NPK, NPK+Lime and NPK treatments. The data (Table 3) thus confirmed that the plants utilized relatively more N, when NPK fertilizers were applied in combination with FYM or Lime than when applied alone. These findings are similar to those observed by Chauhan and Game (2002). The addition of FYM along with fertilizers has been found to significantly improve the N uptake by maize crop (Sharma, 1983; Minhas and Mehta, 1984).

The uptake of phosphorus (Table 4) in NPK+Lime (14.9 kg ha^{-1}), FYM+ $^1/_2$ NPK (13.4 kg ha^{-1}) and FYM+NPK (13.0 kg ha^{-1}) treatments did not differ significantly. Phosphorus uptake by plant in NPK treatment (10.4 kg ha^{-1}) was significantly higher than that observed in Surface soil+FYM, FYM, Forest litter incorporated, Forest litter burned and Surface soil treatments: No significant difference in P uptake was recorded among Surface soil + FYM (5.5 kg ha^{-1}), FYM (4.9 kg ha^{-1}), Forest litter incorporated (4.9 kg ha^{-1}) and Forest litter burned (3.2 kg ha^{-1}) treatments. The lowest P uptake was recorded in Surface soil (2.4 kg ha^{-1}) treatment, which did not differ significantly when compared with Forest litter burned (3.2 kg ha^{-1}). These findings are similar to those observed by Game (1993). The data further showed that the plant utilized appreciably high amounts of P when lime was applied with NPK. Similar results were reported by Datta *et al.* (1983). The addition of FYM along with fertilizers also significantly improved the P uptake by the maize crops. The P uptake by maize varied from 2.4 to 18.0 kg ha^{-1} with an average of 9.30 kg ha^{-1}. Of the total uptake, the grain P constituted on an average 91.4% and among treatments varied from 87.5 to 96.8%. Obviously, the grain P constituted the largest portion of total P uptake by the crop. The P in stover on the other hand accounted for only a small fraction of total P uptake. Among treatments, stover P varied from 3.2 to 12.5% of total P uptake with an average of 8.5%. Similar findings were reported by other workers earlier (Sharma, 1983; Minhas and Mehta 1984; Game, 1993).

The data (Table 5) showed that the K uptake by plant varied from 16.9 to 158.3 kg ha^{-1} with an average of 74.2 kg ha^{-1}. The comparison of the data. further showed that the uptake of K in NPK+Lime, FYM+NPK and NPK did not differ significantly. Similarly, the uptake of K in FYM, Forest litter incorporated, Forest litter burned and Surface soil did not differ significantly. The K uptake in Surface soil+FYM was significantly higher when compared with Surface soil. The uptake of K in FYM+$^1/_2$NPK was significantly higher as compared to the uptake in Surface soil+FYM which showed highest K uptake among non fertilizer treatments. The uptake of K in FYM+NPK+Lime, NPK+Lime, NPK+FYM and NPK was appreciably higher than that recorded in FYM+$^1/_2$NPK. There was no significant difference in K uptake in Surface soil+FYM and FYM treatments. Similar results were obtained by Minhas and Mehta (1984) and Game (1993). The data further showed that lime in combination with FYM and NPK or both did increase K uptake by plant. Similar results were obtained by Datta *et al.*, (1983) who showed that liming has been found to increase the uptake of P, K and Ca + Mg by maize. The data further established that the effect of FYM+NPK, NPK+Lime and FYM+ $^1/_2$NPK on N, P and K uptake was not statistically different. This suggested that for long term fertility management strategy the dose of NPK fertilizer could be reduced when applied in combination with FYM without appreciably affecting N, P and K nutrition of the plants. Such reduction in N, P and K dose however, will not favour best yield harvest. The K uptake in grain varied from 11.3 to 142.1 kg ha^{-1} among the treatment with an average of 65.5 kg ha^{-1}. The K in grain accounted for 66.9 to 92.9% of the K uptake by crop with an average of 83.8%. The K in stover however, varied from 4.8 to 16.2 kg ha^{-1} with an average of 8.74 kg ha^{-1}. The K in stover accounted for 9.2 to 33.1% of K uptake with an average of 16.21%. These findings are in confirmity with the results obtained by Game (1993) during the first year of cultivation on these terraces.

Relative efficiency (%) of various nutrient management practices in respect of grain yield

The computation of relative efficiency (Table 6) of various nutrient management practices based on the yield response over NPK (taking NPK as 100) established that the grain yield in FYM+NPK+Lime, NPK+Lime, FYM+NPK and FYM+ $^1/_2$ NPK was 70.6, 49.0, 18.4 and 10.5 % higher over NPK treatment, respectively. The various nutrient management practices based on their relative efficiency in respect of grain yield could be grouped into three categories. First category includes FYM+NPK+Lime, which produced significantly more than NPK. The second category consists of NPK+Lime, FYM+NPK and FYM+$^1/_2$ NPK, which produced appreciably higher than NPK. The third category includes FYM, Forest litter incorporated, Forest litter burned, Surface soil+FYM, Surface soil and Control which either produced significantly less than NPK or nothing. From the data (Table 6) it can be concluded that among combinations FYM+NPK+Lime was the best practices in respect of yield and N, P and K uptake by maize on terraced land followed by NPK+Lime and FYM+NPK. It can also be concluded that on terraced land the application of FYM+$^1/_2$NPK appears to be viable proposition for long term fertility management strategy as the yield in this treatment was higher than NPK treatment. Further, the data also established that Surface soil+FYM performed better in respect of grain yield than FYM. Addition of FYM produced higher grain yield than Forest litter incorporated, Forest litter burned and Surface soil. The data established that the incorporation of Forest litter on terraced land for long term management was better than Forest litter burned though not as good as addition of FYM.

REFERENCES

Barrows, H.L and V.J. Kilmer. 1963. Plant nutrient loss from soil by water erosion. *Adv. Agron.* 15: 303-316.

Bhatia, K.S. and K.K. Shukla. 1978. Effect of continuous use of fertilizer and manure and fertility status of eroded alluvial soil. *Ind. J. Soil Conserv.* 6:94-97.

Chauhan, B.S. and Tadu Game. 2002. Effect of various management practices on soil fertility and performance of maize (*Zea mays* L.) on newly constructed bench terraces. *Ind. Agri.* 46:55-63.

Datta, M.N., R.K. Gupta and R.N. Prasad. 1983. Response of wheat and maize to lime in acid soil of Nagaland. *J. Ind. Soc. Soil Sci.* 31: 236-240.

Donahue, R.L., R.W. Miller and J.C. Sickluna. 1987. *Soils—An Introduction to Soils and Plant Growth.* Printice Hall of India Pvt. Ltd., New Delhi.

Game, T. 1993. Effect of fertility management practices on the performance of maize (*Zea mays* L.) on newly constructed bench terraces. Unpublished M.Sc. (Ag) thesis submitted to NEHU, Shillong.

Jackson, M.L. 1973. *Soil Chemical Analysis.* Printice Hall India Pvt. Ltd. New Delhi.

Minhas, R.S. and R.L. Mehta. 1984. Effect of continuous application of fertilizers on crop yield and some soil chemical properties under wheat–maize rotation. *J. Ind. Soc. Soil Sci.* 32: 749-751.

Pande, R.C., V.S. Rajput, O.P. Singh and H.C. Jain. 1970. Response of maize to varying levels of N, P and K. J. Soil and Water Conserv. In India. 18: 53-61.

Roy, R.K. and K.P.S. Singh. 1986. Response of crop corn (*Zea mays* Everta) to plant population and nitrogen. *Ind. J. Agron.* 31(1): 89-92.

Russell, E.W. 1973. *Soil Conditions and Plant Growth.* Longman Group Ltd., London.

Sharma, J.P. 1983. Economy in fertilizer use through organic manures in growing maize. *Ind. J. Agron.* 25:154-155.

Suri, V.K. and K.P. Goswami. 1984. Influence of soil released carbon dioxide on field grown corn. Soils and fertilizer. *Abst.* 47 (1-12). *Van Vigyan* (1982) 20: 5-12.

Table 1. Physico-chemical characteristics of 0-15 cm plough layer of the experimental site before and after terracing*

	Soil properties	Before terracing	After terracing
1.	Sand (%)	40.2	34.8
2.	Silt (%)	27.9	28.2
3.	Clay (%)	29.7	25.3
4.	p^H	4.8	4.4
5.	Bulk density (g cc^{-1})	1.2	1.3
6.	Water holding capacity (%)	50.7	47.0
7.	Organic carbon (%)	2.2	1.7
8.	Available N (kg ha^{-1})	564.5	393.6
9.	Available P (kg ha^{-1})	4.1	2.9
10.	Available K (kg ha^{-1})	166.5	138.6

*(Adopted from Chauhan and Game, 2002).

Table 2. Effect of various nutrient management practices on the stover, grain and dry matter yield

Treatments	Grain yield (kg ha^{-1})	Stover yield (kg ha^{-1})	Dry matter yield (kg ha^{-1})
Control	00.0	00.0	00.0
FYM	1754.3	1235.0	2989.3
NPK	4598.0	2522.0	7120.0
FYM + NPK	5442.9	2158.5	7601.4
NPK + Lime	6848.2	1571.5	8419.7
FYM + NPK + Lime	7842.6	2858.3	10700.9
FYM + $^1/_2$ NPK	5079.3	1760.8	6840.1
Alder litter incorporated	1589.7	1630.3	3220.0
Alder litter burned	956.3	1190.3	2146.6
Surface soil	715.7	1057.0	1772.7
Surface soil + FYM	1982.3	1804.3	3786.7
S Em ±	270.5	884.8	157.8
CD at 5%	516.0	335.3	1096.3

Table 3. Effect of various nutrient management practices on the content and uptake of N by maize

Treatments	N content (g kg^{-1})			N uptake (kg ha^{-1})		
	Grain	Stover	Total	Grain	Stover	Total
Control	00.00	00.00	00.00	00.00	00.00	00.00
FYM	13.13	10.12	11.60	22.70	13.20	36.00
NPK	13.30	10.08	11.50	62.50	25.10	87.60
FYM+NPK	12.30	11.23	11.80	67.00	25.40	92.30

NPK+Lime	11.25	9.30	10.30	76.90	14.70	91.60
FYM+NPK+Lime	12.20	9.45	10.80	99.20	27.10	126.20
FYM + $^1/_2$ NPK	12.70	10.50	11.60	64.40	18.90	83.30
Forest litter incorporated	13.46	10.80	14.40	21.20	17.70	38.90
Forest litter burned	11.10	9.10	10.10	10.60	10.50	21.10
Surface soil	10.80	8.90	9.90	07.40	9.2	16.70
Surface soil+FYM	11.20	8.90	10.10	22.30	16.90	39.20
S Em ±	NS	NS	NS	6.90	NS	9.00
CD at 5%	NS	NS	NS	21.90	NS	29.50

Table 4. Effect of various nutrient management practices on the content and uptake of P by maize

Treatments	*P content (g kg⁻¹)*			*P uptake (kg ha⁻¹)*		
	Grain	*Stover*	*Total*	*Grain*	*Stover*	*Total*
Control	0.00	0.00	0.00	0.00	00.00	00.00
FYM	2.50	0.30	1.40	4.40	0.49	4.90
NPK	2.30	0.39	1.30	10.40	0.98	11.30
FYM+NPK	2.60	0.40	1.40	13.00	0.96	13.90
NPK+Lime	2.30	0.35	1.33	14.90	0.53	15.40
FYM+NPK+Lime	2.10	0.34	1.20	17.00	0.95	18.00
FYM + $^1/_2$ NPK	2.60	0.37	1.50	13.40	0.65	14.00
Forest litter incorporated	2.70	0.36	1.50	4.30	0.60	4.90
Forest litter burned	3.00	0.32	1.70	2.80	0.37	3.20
Surface soil	2.90	0.27	1.60	2.10	0.27	2.40
Surface soil+FYM	2.50	0.35	1.40	4.90	0.61	5.50
S Em ±	NS	NS	NS	0.75	NS	0.75
CD at 5%	NS	NS	NS	2.44	NS	2.44

Table 5. Effect of various nutrient management practices on content and uptake of K by maize

Treatments	*K content (g kg⁻¹)*			*K uptake (kg ha⁻¹)*		
	Grain	*Stover.*	*Total*	*Grain*	*Stover*	*Total*
Control	00.00	0.0	00.00	00.00	00.00	00.00
FYM	17.00	4.0	10.60	30.30	4.80	35.20
NPK	21.00	5.0	13.00	98.60	12.90	111.50
FYM+NPK	17.40	5.0	11.00	94.30	9.50	103.80
NPK+Lime	18.20	5.0	11.20	112.80	8.60	121.40
FYM+NPK+Lime	17.80	6.0	11.90	142.10	16.20	158.30
FYM + $^1/_2$ NPK	16.50	5.0	11.50	89.30	9.00	98.30
Forest litter incorporated	16.80	5.0	10.70	26.40	7.70	34.10
Forest litter burned	15.80	5.0	10.70	16.10	5.60	21.80
Surface soil	17.20	5.0	10.60	11.30	5.60	16.90
Surface soil+FYM	17.48	4.0	10.80	34.10	7.50	41.50
S Em ±	NS	NS	NS	5.07	NS	5.91
CD at 5%	NS	NS	NS	16.57	NS	19.30

Table 6. Relative efficiency (%) of various nutrient management practices on grain yield

Treatments	*Relative efficiency (%) of grain yield*
Control	00.0
FYM	38.2
NPK	100.0
FYM+NPK	118.4
NPK+Lime	148.9
FYM+NPK+Lime	170.6
FYM + $^1/_2$ NPK	110.5
Forest litter incorporated	34.6
Forest litter burned	20.8
Surface soil	15.6
Surface soil+FYM	43.1

24

Integrated Nutrient Management and Sustainable Agriculture—An Overview

*A.K. Singh, P.K. Singh and S.K. Sharma**

For a long time, Indian farmers by and large, ignored to maintain the fertility of the soil. Our earlier literature did contain references to the need of manuring the fields and good farmers have been adding available quantities of FYM to their lands. However, when the Royal Commission visited this country (1929), it did remark that Indian soils had been depleted of their fertility to rock bottom. Perhaps that was the situation in most part of the world because 'Alternative Agriculture', a U S publication (1930) stated that crop yield in India, U K, U S and Argentina were about the same (Sekhon, 1995). At that time the importance of farmyard manure and green manuring of legumes was widely known. But the change had started in the direction of the use of chemicals in agriculture in the end of 18th century when Chilean salt petre ($NaNO_3$) had been discovered. In 1840 Justus Von Liebing delivered a lecture in UK and suggested that the plants absorbed nutrient from the soil as ions and that there were 10 essential elements enunciated

* Dept. of Agril. Chemistry and Soil Science, SASRD, Nagaland University, Medziphema Campus, Medziphema, Nagaland 797106.

the Law of Minimum. In 1843, Lawes and Gilbert patented the manufacture of single super phosphate. In 1865, the mining of potassium started when it was accidentally discovered that uses of KCl a by-product of common salt industry was profitable in agriculture. In 1905, a monumental change came when Haber synthesized N_2 and H_2 in the laboratory to produce NH_3. Haber and Bosch won the noble prizes fifteen years later, for perfecting the technology of ammonia reactions which put the fertilizer industry on its course to manufacture nitrogenous fertilizers by 1930.

After independence of India in the early 50s. a 'Grow-more Food Campaign' was started. Work on soil fertility investigation took in form of simple fertilizer trials on cultivators fields and demonstrated the profitability of using fertilizers. Since 1950 population of India increased at a rate of 2.15%. it coincided with a food grain production (primarily wheat and rice) surge at a rate of 2.67% or 3.06 MT/year. Backed up with this unique achievement, India has become self-reliant in cereal production. The future routes to fulfil the food needs of rising population (growth rate range between 1.5 and 1.8% per year or equivalent of 16 to 17 million person/year) compensate at a food grain production growth rate of 1.95% (Kumar, 1998). In the recent decade rate of food grain productivity has shown falling trends (2.97% in 1980s Vs 2.14% in 1990s). Declining pattern in productivity growth during 1990s against that during 1980s is occurred against the background of rising rate of growth in irrigation (1.50 m ha Vs 1.23 m ha) intensity of fertilizer use (76.0 kg/ha Vs 46.5 kg/ha) and spread of area under high yielding varieties (37 m ha Vs 32 m ha). While the area under foodgrain production is more or less static (123 m ha/year), the growth in population continues to bloat unchecked (16 to 17 million person/year). This situation is hardly expected to change in future.

Enhancing the foodgrain production from 50 million tonnes in 1950 to 212 million tones in 2001-2002, largely due to growing high yielding varieties of cereals on irrigated land with chemical fertilizers is a laudable achievement by India. But potentials yields of different crops have not been realised in India. For example, yield gaps of rice and wheat in India and China increased enormously. Both the countries started modernization of agriculture around 1950, rice yields during 1992-93 in China were 59.6 q/ha against 26.9 q/ha in India. The corresponding figure for wheat were 35 and 20 q/ha. Accelerated accretions of the nutrients from mineral fertilizers (NPK) and crop and animal residues have contributed to the success story of the Chinese agriculture. In India, increased usage of chemical fertilizers in an unbalanced manner has created problem of multiple nutrient deficiencies, diminishing soil fertility and unsustainable crop yields Lessons learnt from the past mistakes have made the scientist wiser and various agencies and institutions including FAO have started working on a concept broadly termed as "Integrated Nutrient management" (INM). INM is actually technical and managerial component of achieving the objectives of integrated plant nutrition systems (IPNS) under farm situations. Development of the Integrated Plant Nutrition System (IPNS) for different farming situations aims at use of chemical fertilizers, organic manures and biofertilizers in an integrated manner. The basic principle of IPNS is the maintenance of soil fertility, sustaining agricultural productivity and improving farmers profitability through the judicious and efficient use of mineral fertilizers, organic manures and biofertilizers.

Integrated Nutrient Management and Sustainable Agriculture

Sustainable agriculture is the successful management of resources for agricultural production to satisfy the changing human needs, while maintaining or enhancing the quality of the environment and conserving natural resources. The ultimate goals or the ends of the sustainable agriculture is to develop farming systems that are productive and profitable, conserve the natural resource base, protect the environment and enhance health and safety in the long run.

World Commission on Environment and Development (1987) described a system as 'sustainable' provided today's development accruing from it did not come at the expense of tomorrow's developmental prospects. The traditional agricultural systems that met the tests of sustainability in the past have not been able to respond adequately to modern rate of growth in demand for agricultural commodities as demanded by the current population pressure of human and animals. The need of the time is sustainability of agriculture at enhancing rate of productivity. "Enhanced rate of productivity requires soil quality be either enhanced or atleast sustained at its present level. The post 'Green Revolution' experience has demonstrated that enhanced use of fertilizers and plant protection chemicals resulted multinutrient deficiencies (e.g. S, Zn, Mn and occasionally Fe and B) and stagnant or declining yields. It is estimated that the gap between nutrient removal by crops and addition through fertilizers in India has remained and will remain at a fairly constant level of 8-10 million tonnes per annum (Tandon and Narayan 1990). Such negative balances are depleting the soils of their finite reserves and acute deficiencies will be difficult to correct until or unless some balance view is taken about the problem. One of the most comprehensive strategy is the 'Integrated Nutrient Management' (INM).

The INM helps to restore and sustain soil fertility and crop productivity. It may also help to check the emerging deficiency of nutrients other than N, P and K. Further it brings economy and efficiency in fertilizer use and favorably affects the physical, chemical and biological environment of soil (Singh and Yadav, 1992).

Components of Integrated Nutrient Management

Balanced and efficient fertilizer application is essential for the increased yields and for replenishment of the larger removal of soil nutrients. The Integrated Nutrient Management objective is to emphasize aspect like (a). Maximizing fertilizer use efficiency. (b). Application of nutrients from all possible sources. (c). Retention of soil nutrients and (d). Improvement in soil physico-chemical properties.

Many experiments conducted on cultivators field as well as fixed plot experiments have revealed sustained productivity through balanced nutrient supply under intensive cultivation. Excess removal of nutrients by intensive cropping has led to multiple nutrient deficiencies. Fertilizer application depends on the native soil fertility level and quantity needed by the crops. Indian soils supply on an average about 78 kg/ha of N, 14 kg/ha of P_2O_5 and 76 kg/ha of K_2O to continuous cropping without external application (Palaniappan and Annadurai 1999). The approximate amount of major nutrients removed by few crops are presented in table-1. Hence nutrients have to be applied at the required quantities to an optimum level for sustaining the desired productivity.

Use Efficiency of Fertilizers

Use efficiency of fertilizers in India continues to be very low resulting in wastage of financial resources. For example, N use efficiency seldom exceeds 40% under lowlands and 60% under upland conditions. In best managed package of practices, the efficiency of P and Zn fertilizers hardly exceeds 20% and 2%, respectively. Unutilized fertilizer N has a potential of contaminating atmosphere with N_2O and polluting ground water with nitrate. Excessive P application has been linked with heavy metal (Cd, Pd) accretion to the soil.

Rice alone uses 40% of the total N used in India. Even a 10% increase in the efficiency can lower the requirement by about 1.5 million tonnes annually. Considerable research on the use of nitrification inhibitors, slow release N fertilizers, urea super granules (USG) and briquettes has revealed increased N use efficiency in rice by 15-30% compared to conventional urea. Neem cake treated urea, USG and gypsum or rock phosphate coated urea increased rice yields by 15-30%. In rice, deep placed USG on an average, has resulted in 33% saving of N as compared to prilled urea(PU), besides giving 15-20% more yield, especially in heavy soils. The nitrogen recovery of rice by using USG is as 48-75% as against 23-33% recovery with PU (Savant and stangfel, 1990). Even in maize and wheat neem urea has shown promising results (Prasad *et al.*, 1990).

A large number of innovations in modifying the nitrogen fertilizer materials in form of slow release fertilizers and nitrification inhibitors have been made to reduce N loss through denitrification, leaching and volatilization processes but nothing spectacular has happened. With respect to P use efficiency also nothing noteworthy has happened although the efficiency has been found to increase with organic matter application and by keeping the soil moisture at optimum condition.

Organic Manures

India is endowed with enormous potential for plant nutrients present as biological and industrial by-products. The total annual nutrients ($N+P_2O_5$ + K_2O) potential of these so called wastes material is of the order of 19.11 million tonnes, out of which cattle dung manures alone accounts 6.88 million tonnes (Table-2). According to Tandon (1992), addition of one tonne FYM substituted 3.6 kg (N : P_2O_5 : K_2O :: 2:1:1) and organic manures act as excellent storehouse of nutrients. Higher sustained and stable yield of rice and wheat in china could be clearly linked to supplementation of nutrients through the organic sources.

Experimental results on calcareous soils of pusa, Bihar showed that the integrated use of FYM @ 12T/ha + 80 kg N/ha gave as much rice yield as did the 120 kg/ha as chemical fertilizer (Prasad 1994). On acidic red loam soils of Ranchi, supply of entire N through FYM maintained a moderate wheat productivity of around 3T/ha against no grain where N was supplied through ammonium sulphate for 33 years (Mathur *et al.*, 1989). Long term fertilizer experiments (LTFE) of ICAR from different centres in India revealed that annual addition of FYM @ 10-15 T/ha to the Kharif crop along with regular applications of 100% NPK gave higher crop yields as compared to 150% NPK dose. Organic manures besides supplying essential nutrients in balanced ratio through relatively slow release and stimulating soil flora and fauna, it improve the soil physical environment by way of (i) Improving soil structure and water holding capacity (ii) Moderating soil surface temperature and (iii) Reducing soil losses due to erosion. Organic matter decomposition produces ligands capable of complexing nutrient elements. Complexed elements (Chelate) remain more available to plant roots because complexation shields them against immobilization in soils. Results of several long-term experiments, continuing for almost 30 years have proven beyond doubt that organic manure treatment is necessary to sustain productivity and to keep the fertilizer related pollution under control (Nambiar, 1995; Swarup *et al.*, 1998).

Green Manures and Crop Residues

Incorporation of green manures with legumes shrubs or tree

lopping for sustainable health of soil has been a age-old practices. Green manuring is a well-known approach to soil amelioration and nutrient supply. However, its acceptance lags behind the acknowledged benefits. The competition for land between a green manure and the main crop is the biggest hurdle in its acceptance. Legumes that produce grain for sale and non-grain part for green manuring attract the farmers.

In India substaintial amounts of crop residues are produced.(Table 3). Major crops of India, namely rice, wheat, sorghum, pearl millet and maize together yield approximately 235 million tonnes of straw/stover. The nutrients potential of these crops alone comes to 1.13, 1.41 and 3.54 million tonnes of N, P_2O_5 and K_2O, respectively (Chhonkar, 1995). As per estimates of Tandon (1992), the total nutrient potential of crop residues in India is 7.15 million tonnes per annum. However, expansion of agriculture associated with enhanced cropping intensities and excellent response of miracle varieties to chemically fixed nutrients, pushed this practice to back. Adverse effects became visible soon in the form of declined crop productivity and soil health.

Biofertilizers

In 1834, the French chemist Baussingault gave the concept of Biological Nitrogen Fixation (BNF) by legumes. The practical exploitation of the BNF began to take shape when M.W. Beijerinck, a Dutch microbiologist isolated N-fixing bacteria from root nodules of legumes and named it *Bacillus radicicola* (now known as *Rhizobium* sp). Beijerinck also isolated *Azotabacter* in 1902 and *Azospirillium* (then *Spirillium*) in 1925 (Motsara *et al.*, 1995). Commercialization of legume inoculants was initiated in 1895 when the product sold under the trade name "Nitragin" in the USA. The production of *Rhizobium* inoculant in India was started in 1934. Its commercial production was taken up in 1964 when soybean was introduced in India.

With the initiation of National Project on 'Use and Development of Biofertilzers' biofertilizers utilization has increased from mere 900 tonnes in 1989-90 about 12,000 tonnes in 1999-2000 (Yadav and Raychaudhary, 1999). Nowadays promising stains of N- fixing bacteria viz, *Rhizobium*, BGA, *Azolla*-

Anabenae association and other free living organisms like *Azospirillium* and *Azotobacter* have been developed and are being utilized as biofertilizers. *Rhizobium* in legumes and *Azotobacter* and *Azospirillium* biofertilizer in non legumes have been found to be replacing 25-30% of chemical nitrogen when used in combination with chemical fertilizers. While in fields where no significant quantity of chemical fertilizers are used, they have been found to be increasing the yield by 15-30% which is comparable to 20-35 kg of applied nitrogen. Apart from nitrogen fixing ability, *Azospirillium* is known to produce auxins, like cytokinins and gibberellins.

Azotobacter have been reported for producing vitamins of B group, nicotinic acid and panothemic acid, biotin, heteroauxin and gibberellines. *Azotobacter* has ability to produce antifungal antibiotics and fungistatic compound against pathogens like *Fusarium, Alterneria, Trichoderma* etc (Lakshmi-Kumari, 1975). In a recent review of worldwide crop responses to inoculation with *Azotobacters* and *Azospirillium*, the results indicated that responses varied with crops, cultivers, locations, seasons, agronomic practices, bacterial stains, level of soil fertility and interaction with soil microflora. Of the trials, statistically 60% significant yield increase were obtained in USSR, Israel and India (Wani, 1990). Gaur and Singh (1982) have estimated that 1.90 MT of N could be fixed by *Rhizobium, Azospirillum* and Blue green algae.

The Azolla and blue green algae (BGA) are well known for their contribution to nitrogen economy in low land rice cultivation. *Azolla- Anabaena* association on being used as basal green manure or as dual crop can contribute 40-60 kg of nitrogen per hectare per crop. (Kannaiyan, 1994). The BGA are distributed worldwide and contribute to the soil fertility in many agricultural ecosystems. More than 125 stains of N-fixing free-living BGA are common in flooded paddy fields. The predominant species found at CRRI were *Aulosia, Nostoc, Anabaenea, Cylindrospermum, Aphanothece* and *Gloeotrichia*. One tonne of fresh BGA contains about 1-2 kg N and 500 kg dry BGA contains about 15-20 kg N/ha. On an average, a BGA corresponds to 20-25 kg N/ha (Tondon, 1992).

Indian soils are very much deficient in phosphorus and when water soluble phosphorus is added in the form of fertilizers to soils, it dissolves in soil water and quickly reacts with compounds of Al, Fe, Ca, etc. Due to fixation problem only 25-30% applied phosphate is available to the crop plants. The efficient P-solubilizing microorganisms and arbuscular mycorrhiza have ability to increase the availability of phosphorus from insoluble sources of phosphorus as well as from labile pool (slowly available phosphates) and non-labile pool. Gaur (1990) reported that grain yield of wheat significantly increased by inoculation of either *Penicillium striata, Aspergillus awamori, Penicillium digitatum* or *Bacillus polymyxa* without any fertilizer input. The maximum increase was 37.8% over control was observed with *Aspergillus awamori*. Phosphate solubilizing biofertilizers (Phosphetika) have been found to be solubilizing 10-15 kg of soil phosphorus per hectare per season (Yadav and Raychaudhari, 1995).

Arbuscular mycorrhiza (AM) have received considerable attention in recent years. AM colonize roots of agricultural, horticultural and forestry plants except those plants belongs to family *Crucifarae, Chenopodiaceae* and *Cyperaceae*. The presence of efficient AM fungi improves phosphorus nutrition of crops, enhances water transport, decreases transplant injury, promotes transplant in wasteland and reduces the soil borne diseases. AM have also been reported to improve the uptake of Zn and Cu (Singh and Gupta, 2001). In term of plant growth, an increase of 20-30% in biomass has been reported.

Conclusion

In global terms, India today has 16% human population, 15% of farm animal population, 2% of geographical area, 1% of rainfed area, 0.5% of forests and 0.5% of grazing land. The demand for food and water will increase every year. At the same time, the ecological foundations essential for sustained advances in biological productivity, such as land, water, forest, biodiversity and the atmosphere are experiencing degradation and depletion (Swaminathan, 1999). Agriculture is challenged to develop strategies to conserve non-renewable natural resources (soil) to sustain life on earth. Mismanagement and neglect can ruin these fragile resources and become a threat to human survival (Lal and Pieree, 1991). Soil degradation was thought to be responsible for the collapse of the Harappan civilization in western India, Mesopotamia in Asia Minor and Mayan culture in Central America. In 21st century loss of productive agricultural land is a the most pressing concern for the ever growing population.

Maximization of food grain production per unit of arable land is our national priority. Every increased demand for agriculture product has to come from more intensive cultivation with increased and balanced use of fertilizers. Integrated nutrient management is viable strategy advocating accelerated and enhanced use of chemical fertilizer with matching addition of organic manure, biofertilizers and crops encouraging biological nitrogen fixation. Certain environmental groups are advocating strongly.for Low External Input Sustainable Agriculture (LEISA). Although LEISA as a concept may be new to developed Countries but traditional low yielding agriculture practiced in India during the pre-green revolution period has been based on this model. Its disastrous effects still find expression on the faces of those who experienced hunger in the early sixties. During post revolution period, the question of unsustainability of the productivity of different cropping systems and environmental pollution associated with use of chemical fertilizers have given rise to what is known as "Integrated Nutrient Management". Although chemical fertilizers have been linked with soil and water pollution, their application rates in India are much below the world average and it could be doubled. Therefore, enhanced use of chemical fertilizers with matching addition of organic manures, crop residues and biofertilizers can provide food and nutritional security, sustainability of agriculture along with environmental safety.

REFERENCES

Bhardwaj, K.K.R: (1985). Recycling crop residues promotes nitrogen econmy. *Indian Farming,* 33, 17-19.

Chhonkar, P.K. (1995). Recycling of Organic wastes for plant nutrient management. Proc. Seminar Soil Nutrient Management, Ministry of Agriculture and IARI, New Delhi, June 26, pp. 11-18.

Gaur, A.C. and Singh, R. (1982). Integrated nutrient supply system. *Fertilizer News* 27: 87-89.

Gaur, A.C. (1990). *Phosphate solubilizing micr511organisms as biofertilizer.* Omega Scientific Publishers, New Delhi.

Juwarkar, A.S., Shande, A., Thawale, P.R., Satyanarayanan,S., Deshbratar, P.B., Bal, A.S. and Juwarkar, A. (1992). Biological and industrial wastes as sources of plant nutrients. Tandon, H.L.S. (Ed). (1992). *Fertilizers, Organic Manures, Recyclable wastes and Biofertilizers,* FDCO, New Delhi, pp. 72-90.

Kannaiyan, S. (1994). Azolla-Anabaena symbiosis- A potential biofertilizer for rice. In *Environment and Biotechnology.* Eds. H.S. Sohal and A.K. Srivastava, pp. 37-57.

Kumar, P. (1998). Food demand and supply projection for India. Agricultural Economics Policy Paper, IARI, New Delhi, 98-101.

Lakshmi-Kumari, M., Vijaya Lakshmi, K. and Subbha Rao, N.S. (1975). Interaction between *Azotobacter* sp. and fungi. *In vitro* studies with *Fusarium maniforme* Phytoph. Z. 75, 27-30.

Lal, R. and Pierce, F.J. (1991). The vanishing resources. In "Soil Management for Sustainability". Soil and Water Conservation Society, Ankeny, IA, pp. 1-5.

Mathur, B.S., Sarkar, A.K., Singh, K.P. and Lal, S.(1989). SSAC (BAU) *Research Bulletin* 22, Birsa Agril. Univ. Ranchi.

Modgal, S.C., Singh, Y and Gupta, P.C.(1995). Nutrient management in rice-wheat cropping system, Fertilizer News, 40: 49-54.

Motsara, M.R., Bhattacharyya, P. and Srivastava, B. (1995). *Biofertilizer, Technology, Marketing and Usage.* FDCO, New Delhi..

Nambiar, K.K.M. (1995). In *Agricultural Sustainability. Economic Environment and Statistical Considerations* (Barnett, V., Pyne, R. and Steiner, R. eds). John Wiley and Sons, New York, USA, pp. 133-168.

Prasad, B. (1994). Integrated nutrient management for sustainable agriculture. *Fertilizer News,* 39: 19-25.

Prasad, R. (1990). Nitrogen management in soil fertility and fertilizer use. IFFCO, New Delhi. pp. 41-51.

Palaniappan, S.P. and Annadurai, K. (1999). *Organic Farming,* Scientific publishers, Jodhpur, India.

Savant, N.K. and Stangfel (1990). Deep placement of urea super granules in transplanted rice. *Principles and Practices.* Fertilizer Research, 25: 1-83.

Sekhon, G.S. (1989). Nutrient balances in the soils and crop productivity. *Fertilizer News* 34: 358-360.

Sekhon, G.S. (1995). Management of nutrient supply to crops in India. Proc. Seminar. 'Soil nutrient management' Ministry of Agriculture and IARI, New Delhi, June 26, pp. 8-10.

Sekhon, G.S. (1998). Nutrient balances in soils and crop productivity, *Fertilizer News*, 34:358-360.

Singh, G.B. and Yadav, D.V. (1992). Integrated nutrient supply system in sugarcane and sugarcane based cropping system, *Fertilizer News* 37: 15-27.

Singh, A.K. and Gupta, R.C. (2001). Importance of Vascular arbuscular mycorrhiza in increasing agricultural productivity. Seminar abstract "Approaches for increasing agricultural productivity in hill and mountain ecosystem. ICAR Research Complex, Meghalaya, October 18-20, pp. 4-5.

Swaminathan, M.S. (1999). The challenges ahead. The Hindu Survey of Indian Agriculture.

Swarup, A., Reddy, D.D. and Prasad, R.N. (1998). Proc. of National Workshop on Long Term Soil Fertility Management through Integrated Plant Nutrient supply. Indian Institute of Soil Science, Bhopal.

Tandon, H.L.S. and Narayan, Pratap (1990). Fertilizers in Indian Agriculture—Past, Present and Future, FDCO, New Delhi.

Tandon, H.L.S. (1992). Fertilizers, organic manures, recyclable wastes and bio-fertilizers. FDCO, New Delhi, pp. 15.

Wani, S.P. (1990). Inoculation with associative nitrogen fixing bacteria. Role in cereal grain production improvement. *Indian J. Microbiology* 30, 363-393.

Yadav, A.K. and Raychaudhuri, S. (1999). Exploiting Biofertilizers in North Eastern Reggion. RBDC, Imphal.

Table 1. Quantity of nutrients removed by major field crops

Crop	*Yield Kg/ha*	*Nutrient removed (kg/ha)*		
		N	P_2O_5	K_2O
Rice	1482-8000	31-167	13-69	66-358
Wheat	1998-6000	54-163	30-90	72-216
Sorghum	567-6000	26-139	9-48	44-231
Maize	1122-4000	48-170	20-70	44-156
Groundnut	847-2250	26-69	11-29	23-61
Cotton(lint)	67-800	41-196	31-150	132-625
Sugarcane	59.7-120 tonnes	102-205	37-74	203-408

Source: Sekhon, 1989.

Table 2. Nutrient potential of biological wastes

Type of waste	*Total quantity available*	*Total nutrients ,000T/ year* N	P_2O_5	K_2O	Total
1. Cattle dung manure	279.8	2813.3	1999.7	2069.3	6882.3
2. Crop residue	273.3	1283.1	1965.6	3903.9	7152.6
3. Forest Litter	18.7	99.7	37.4	99.7	236.8
4. Rural Compost	285.0	1431.2	861.5	1422.7	3715.4
5. City refuse	14.0	98.0	84.0	112.0	294.0
6. Sewage sludge	0.5	5.1	2.9	2.8	10.8
7. Pressured	3.2	33.3	79.4	55.4	168.1

Source: Juwarkar *et al.*, 1992.

Table 3. Estimates of the availability of some crop residues in India and their plant nutrient potential

Crop	*Residue yield (,000 tonnes)*	*Nutrient %* N	P_2O_5	K_2O	*Nutrient potential (,000 tonnes)* Total	*Utlisable**	*Fertilizer equivalent***
Rice	110,495	0.61	0.18	1.38	2,398	799	399
Wheat	82,631	0.48	0.16	0.18	1,504	501	250
Sorghum	12,535	0.52	0.23	1.34	262	87	43
Maize	11,974	0.52	0.18	1.35	252	844	42
Pearl millet	6,967	0.45	0.16	1.14	121	40	20
Total	224,602				4,537	1511	754

* One third of the total NPK potential assuming that two-thirds of the total residue is used as animal feed on national basis.

** 50% of the utilisable NPK assuming 50 % mineralization of NPK per season

Source: Bhardwaj, 1995.

25

Zabo and Alder Agriculture—Indigenous Farming Systems of Nagaland

S.D. Rao, Anamika Sharma**, Chandan Rajkhowa*** & Joseph kikon*****

ABSTRACT

Chakhesang tribe of *Kikruma* village in the *Phek* district of *Nagaland* practices *Zabo* system of farming. The system is a combination of agriculture, forestry and animal husbandry with well-founded conservation base for soil erosion control, water resource development and water management as well as protection of environment. The rainwater is collected from the catchments of protected hilltops of above 100% slopes in a pond with seepage control. Silt retention tanks are constructed at several points before the run- off water enters in the pond. The practice of using *alder trees* for raising crops like maize and millets is

* Scientist, Agril. Entomology, ICAR Res. Complex, Nagaland Centre.

** T-5, Trg. Asstt, Hort., KVK Nagaland Centre

*** Joint Director, ICAR Research Complex, Nagaland Centre.

**** T-1, Lab Asst. Ento., ICAR Res.Complex, Nagaland Centre.

time tested practice among the farmers of *Angami, Chakhesang, Chang, Yimchunger* and *Konyak* tribes of Nagaland. The alder agriculture fields are generally located at the altitudes between 1000 to 2000 msl. The alder is used for raising the primary crops of maize, Job's tear, millets, potato and wheat and the secondary crops of chilli, pumpkin and *taro* (Colocasia). The available information and preliminary trials by the State Government showed that if a village with 100 families could set aside about 120 ha. of land to grow alder trees, all families would be able to get sufficient firewood every year.

Introduction

Nagaland is one of the seven sisters states located in eastern part of North East India. The state is located in latitude between 25°6′ and 27°4′ north of equator and between the longitudinal lines of 93°20′E and 95°15′E and having a geographical area of 16, 579 sq.km. The state is predominantly a hilly area consisting of high, mid and low hills with limited plain areas of foothills. The hills are interspersed with plateau, valley, rivers and streamlets. The altitude of the hills varies between 194 meters and 3048 meters. There is an area of 8, 62,532 ha. of land under forest cover, this represents 55.80% of total land mass although it has dwindled severely due to pressure for timber fuel and traditional jhum cultivation. In this state 42.3% of total work force engages in agricultural activity as compared to 31% of non-Himalayan region. Nagaland is thinly populated area with population of around 20 lakhs and density of 120/sqkm. There is high pressure on agricultural land in the hilly region due to 17.29% of net cultivated area as compared to 47% in the whole country. The land has diverse vegetation with plethora of flora and fauna of great economic importance. In this humid hilly state a number of traditional farming systems are practicing since time immemorial. Among them, *Zabo* **and** *Alder* based agriculture are of prime importance.

Zabo System

Zabo system of farming is practiced by *Chakhesang* tribe of *Kikruma* village in the *Phek* district of Nagaland (Sonowal et al., 1989). The system is a combination of agriculture, forestry and animal husbandry with well-founded conservation base for soil erosion control, water resource development and water management as well as protection of environment. The rainwater is collected from the catchments of protected hilltops of above 100% slopes in a pond with seepage control. Silt retention tanks are constructed at several points before the run- off water enters in the pond. The cultivation fully depends on the amount of water stored in the pond. In some pockets of Nagaland such type bench terraces are seen even on very poor lands having 10 to 15 cm soil depth. Even the soil is brought from outside and 10 to 15 cm soil depth is maintained in those portion of terraces where underlying rocks are exposed while making the bench terraces on steep slopes. The land is primarily utilized for rice.

Alder Agriculture

The alder tree found in the hills of eastern Himalayan region is botanically known as *Alnus nepalensis,* belongs to family Betulaceae of Dicotyledonous. The plant is a deciduous and non-leguminous nitrogen fixer. Hence, it plays important role in nutrient recycling on farmlands. The tree is valuable for firewood and medium timber.

The practice of using alder trees for raising crops like maize and millets is time tested practice among the farmers of *Angami, Chakhesang, Chang, Yimchunger* and *Konyak* tribes of Nagaland (Gokhale *et.al.*, 1985). The alder agriculture fields are generally located at the altitudes between 1000 to 2000 msl. The alder is used for raising the primary crops of maize, Job's tear, millets, potato and wheat and the secondary crops of chilli, pumpkin and *taro* (Colocasia). The practices of alder agriculture are as follows:

a) Pollarding

Initially, six to ten years old trees are cut off from main trunk horizontally at a height of two meters from the ground during the month of December and January. The age of trees are judged by observing development of fissures on the main trunk. Before this age, alder cannot tolerate pollarding. The trees sprout 50 to 150 coppices in one year. The entire coppice shoots except five or six on the top of the main trunk are cut at its base. Remaining shoots are allowed to grow and attain heights of about 6 m having a diameter of 15-20cm in three to four years, when it is again pollarded. These shoots are stripped of most of the leaves and sub branches, leaving just a few leaves at the tips. The fallen branches are further stripped and cut down to a convenient size and stacked nearby for firewood. Pollarding is done with sharp edge *dao* so that no crack develops on the cut surface to allow pathogens and insect pests to infect the plants. It is said that a farmer tends an alder tree as if he is giving his son a hair cut. If the tree is not very old or it is in the area where frost is common, pollarding is always done from November to January and a slab of stone to protect it from frost covers the fresh cut. Otherwise frost may kill the tree. Only the young shoots at the end of trunk one left to grow. Regular pollarding at the end of every 4 to 6 years seems to make the tree to live longer. In *Khonoma* village of Kohima district, there are alder trees, which are more than 200 years old and still sprout abundant coppices. The leaves and small twig left over the ground after the twigs separated for firewood are gathered and burnt at a safe distance from the trunks. The ashes are spread over the ground and mixed with soil.

b) Crop production

After the trees have been pollarded during the month of December and January, seeds of primary crops viz. maize, millets, Job's tear and potato are sown in line during the month of February, March and April. During same period, seeds of secondary crops viz. chillies, pumpkin and *taro* are sown in between the line of primary crops. Before sowing, the leaves and dry twigs of alder are heaped away from the trunk and burnt at a distance. The ashes are spread over the ground and the soil filled to receive the seeds of intended crops. Again after the harvest of crops during October and November, cut off coppice shoots yield second crop of firewood and crop residue, are gathered in small heaps and burnt in December. After second crop, alder trees are left to grow on their own without any further tending and the fields remain fallow for another 2 to 4 years. By this time coppices would be 4 to 6 years old and ready for pollarding and agriculture again. The 4-year-old coppice is lopped off neatly at its base from the main trunk to yield firewood.

c) System potential

The available information and preliminary trials by the State Government showed that if a village with 100 families could set aside about 120 ha. of land to grow alder trees, all families would be able to get sufficient firewood every year and at the same time raised crops such as maize, Job's tear, millets, potato and wheat under the alder in about 30 ha every year. The present yield level of food crops can be raised to a higher level by adopting proper alder tree planting geometry, land development, such as terracing, moderate use of fertilizers and stopping burning of alder leaves and crops residue.

The firewood from alder is easy to split and burns even when it is not full dry. For this reason, the housewife's prefers it to other firewood.

In the *Konyak* area (Mon district), where the alder tree is used, terracing is not done but trunks of trees are laid across the slopes to slow down the water run off. However, in *Khonoma* village people have resorted to even terracing the alder fields to further reduce soil erosion and to retain soil fertility. Spreading nature of alder roots also help to retain and keep intact the soil on hill slopes.

Literature Cited

1. Sonowal, D.K., Tripathi, A.K.& Kirekha, V. (1989). Zabo—An Indigenous Farming System of Nagaland. *Indian Journal of Hill Farming,* 2(1). 1-8.
2. Gokhale, A.M., Zeliang, D.K, Kavi Chesan, R. & Angami, T. (1985). The use of alder trees, pub. State Council of Educational Rseaearch and Training, Education Dept., Govt. of Nagaland, Kohima.

26

Regulated Market in India

*Bendangmenla Tzudir**

Introduction

- The establishment of regulated market have resulted in the removal of defects and malpractices in the marketing system of agricultural products under traditional system.
- In 1938, a Bill was passed by the Directorate of Marketing and Inspection for the regulation of markets.
- Regulated market—Elimination of the unhealthy & unscrupulous practices, reducing marketing charges & providing facilities to producer-sellers in the market.

Objectives

- ✓ To prevent the exploitation of farmers.
- ✓ To make the marketing system most effective and efficient.
- ✓ To provide incentive prices to farmers.
- ✓ To promote an orderly marketing of agricultural produce.

* Department of Agricultural Economics, NU: SASRD, Medziphema.

Important Features of Regulated Market

- *Market Committee:* It is established to look after the proper functioning of the regulated market.
- *Weightment of Produce:* This eliminates short weights and malpractices arising when weighing with hand balance.
- *Grading of Produce:* The produce in the regulated market is expected to be sold only after grading.
- *Market News Service:* Market prices are disseminated properly and correctly through various media.
- *Method of Sale:* The sale of agricultural produce is undertaken either by open auction or by the close tender method.
- *Settlement of Disputes:* Disputes arising between producer-seller and traders are solved by the sub-committee of the market committee.
- *Eliminating Malpractices:* The establishment of regulated markets have resulted in removal of a number of malpractices.
- *Market levies or fees:* Market levies or fees are charged on the basis of value of volume of a commodity bought and sold in the market.

Advantages of Regulated Market

1. Market charges are clearly defined and specified.
2. Market practices are regulated and undesirable activities are brought under control.
3. Correct weighment is ensured by periodical inspection and verification of scales and weights.
4. Suitable arrangement for the settlement of disputes is provided.
5. Reliable and up to date market news are made available to the farmers.
6. Suitable quality standards and standard terms for buying and selling are conveniently enforced.
7. Reliable statistics of arrivals, stocks, prices are maintained.
8. Numerous facilities are provided.

9. Open auction method is strictly followed.
10. Propaganda for agricultural improvement is more conveniently carried out.

Progress of Regulated Market in India

Table 1. Progress of Market Regulation in India

Year	*Number of Regulated Markets*	*Regulated Markets as per cent of total Wholesale Assembling Markets*
1951	236	3.23
•	470	6.44
•	715	9.80
1966	1,012	13.87
1976	3,528	48.37
1980	4,446	60.96
1986	5,766	79.06
1990	6,217	85.25
1991	6,640	91.05
1992	6,738	92.39
1993	6,752	92.58
1994	6,809	93.36
1995	6,836	93.73
1996	6,968	95.54
2000	7,077	97.04
2001	7,161	98.19

Sources: *Indian Agriculture* (in Brief), (Various Issues), Directorate of Economics and Statistics, Ministry of Agriculture, Government of India, New Delhi & *Economic Survey*, (Various Issues), Ministry of Finance, Government of India, New Delhi.

Table 2. State-wise area served by Regulated Markets

S.No.	*State/Union Territory*	*Geographical Area ('000 Sq. Km)*	*Number of Regulated Markets*	*Area covered by each Regulated Markets (Sq. Km.)*
1.	Andhra Pradesh	275	861	319
2.	Arunachal Pradesh	84	-	-
3.	Assam	79	35	2257
4.	Bihar (including Jharkhand)	174	813	214
5.	Goa	4	8	500
6.	Gujarat	196	396	495
7.	Haryana	44	284	155
8.	Himachal Pradesh	56	35	1600
9.	Jammu & Kashmir	222	-	-

Present Status of Regulated Market in India

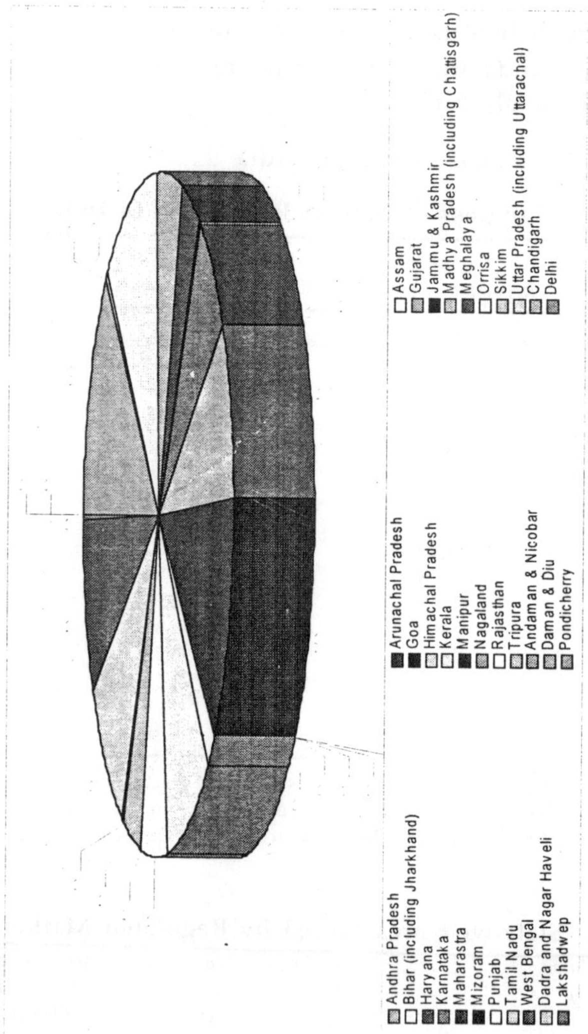

Fig 1 : Number of wholesale assembling makets, rural periodic markets and regulated markets in states of India

10.	Karnataka	192	473	406
11.	Kerala	39	-	-
12.	Madhya Pradesh (Including Chattisgarh)	443	616	719
13.	Maharastra	308	857	359
14.	Manipur	22	-	-
15.	Meghalaya	22	-	-
16.	Mizoram	21	-	-

17.	Nagaland	17	-	-
18.	Orissa	156	144	1083
19.	Punjab	50	675	74
20.	Rajasthan	342	412	830
21.	Sikkim	7	-	-
22.	Tamilnadu	130	270	481
23.	Tripura	10	21	476
24.	Uttar Pradesh (including Uttaranchal)	294	645	456
25.	West Bengal	89	587	152
26.	Andaman & Nicobar	8	-	-
27.	Chandigarh	0.1	2	53
28.	Dadra & Nagar Haveli	0.5	-	-
29.	Daman & Diu	0.1	-	-
30.	Delhi	1.5	21	71
31.	Lakshadweep	0.3	-	-
32.	Pondicherry	0.5	6	83
	Total	**3287**	**7161**	**10783**

Source: Agricultural Marketing Statistical Abstract (2001), NIAM, Jaipur (Rajasthan) & Directorate of Marketing and Inspection, Ministry of Agriculture, Faridabad.

Problems of Regulated Market

- Emphasis is mostly on construction activities and on collection of market fees.
- Several weaknesses and malpractices are still reported.
- Bureaucratization in the management of the regulated markets.
- Lack of qualified staff to manage.
- Most producers refrain from bringing their commodities to these regulated markets.
- The regulated markets have indirectly led to the monopolization of trade.

Conclusion

✓ Provide efficient organized marketing systems.

✓ Increase production as well as income of the farmer.

✓ Helps to improve rural economy of the region.

27

Evaluation of fungicides *in vitro* against the growth of *Cercospora capsici* : the casual organism of chilli leaf spot disease

Ruokuovilie Mezhatsu; L. Daiho and D.N. Upadhyay*

Abstract: In the present experiment, *in vitro* test with Bavistin (0.1%), Fytolan (0.3%) and Indofil M-45 (0.2%) against the growth of *Cercospora capsici* by poison food technique showed significant effect. Bavistin was found most effective against the radial growth with mean value of 24.27 mm, followed by Indofil M-45 with 27.17 mm and lesser but significant control by Fytolan with 28.63 mm as against 41.78 mm in the control.

Key words: In vitro, poison food technique, radial growth and *Cercospora capsici*.

Chilli is the most important ground spice item exported from India. India earned about Rs. 9665700/- through export of 815.66 tonnes of dry chilli during 1984-85 (Anon., 1986). But the production of chilli in India is hampered by a number of diseases. Among the diseases, *Cercospora capsici* causing leaf spot

* Department of Plant Pathology, Nagaland University, School of Agricultural Sciences and Rural Development, Medziphema-797106, Nagaland, India.

disease is one of the major problem in production due to complete defoliation of leaves. Therefore, an experiment was carried out in the laboratory to see the relative efficacy of the selected fungicides on its growth by poison food technique.

Materials and Method

The present experiment was carried out in the school of Agricultural Sciences and Rural Development, Nagaland University, Medziphema, Nagaland, India, during 2000 to see the relative efficacy of the selected fungicides by poison food technique.

Leaf spot caused by *C. capsici* were observed on *Capsicum annuum* plants in the Experimental farm. They were collected and brought to the department for isolation. Diseased leaves were then surface sterilized with 0.4% sodium hypochloride for 2 minutes to remove non-causal micro-organisms. They were washed in distilled water and cut into small pieces through the infected spots and transferred to poptato dextrose agar (PDA) medium in petri-plates of 75 mm in diameter. After 3 days, the growing tips of the mycelia were again transferred to PDA slants to make pure culture and incubated at 25±2□C till conidia formation. The stock cultures were maintained on PDA slants in refrigerator at 5□C and the pathogen was sub-culture at regular interval for maintaining the live culture for further studies.

Young cultures of 7 days old, grown on PDA medium was used for inoculation. The size of inoculum was standardized by a cork borer having an internal diameter of 5 mm. The cut inoculum from the PDA medium was taken upon by the loop of inoculating needle and placed at the center of the plate in an inverted position, so that the inoculum come in direct contact with the surface of the medium. The inoculation was done using Laminar air flow. After inoculation, the culture plates were incubated at 25±2°C in BOD incubator.The selected fungicides tested against the growth of *C. capsici* were- Bavistin at 0.1%, Fytolan at 0.3% and Indofil M-45 at 0.2% respectively were used. The tested fungicides were maintained in tri-plicates with one control set.Slides were prepared from 7 days old fungal culture and host plant and morphological characters were recorded under the microscope. The length and breadth of the conidia and conidiophores were measured with the help of ocular micrometer. The mycelial growth of the fungus in petri-plates was measured by taking the average of the longest and shortest linear growth of the fungus. Radial growth of the fungus colonies was measured in tw2o straight directions at right angles to each other along the diameter of the developing colony. The observations were recorded at an interval of 24, 48 and 72 hours after inoculation. The radial growth was recorded in millimeter.

Result and Discussion

The fungal structures observe were similar to the characters described by Heald and Wolf. The mycelia were coarse, hyaline to coloured and septate. In older hyphae, colour tends to shade of olive or brown, conidiophores were pale to dark pigmented, septate, single or in fascicles, smooth or geniculate, measured 25.78-51.56 x 4.29-6.45 mm. Conidia obclavate or needle shaped, hyaline, multi-celled, base truncate and tip acute, measuring 38.67-64.45 x 3.22-4.29 mm in length and diameter respectively. Similar morphological characters of C *capsici* had been reported by Perez Sendin et al., (1982), Sung et al., (1984) and Meon in 1990.Selected fungicides namely-Bavistin, Fytolan and Indofil M-45 against growth of *C. capsici* by poison food technique and the data collected are presented in the table.

Table: Relative efficacy of fungicides against the growth of *Cercospora capsici.*

Sl. No.	*Name of fungicide*	*Concentration used*	*Radial growth of the fungus (in mm)**			
			24 hr	*48 hr*	*72 hr*	*Mean*
1	Bavistin	0.1%	10.20	27.40	35.20	24.27
2	Fytolan	0.3%	13.30	32.60	40.00	28.63
3	Indofil M-45	0.2%	11.50	31.70	38.30	27.17
4	Control	——	15.25	39.80	70.30	41.78

C.D. for treatment means at 5% 1.15 1.42 2.16

* Average of 3 replications.

In the present experiment, *in vitro* test with selected fungicides against *C. capsici* showed significant effect. Out of 3 fungicides used, Bavistin was found most effective in reducing the radial growth of the fungus with mean growth value of

24.27 mm against 41.78 mm in control. Sharma and Sohi (1984), also reported that spraying of Bavistin at 15 and 20 days intervals gave the best control of *C. capsici*. Indofil M-45 was found second best with 27.17 mm and Fytolan 28.63 mm as against 41.78 mm in control. Similar type of results was also being reported by Jharia et al., (1977); Gonzalez and Garia (1987) by using Dithane M-45 and Fytolan against *C. capsici*. Sharma and Sohi (1979), reported that used of Bavistin (0.1%) and Fytolan (0.3%) effectively control the *C. capsici*. Effective control of *C. capsici* by using Dithane M-45 and Bavistin was also reported by Raw and Shanmugam in 1983.

REFERENCES

1. Anon. (1986) : *Indian Cocoa, Arecanut and Spices Journal* 8:1-9.
2. Gonzalez, M. and Garia, E. (1987) : Chemical control of Cercospora disease of *Capsicum*. *Arotunia de Cuba* 19 (2) 25-30.
3. Jharia, H. K.; Khare, M.N. and Amar Chand (1977) : Efficacy of fungicides in the control of fungal diseases of chillies. *Indian Phytopath.* 30 (6) 341-343.
4. Meon, S. (1990) : Infection of chilli by *Cercospora capsici*. *Pertanika* 13 (3) 321-326.
5. Perez Sendin, M. De L.A.; Gonzalez, M and Barriors, J. (1982). Sporulation of *Cercospora capsici* in different culture media. *Ciecias de la Agriculture* 12 : 23-29.
6. Raw, A.V. and Shanmugam, N. (1983) : In proceedings of National Seminar on the production technology of Tomato and Chillies, Coimbatore, India, 163-164.
7. Sharma, S.R. and Sohi, H.S. (1979) : Studies on chemical control of Cercospora left spot of chilli. *Indian Institute of Hort. Res.*, Bangalore 11 (1) 30-34.
8. Sharma, S.R. and Sohi, H.S. (1984) : Control of Cercospora leaf spot of chilli with Bavistin. *Pesticides* 18 (4) 21-23.
9. Sung, J.M.; Cho, D.J.; Cho, E.K. and Kand, S.W. (1964) : Undescribed fungal leaf spot disease of pepper caused by *Cercospora capsici* in Korea. *Korean J. Mycol. II* : 329-330.

28

Evaluation of fungicides *in vitro* against the growth of *Colletotrichum capsici* : the casual organism of Chilli fruit rot disease

Ruokuovilie Mezhatsu; L. Daiho and D.N. Upadhyay*

Abstract: In the present experiment, *in vitro* test with Bavistin, Fytolan and Indofil M-45 against *Colletotrichum capsici* by poison food technique had a significant effect. The best fungicides tested was Bavistin against the growth of the fungus followed by Indofil M-45 and Fytolan was observed.

Keywords: *Colletotrichum capsici, in vitro,*Potato dextrose agar medium (PDA), Petri-plates, Slants,Setae and conidia.

Chilli is an important spice crop and widely grown in India. It is worth undertaking on the problem which constraint its maximum production and suggest remedial measures for more production and improve the National economy. Colletotrichum fruit rot is the most important fungal disease in terms of economic loss in production. Therefore, it was felt pertinent to carried out an experiment with few selected fungicides against

* Department of Plant Pathology, Nagaland University, School of Agricultural Sciences and Rural Development, Medziphema-797106, Nagaland, India.

the growth of *Colletotrichum capsici* by poison food technique to work out the relative efficacy of the fungicides.

Materials and Method

The present *in vitro* test was carried out in the School of Agricultural Sciences and Rural Development, Medziphema, Nagaland, India, during 2000 to see the relative efficacy of the fungicides used.

Fruit rot of chilli infected by C. *capsici* were collected from the Experimental farm and brought to the department for isolation. The collected fruits were surface sterilized with 0.4% sodium hypochloride for 2 minutes and washed with distilled water. They were cut into pieces with blade through the infected spots and placed it on potato dextrose agar (PDA) medium in petri-plates of 75 mm diameter. The mycelia of the fungus after 3 days were again transferred to PDA slants to make pure culture and incubated at 25±2°C till conidia formation. The stock cultures were maintained on PDA slants in refrigerator at 5°C and the pathogen was sub-culture at regular interval for maintaining the live culture for further studies.

For inoculating on the solid media in petri-plates,young cultures of 7 days old, grown on PDA medium was used for inoculation. The size of inoculum was standardized by a cork borer having an internal diameter of 5 mm. The cut inoculum from the PDA medium was taken upon by the loop of inoculating needle and placed at the center of the plate in an inverted position, so that the inoculum come in direct contact with the surface of the medium. After inoculation, the culture plates were incubated at 25±2°C in BOD incubator. Slides were prepared from 7 days old fungal culture and host plant and morphological characters were recorded. The length and breadth of the conidia and setae were measured with the help of ocular micrometer by calibrating in the microscope. The mycelial growth of the fungus in petri-plates was measured by taking the average of the longest and shortest linear growth of the fungus. Radial growth of the fungus colonies was measured in two straight directions at right angles to each other along the diameter of the developing colony. The observations were taken at an interval of 24, 48 and 72 hours after inoculation and the radial growth of the fungus was recorded in millimeter.

The selected fungicides tested against the growth of *C. capsici* were- Bavistin (0.1%), Fytolan (0.3%) and Indofil M-45 (0.2%) respectively were used. The tested fungicides were maintained in tri-plicates with one control set.

Result and Discussion

The pathogen causing fruit rot of chilli was isolated and identified as *Colletotrichum capsici* (Syd.) Butler and Bisby (1931). Mycelia were hyaline when young, later becoming brownish with age and septate. Conidia falcate, fusiform, single celled, hyaline in single but pink or salmon coloured in masses, measured 18.23-25.78 x 6.45-9.89 mm. Setae are dark brown, rigid, septate and tapering towards the apex, straight or curved, measuring 51.56-128.90 x 4.29-6.45 mm. The fungus colony was observed circular, dense, at first white, becoming grey as culture age. Similar cultural characters had been reported by Chowdhury (1957); Mazlan and Sariah (1980); Mishra and Gupta (1994) and Kumar and Mahamood in 1984.

The fungicides tested in *in vitro* were Bavistin, Fytolan and Indofil M-45 against the growth of *C. capsici* by poison food technique. The average growth of the fungus was recorded and the data obtained are presented in the table below.

Table : Efficacy of the fungicides against the growth of *Colletotrichum capsici*

Sl. No.	*Name of fungicide*	*Concentration used*	*Radial growth of the fungus (in mm)**			
			24 hr	*48 hr*	*72 hr*	*Mean*
1	Bavistin	0.1%	12.20	24.00	36.20	24.13
2	Fytolan	0.3%	15.13	32.33	47.31	31.59
3	Indofil M-45	0.2%	13.30	28.12	41.44	27.62
4	Control	——	23.80	47.32	70.60	47.24
C.D. for treatment means at 5%			1.62	2.05	2.71	

* Average of 3 replications.

The fungicides were effective against the growth of the fungus. Treatment with Bavistin was found most effective with 24.13 mm mean radial growth as against 47.24 mm in control. Effect of Bavistin on *C. capsici* had been reported by Kore and Apet (1989) and Chrakravarty *et al.*, (1981). This was followed by Indofril M-45 with 27.62 mm mean radial growth. Complete inhibition of spore germination of *C.capsici* by Dithane M-45 at 100 ppm was also reported by Gupta et al., (1974); Thind and Jhooty (1987). The least effect among the three fungicides against the fungus was shown by Fytolan with 31.59 mm mean growth over the control as above. Similar type of results was also being reported by Avdhesh Narian and Panigrahi in 1971, using Blitox-50 with 1% concentration against *C. capsici*. Perane and Joi (1989), confirmed that seed treatment with Bavistin and spray with Fytolan, Blitox and Bavistin were more effective against *C.capsici* than either alone.

REFERENCES

1. Avdhesh Narian and Panigrahi, C. (1971) : Efficacy of some fungicidal compounds to control *Colletotrichum capsici* in vitro and in vivo. *Indian Phytopath.* 24: 593-596.
2. Butler, E.J. and Bisby, G.R. (1931) : The fungi of India. *Imper. Council Agril. Res. Sci. Monograph-1*, 18 : 237.
3. Chakravarty, D.K.; Khatua, D.C. and Giri, D.N. (1981) : Evaluation of some chemical dips for control of post harvest anthracnose of chilli fruits. *Indian J. Mycol. And Pl. Pathol.* 11 (2) 243-245.
4. Chowdhury, S. (1957) : Studies on the development and control of fruit rot of chillies. *Indian Phytopath.* 10 : 55-59.
5. Gupta, R.B.L.; Singh, G. and Mathur, R.L. (1974) : Relative efficacy of fungicides against some fruit rot pathogens of chillies in vitro. Indian Phytopath. 27 : 421-422.
6. Kore, S.S. and Apet, K.T. (1989) : Adaptation of *Colletotrichum capsici* to fungicides. *Journal of Maharashtra Agric. Univ.* 4 (1) 103-104.
7. Mazlan, S. and Sariah, M. (1980) : Anthracnose of chilli in Malaysia; biology of the pathogen and varietal susceptibility. *Pertanika* 3 (1) 47-52.
8. *Mishra, A. and Gupta, O.* (1994) : Influence of environment on growth and sporulation of *Colletotrichum dematium*. *Indian J. Mycol. And Pl. Pathol.* 24 (2) 85-87.
9. Perane, R.R. and Joi, M.B. (1989) : Control of fruit rot and die-back of chilli by seed treatment and spray. *Journal of Maharashtra Agric. Univ.* 14 (3) 368.
10. Thind, T.S. and Jhooty, J.S. (1987) : Relative performance of some fungicides in controlling anthracnose and black rot of chillies. *Indian Phytopath.* 40 (4) 543-545.

29

Screening of chilli cultivars against leaf spot and fruit rot diseases caused by *Cercospora capsici* and *Colletotrichum capsici*

Ruokuovilie Mezhatsu; L. Daiho and D.N. Upadhyay*

Abstract : Three chilli cultivars viz. Krishna, Gagan and Jyothi were screened against *Cercospora capsici* and *Colletotrichum capsici* under field condition. All three cultivars were found moderately resistant to *Cercospora capsici* from 6-10% infection whereas, Krishna was found highly resistant to *Colletotrichum capsici* (0-1% infection), Gagan was found moderately resistant to fruit rot with 6-10% infection and Jyothi was found moderately susceptible with 11-25% infection respectively.

Keywords: Colletotrichum capsici, Cercospora capsici, Krishna, Gagan, Jyothi and Cultivars.

Chilli is the leading spice crop of India. It has been cultivated all over the country. The chief uses of chilli through out the

* Department of Plant Pathology, Nagaland University, School of Agricultural Sciences and Rural Development, Medziphema-797106, Nagaland, India.

world is as spices on account of its pungency and pleasant flavour. Chilli is used as a major ingredient in curry powder in culinary preparations. It is also used in many pharmaceutical preparation, carminatives, tonic and stimulants (Pruthi, 1979). However, the production of chilli is hampered by a number of diseases. Among the diseases, leaf spot and fruit rot are the major problems of chilli causing great economic loss in production (Rathaiah, 1987). Therefore, an effort was made to screen out the resistant chilli cultivars against these diseases to attain maximum production without used of fungicides.

Materials and Method

The present research work was carried out in the Experimental farm of School of Agricultural Sciences and Rural Development, Medziphema, Nagaland, during 1999-2000.

Seeds of three chilli cultivars viz; Krishna, Jyothi and Gagan were obtained from " Asian seeds corporation" New Delhi. Seeds were soaked in water for over night before sowing into the nurseries. Seedlings were transplanted to the main field after 3-4 weeks of sowing in the nurseries. The tested cultivars were maintained in tri-plicates with one control set.

A scale with index values of 0-9 was followed , as used by Mayee and Datur (1986). The index values are given below.

Scale	Description	Degree of resistance.
0	0-1% infection	Highly resistance (HR)
1	2-5% infection	Resistant (R)
3	6-10% infection	Moderately resistant (MR)
5	11-25% infection	Moderately susceptible (MS)
7	26-50% infection	Susceptible (S)
9	51% and above	Highly susceptible (HS)

Result and Discussion

The results of chilli cultivars reaction to *Cercospora capsici* and *Colletotrichum capsici* under field condition are presented in the table.

Table: Reaction of chilli cultivars to *Cercospora capsici* and *Colletotrichum capsici*

Sl. No.	Chilli cultivars	Disease incidence (%)	
		Cercospora capsici	Colletotrichum capsici
1	Krishna	MR (5.68)	HR (0.78)
2	Gagan	MR (6.20)	MR (6.78)
3	Jyothi	MR (5.22)	MS (11.58)

When chilli cultivars were screened against leaf spot and fruit rot diseases; Krishna, Gagan and Jyothi were found moderately resistant to *Cercospora capsici* from 6-10% infection whereas, Krishna was found highly resistant to *Colletotrichum capsici* (0-1% infection), Gagan was found moderately resistant to fruit rot with 6-10% infection and Jyothi was found moderately susceptible with 11-25% infection. Out of 298 genotypes of *Capsicum spp.* evaluated, 8 were found resistant to *Cercospora capsici* and 6 were found resistant to *Colletotrichum capsici* (Ullsa et al., 1981). Rathaiah (1983), worked on different cultivars of chillies and found that Suryamukhi was tolerant to *C. capsici* and *C. capsici* and gave the highest mean yield. Out of 370 Capsicum lines tested, 27 exhibited consistent resistant to *Cercospora. capsici* in two or more seasons (Despande et al., 1984). In 1980, Mazlan and Sariah, reported that C10 was the most susceptible and C1 was most tolerant of four *C. annuum* cv. studied. Some cvs. of chillies were resistant to die-back being susceptible to fruit rot and vice versa (Perane and Joi, 1989).

REFERENCES

1. Despande, A.A.; Rawal, R.D.; Singh, D.P. and Pathak, C.S. (1984): Chilli pepper genotypes resistant to Cercospora leaf spot and powdery mildew. *Tropical pest management* 30 (4) 470-471
2. Mayee, C.D. and Datur, V.V. (1986) : Phytopathometry; *Technical Bulletin-1,* Maharashtra Agric. Univ., Parbhani, India p.146.
3. Perane,R.R. and Joi, M.B. (1989) : Control of fruit rot and die-back of chilli by seed treatment and spray. *Journal of Maharashtra Agric. Univ.,* 14 (3) 368.
4. Pruthi,J.S. (1979) : *Spices and condiments* (2nd Edn.), pp.40-47. National Book Trust of India, New Delhi.
5. Rathaiah, Y. (1983) : Yields and reaction to fruit rot and Cercospora

leaf spot of chilli cultivars. *Jr. Res. Assam Agric. Univ.* 4 (1) 31-33.

6. Ullsa, B.A.; Rawal, R D.; Sohi, H.S.; Singh, D.P. and Joshi, M.C. (1981) : Reaction of sweet pepper genotypes to anthracnose, Cercospora leaf spot, and powdery mildew. *Plant Diseases* 65 (7) 600-601.

30

Studies on management of fruit rot of Chilli (*Capsicum annuum* L.)

Ruokuovilie Mezhatsu; L. Daiho and D.N. Upadhyay*

Abstract : Maximum fruit rot of chilli caused by *Colletotrichum capsici* was observed in september with temperature 29°C and relative humidity of 75.9% at Medziphema,

Nagaland. Among the fungicides tested against the disease, Bavistin (0.1%) was found the best in controlling Colletotrichum fruit rot resulting in increased in yield followed by Indofil M-45 (0.2%). Fytolan (0.3%) was found less effective against the pathogen as compared to the former two fungicides. The symptoms and cultural characters were also discussed. Among the three varieties tested against the disease, Krishna was found resistant, Gagan moderately resistant and Jyothi moderately susceptible.

Keywords : Colletotrichum capsici, Bavistin, Fytolan, Indofil M-45, Krishna, Gagan and Jyothi.

Chilli is the leading spice of India. Among the spices consumed per head in India, dried chilli contributes the major

* Department of Plant Pathology, Nagaland University, School of Agricultural Sciences and Rural Development, Medziphema-797106, Nagaland, India.

share. Chilli is cultivated all over India and it occupied about 9,07,800 ha. With production of 8,01,500 tonnes during 1989-90 and 6,91,00 tonnes during 1990-91 (Anon.1992). India earned about Rs. 9,66,57,00/- through export of 815.66 tonnes of dry chilli during 1984-85 (Anon. 1986). However, the maximum production of chilli is hampered by a number of diseases. Among the diseases, fruit rot of chilli is the most severe problems causing great economic loss in production (Rathaiah, 1987). Serious fungal diseases of chilli, mostly on ripened fruits, are encountered in the Southern and North-Eastern states of India during the rainy season (Sankaralingam et al., 1983). Therefore, it was felt pertinent to carry out a detailed investigation on fruit rot disease of chilli and their management.

Materials and Method

The present investigation on management of fruit rot of chilli with few selected fungicides was carried out in the Experimental farm of School of Agricultural Sciences and Rural Development, Medziphema, Nagaland, during 2000-2001.

For determining the efficacy of fungicides used against the pathogen under investigation were Bavistin (0.1%), Indofil M-45 (0.2%) and Fytolan (0.3%) respectively. The first spray was applied at 112 days after sowing and followed by 3 more sprays were given at an interval of 15 days.

In the field trial, the seeds were soaked in water for over night before sowing in the nurseries. Seedlings were then transplanted in the main field after 3-4 weeks of sowing. The chilli cultivars tested were maintained in tri-plicates with one control set..

The disease incidence was recorded at 10 days interval starting from the first disease appearance till the final picking. Diseased fruits from each plot was selected randomly for recording disease incidence. Total number of fruits infected by the fungus was counted and the disease incidence was calculated by the following formula.

$$\text{Disease incidence} = \frac{\text{No. of fruit infected in sample population} \times 100}{\text{Total No. of fruits in sample population.}}$$

Results and Discussion

The pathogen causing fruit rot of chilli was isolated trom the diseased chilli fruit and culture on PDA medium in the petri-plates. The causal organism was identified as *Colletotrichum capsici* (Sid.) Butler and Bisby (1931).

The prevailing climatic condition during the period of investigation on disease incidence was recorded on monthly basis. The maximum temperature range from 25.54-31.05□C and minimum from 17.58-27.50□C. The maximum disease incidence was recorded at 29□C and relative humidity at 75.90% in the month of September. The optimum temperature for growth of *C.capsici* lies around 27-30□C and R.H.at 92-100% was reported by Chowdhury (1957); Mazlan and Sariah, (1980); Mishra and Om Gupta, (1994) and Astuti and Suhardi in 1986.

The characteristic symptoms of fruit rot of chilli was observed circular, sunken and elliptical or oblong spot with black margins. Badly infected fruits lose their normal colour and turn straw coloured. In advanced stage of the disease, concentric markings with black fruitifications representing the fungal acervuli were observed. Similar type of result had been reported by Chowdhury (1957) and Rangaswami (1994). The spotted fruits drop off prematurely resulting reduced in yield (Basak, 1994). In severe cases, it attacks the fruit stalk and spread along the stem causing die-back symptom. The spot on the fruit measured 5-10 mm in diameter and 10-45 mm in length.

The selected fungicides were sprayed after the first disease incidence appeared, followed by 3 more sprays at 15 interval. The disease incidence was recorded at 1o days interval by counting the number of fruits infected and total number of fruits in a sample population, randomly selected. The data recorded are presented in table below.

Table : Effect of fungicides on fruit rot disease on different chilli cultivars.

Fungicides used	*Chilli cultivars*	*Disease incidence (%) Days after transplanting*					
		70	*80*	*90*	*100*	*110*	*120*
Bavistin	Krishna	0.00	0.00	0.22	0.00	0.00	0.00
(0.1%)	Gagan	1.11	3.13	3.71	2.55	1.53	0.00
	Jyothi	0.08	3.86	5.87	3.29	1.05	0.00

Fytolan	Krishna	0.00	0.00	0.16	0.84	0.35	0.00
	Gagan	2.76	4.06	4.67	3.93	2.17	1.27
	Jyothi	0.93	9.89	7.05	5.69	2.71	0.00
Indofil M-45	Krishna	0.00	0.00	0.25	0.20	0.00	0.00
(0.2%)	Gagan	1.12	3.32	4.02	3.11	2.06	0.00
	Jyothi	1.04	5.38	6.60	4.07	1.46	0.00
Control	Krishna	0.00	0.00	1.42	2.00	1.84	0.25
	Gagan	3.62	4.44	5.01	8.80	8.08	3.52
	Jyothi	4.63	10.83	11.79	24.76	27.41	1.63
C.D. at 5% for fungicides		0.17	0.39	0.35	0.37	0.24	0.16
C.D. at 5% for cultivars		0.15	0.34	0.31	0.32	0.21	0.14
C.D. at 5% for fungicides x cultivars		1.29	0.68	0.61	0.63	0.41	0.27

* Average of 3 replications.

Effect of Bavistin on fruit rot of chilli cultivars under studied were found significant. On Krishna, per cent infection was found 0.00-0.22% over 0.25-2.00% in control, Gagan with 1.11-3.71% as against 3.52-8.80% control and Jyothi was found 0.08-5.87% over 1.63-27.41% in control. Treatments with Fytolan was alos found to be significant, with its application. Disease incidence on Krishna was observed 0.00-0.84% as against 0.23-2.00% in control, Gagan 1.27-4.67% over 3.52-8.80% control and Jyothi was found 0.93-9.89% as against 1.63-27.41% in control. Spray of Indofil M-45 was found significant against the fruit rot of chilli. The effect on Krishna was found 0.00-0.25% infection, Gagan 1.12-4.02% and Jyothi with 1.04-6.60% as against 0.25-2.00%,3.52-8.80 and 1.63-27.41% infection respectively in control.

The results revealed that all fungicides and chilli cultivars were found highly significant over the control. The interaction of fungicides and cultivars were also found significant.

Bavistin was confirmed the best in controlling the disease and increased in yield, followed by Indofil M-45 and Fytolan. Similar types of results was reported by Jharia et al., (1977) and Datur et al., (1990) by spraying of Dithane M-45 , Fytolan and Bavistin could effectively control *C. capsici* and increased yield. Effective controlled of *C. capsici* by Dithane M-45 applied 5-6 times at 15 days interval from the first appearance of the disease and increased yield (Raju et al., 1982; Raju and Rao, 1985; Gupta et al., 1974 and Thind and Jhooty, 1987). Bavistin performed the best for the control of *C. capsici* on chilli fruit rot (Kumar and Mahamood, 1986 and Azad, 1992). Spraying of Fytolan and Bavistin at 15 days interval controlled *C. capsici* and increased yield (Jayasekhar et al., 1987; Eswaramurthy et al., 1998 and Perane and Joi, 1989). Also, used of Bavistin and Dithane M-45 in controlling *C. capsici* on Fruit rot of chilli by Mishra (1988); Raju and Rao (1989) and Datur (1996). Among the cultivars, Krishna was found least affected by fruit rot disease, followed by Gagan. However, Jyothi was observed more susceptible to the disease. Similar result had been reported by Ullsa et al., (1981); Rathaiah (1983) and Perane and Joi (1989).

REFERENCES

1. Anon., (1986) : *Indian coaca, Areconut and Spices Journal* 8: 1-9
2. Anon., (1992) : ***Status paper on Spices***. Spices Board Ernakulam, Cochin p. 465.
3. Azad, P. (1992) : Efficacy of certain fungitoxicants against *Colletotrichum capsici* (Syd.) Butler and Bisby, the incitant of ripe rot of chilli. *Jr. Assam Sci. Soc.,* 34 (2) 34-39.
4. Basak, A.B. (1994) : A comparative study on dry weight loss due to major fruit rot diseases of chilli. *Chittagong University Studies, Science,* 18 (1) 29-131.
5. Butler, E.J. and Bisby, G.R. (1931) : The fungi of India. *Imper. Council Agril. Res. Sci. Monography-I,* 18 : 237.
6. Chowdhury, S. (1957) : Studies on the development and control of fruit rot of chillies. *Indian Phytopath.* 10 : 55-59.
7. Datur, V.V.; Sontakhe, M.B.; Putandare, N.D. and Shinde, N.N. (1990) : fungicidal control of anthracnose of chillies. *Indian J. Mycol. and Pl. Pathol.* 20 (2) 156-158.
8. Datur, V.V. (1996) : Efficacy of growth regulators and fungitoxicants on fruit rot of chilli. *Indian J. Mycol. And Pl. Pathol.* 26 (3) 239-242.
9. Gupta, R.B.L.; Singh, G. and Mathur, R.L. (1974) : Relative efficacy of fungicides against some fruit rot pathogens of chillies *in vitro*. *Indian Phytopath.* 27 : 421-422.
10. Jayasekhar, M.; Eswaramurthy, S. and Nataranjan, S. (1987) : Effect of certain fungicides on chilli fruit rot. *Madras Agril. Journal* 74 (10-11) : 479-480.
11. Jharia, H.K.; Khare, M.N. and Amar Chand (1977) : Efficacy of fungicides in the control of fungal diseases of chillies. *Indian Phytopath.* 30 (6) 341-343.
12. Kumar, S. and Mahamood, M. (1986) : Evaluation of fungicides against *Colletotrichum capsici*, the incitant of die-back and fruit

rot of chilli. *Pesticides* 20 (4) 755.

13. Mishra, D. (1988) : Fungicides control of anthracnose and fruit rot (*Colletotrichum capsici*) of chilli (*Capsicum annuum*). *Indian J. Agric. Sci.* 58 (2) 147-149.
14. Mishra, A. and Gupta, O. (1994) : Influence of environment on growth and sporulation of *Colletotrichum dematium*. *Indian J. Mycol.and Pl. Pathol.* 24 (2) 85-87.
15. Perane, R.R. and Joi, M.B. (1989) : Control of fruit rot and die-back of chilli by seed treatment and spray. *Journal of Maharashtra Agric. Univ.* 14 (3) 368.
16. Raju, K.S.; Rao, G.S. and Subbaya, J. (1982) : Note on fungicidal control of chilli fruit rot. *Haryana J. Hort. Sci.*, 11 (3/4) 264-265.
17. Raju, K.S.and Rao, G.S. (1985) : Effect of combined application of Dithane M-45 with different insecticides to control fruit rot and pest complex on chilli. *Indian J. Mycol. And Pl. Pathol.* 15 (3) 239-246.
18. Rangaswami, G. (1994) : Fungi of South India p. 57. *University of Agril.Sci., Bangalore.*
19. Rathaiah, Y. (1987) : Diseases of turmeric in Assam. **Pesticides.** 21 (8) : 15-17.
20. Rathaiah, Y. (1983) : Yields and reaction to fruit rot and Cercospora leaf spot of chilli cultivars. *Jr. Res. Assam Agric. Univ.* 4 (1) 31-33.
21. Sankaralingam, A.; Suthanthirapandian, I.R. and Ravi Kumar, V. (1983) : *Madras Agriculture Journal* 61 : 889.
22. Thind, T.S. and Jhooty, J.S. (1987) : Relative performance of some fungicides in controlling anthracnose and black rot of chillies in Punjab. *Indian phytopath.* 43 (1) 53-58.
23. Ullsa, B.A.; Rawal, R.D.; Sohi, H.S.; Singh, D.P. and Joshi, M.C. (9181) : Reaction of sweet pepper genotypes to anthracnose, cercospora leaf spot and powdery mildew. *Plant Diseases* 65 (7) 600-601.

31

Studies on management of Cercospora leaf spot of chilli (*Capsicum annuum* L.) with systemic and non-systemic fungicides

Ruokuovilie Mezhatsu; L. Daiho and D.N. Upadhyay*

Abstract : In the present experiment, maximum disease incidence was recorded in August with temperature of 30□C and relative humidity of 74.9% at Medziphema, Nagaland. The disease symptoms and cultural characters are also discussed. All the fungicides were found significant over the control and thereby, increased in yield. Bavistin was found most effective in controlling Cercospora leaf spot disease, followed by Indofil M-45 and Fytolan. Chilli cultivars viz; Krishna, Gagan and Jyothi were found moderately resistant to *Cercospora capsici*.

Keywords : *Cercospora capsici*; Krishna, Gagan , Jyothi, Bavistin, Fytolan and Indofil M-45.

Chilli is cultivated all over India and it occupies about 9,07,800 ha. Chilli is the most important ground spice (chilli

* Department of Plant Pathology, Nagaland University, School of Agricultural Sciences and Rural Development, Medziphema-797106, Nagaland, India.

powder) item exported from India ranging from 7,100 mt to 15,900 mt during the last five years (1994-95 to 1998-99), registering an average growth of 31% per annum. Among the spices consumed per head in India, dried chilli contributes the major share (Cheriankunju, 2000). The maximum production of chilli is however, hampered by a number of diseases and insect pests. Among the diseases, Cercospora leaf spot is one of the major problems in production causing complete defoliation of leaves and flowers resulting great economic loss in yield (Rathaiah, 1987). Therefore, it was felt pertinent to carry out the research work on their management with systemic and non-systemic fungicides.

Materials and Method

The present research work on the management of Cercospora leaf spot with systemic and non-systemic fungicides was carried out in th Experimental farm at School of Agricultural Sciences and Rural Development, Medziphema, Nagaland during 2000-2001.

The fungicides selected for the experiment were Bavistin (0.1%), Fytolan (0.3%) and Indofil M-45 (0.2%). Three chilli cultivars viz; Krishna, Gagan and Jyothi were obtained from the market.

In field trial, the seeds of chilli cultivars were soaked in water for over night before sowing into the nurseries. The seedlings were transplanted to the main field after 3-4 weeks of age. The tested cultivars were maintained in tri-plicates with one control set following randomized block design.

The disease incidence were to record at 10 days interval and spraying of fungicides at 15 days interval starting from the first disease incidence. Diseased leaves from each plot was selected randomly for recording the disease incidence. Total number of 5 leaves per plant infected by the fungus was counted and the percentage infection was calculated by the following formula.

$$\text{Disease incidence} = \frac{\text{Apparent \% of leaf area infected in sample population} \times 100}{\text{Total area of leaf in sample population.}}$$

Results and Discussion

The climatic condition during the period of investigation on Cercospora leaf spot of chilli was maximum from 25.54-31.05□C and minimum from 17.58-27.50□C. The relative humidity was recorded maximum on June with 78.90% and minimum on April with 66.60%. Similar type of result for the growth of *C. capsici* at different temperature had been reported by Perez Sendin et al., (1982); Sung et al., (1984) and Meon (1990).

The causal organism of leaf spot disease of chilli was isolated and identified as *C. capsici*. The nature of the disease symptoms and fungal structures observed were similar to the characters described by Heald and Wolf.

The fungal mycelia were coarse, hyaline to coloured and septate. In older hyphae, colour tends to shade of olive or brown, condiophores were pale to dark pigmented, septate, single or in fascicles, smooth or geniculate, measured 25.78-51.56 x 4.29-6.45 mm. Conidia obclavate or needle shaped, hyaline, multicelled, base truncate and tip acute, measuring 38.67-64.45 x 3.22-4.29 mm.

The characteristic symptom was observed as minute, water soaked lesions on leaf blade which enlarged and developed into chlorotic lesions, angular to irregular in shape, measuring 4-12 mm in diameter and characterized by grayish spot in the center surrounded by dark brown margin. Severely infected leaves drop off prematurely and later, the entire plant withered and died. Similar type of symptoms had been reported by Doolittle (1953); Rangaswami (1994) and Matsuoka et al., (1996).

The first spray of fungicides was given after the first disease incidence was spotted in the field, followed by 4 more sprays at 15 interval. The disease incidence was recorded by visual aid from randomly selected 5 leaves per plant at 10 days interval and the results obtained are presented in table below.

Table : Effect of selected fungicides on leaf spot disease on different chilli cultivars

Fungicides used	*Chilli cultivars*	*Disease incidence (%). Days after transplanting*							
		35	45	55	65	75	85	95	105
Bavistin (0.1%)	Krishna	5.93	0.68	0.52	0.69	0.05	0.00	0.00	0.00
	Gagan	4.31	0.57	0.48	2.41	0.11	0.28	0.00	0.00
	Jyothi	0.00	2.27	0.03	0.19	0.68	0.00	0.00	0.00
Fytolan (0.3%)	Krishna	17.52	2.33	2.43	2.91	3.85	2.56	3.00	0.25
	Gagan	7.16	1.39	2.48	3.52	2.57	2.96	2.35	0.00
	Jyothi	3.13	1.40	1.39	1.52	1.64	2.27	1.79	0.05
Indofil M-45 (0.2%)	Krishna	13.09	1.47	2.59	1.04	0.80	1.73	0.32	0.00
	Gagan	11.03	0.89	1.08	2.64	0.23	0.29	0.00	0.00
	Jyothi	2.59	0.88	0.81	1.64	0.09	1.07	0.00	0.00
Control	Krishna	12.93	3.76	3.04	3.76	5.11	5.49	7.83	9.24
	Gagan	9.87	3.85	2.83	3.55	3.71	5.29	8.79	7.93
	Jyothi	4.96	3.50	2.81	3.09	5.09	5.97	17.85	3.71
C.D. at 5% for fungicides		0.63	0.34	0.32	0.32	0.42	0.36	0.35	0.20
C.D. at 5% for cultivars		0.55	0.29	0.28	0.27	0.36	N.S	0.31	0.17
C.D. at 5% for fungicides x cultivars.		1.09	N.S.	0.55	0.55	0.73	0.62	0.61	0.34

* Average of 3 replications.
N.S. = Not significant.

The effect of Bavistin on different chilli cultivars were found significant. The effect on Krishna was found 0.05- 5.93% over 3.04-12.93% infection in control; on Gagan the disease incidence was found 0.11-4.31% as against 2.83-17.93% infection control and with Jyothi there was least disease incidence with 0.03-2.27% infection as against 3.09-17.85% in control. Fytolan was found less effective against leaf spot disease. Effect of Fytolan on Krishna was recorded 0.25-17.52%, Gagan 1.39-7.16% and Jyothi with 0.05-3.13% disease incidence over the control as mentioned above. Effect of Indofil M-45 against leaf spot disease on Krishna was found 0.32-13.09% infection, Gagan 0.23-11.03% and Jyothi 0.81-2.59% over the control as above.

The results from the above revealed that all selected fungicides were found significantly effective over the control and thereby increased in yield. Bavistin was found most effective in controlling Cercospora leaf spot disease, followed by Indofil M-45. Fytolan was observed less effective but has significant effect. Spraying of Bavistin (0.1%) at 15 and 20 days interval gave the best control of *C. capsici* and increased yields (Sharma and Sohi,1984). Raw and Shanmugam (1983), also reported that spraying of Dithane M-45 and Bavistin at 15 days interval after planting gave good control of *C. capsici* on *Capsicum* cv. Co2 and obtained higher yield of green chillies. Leaf spot disease of chilli could be control by spraying Mancozeb (Suhardi and Biswas Saroyo, 1980). Also spraying Bavistin and Fytolan could effectively control *C. capsici* (Sharma and Sohi,1979) and Dithane M-45 and Fytolan (Jharia et al., 1977; and Gonzalez and Garia,1987). The chilli cultivars tested were found non-significant and moderately resistant to Cercospora leaf spot disease. The interaction between the fungicides and cultivars were found significant over the control. Similar type of results had been reported by Ullsa et al, (1981), that out of 298 genotypes of *Capsicum spp.* Evaluated, 8 were found resistant to *C. capsici*. In 1984, Despande et al., found that out of 370 *Capsicum* lines tested, 27 exhibited consistent resistance to *C. capsici* in two or more seasons. Suryamukhi was tolerant to *C. capsici* and gave the highest mean yield followed by Cluster, Jwala, G4 and G5 (Rathaiah, 1983).

REFERENCES

1. Cheriankunju, M.S. (2000) : *Spice India* 52 (3) 3.
2. Despande, A.A.; Rawal, R.D.; Singh, D.P. and Pathak, C.S. (1984): Chilli pepper genotypes resistant to Cercospora leaf spot and powdery mildew. *Tropical pest management* 30 (4) 470-471.
3. Doolittle, S.P. (1953) : *Year book of Agriculture. Diseases of peppers* p. 469.
4. Gonzalez, M. and Garia, E. (1987) : Chemical control of Cercospora disease of Capsicum. *Arotunia de Cuba* 19 (2) 25-30.
5. Jharia, M.H.K.; Khare, M.N. and Amar, Chand (1977) : Efficacy of fungicides in the control of fungal diseases of chillies. *Indian Phytopath.* 30 (6) 341-343.
6. Matsuoka, K.; Vanti, C.A.; Costa, H. and Pinto, C.M.F. (1996): Diseases caused by fungi in Capsicum and pepper. *Informe Agropecuria (Belo Horizonte)*, 18 (184) 64-66.
7. Meon, S. (1990) : Infection of chilli by *Cercospora capsici*. *Pertanika* 13 (3) 321-325.

8. Perez Sendin, M.De. L.A.; Gonzalez, M. and Barrios, J. (1982): Sporulation of *Cercospora capsici* in different culture media. *Ciencias de la Agriculture* 12 : 23-29.
9. Rangaswami, G. (1994) : Fungi of South India. P. 57. *Univ. Agril. Sci.,* Bangalore.
10. Rathaiah,Y. (1987) : Diseases of turmeric in Assam. ***Pesticides*** 21 (8) 15-17.
11. Rathaiah,Y. (1983) : Yields and reaction to fruit rot and Cercospora leaf spot of chilli cultivars. *Jr. Res. Assam Agric. Univ.* 4 (1) 31-33.
12. Raw,A.V. and Shanmugam, N. (1983) : *In proceedings of National Seminar on the production technology of tomato and chillies,* Coimbatore, India, 163-164
13. Sharma, S.R. and Sohi, H.S. (1979) : Studies on chemical control of Cercospora leaf spot of chilli. *Indian Institute of Hort. Res., Bangalore* 11 (1) 30-34.
14. Sharma, S.R. and Sohi, H.S. (1984) : Control of Cercospora leaf spot of chillies with Bavistin. *Pesticides* 18 (4) 21-23.
15. Suhardi, and Saroyo, B. (1980) : Cercospora leaf spot on red pepper *(Capsicum annuum)*, I. Chemical control. *Bulletin penelitian Hort.* 8 (11) 1-10.
16. Sung, J.M.; Cho, D.J.; Cho, E.K. and Kand, S.W. (1984) : Undescribed fungal leaf spot disease of pepper caused by *Cercospora capsici* in Korea. *Korean J. Mycol.* 12 (2) 75-77.
17. Ullsa, B.A.; Rawal, R.D.; Sohi, H.S.; Singh, D.P. and Joshi, M.C. (9181) : Reaction of sweet pepper genotypes to anthracnose, cercospora leaf spot and powdery mildew. *Plant Diseases* 65 (7) 600-601.

32

An Analysis of Marketed Surplus of Rice in Assam

*D.C. Kalita[1], B.C. Bhowmick, R.S. Saikia & C. Hazarika**

ABSTRACT

The present study was conducted in Assam covering all the six agro-climatic zones of Assam covering a total sample farmers of 300 from three-size groups *viz.*, 82 small (1.01-2.00 ha), 95 medium (2.01-4.00 ha) and 123 large (above 4.00 ha) being selected through multistage stratified random sampling procedure. The data related to the year 1996-97. Marketed surplus was calculated as the quantity of production that was sold out in the market. For analyzing the factors effecting marketed surplus, multiple regression analysis was done. The per hectare marketed surplus was highest for the small group, the amount being 7.26 qt followed by 5.14 and 2.99 qt respectively for medium and large group of farmers which

1 Lecturer, Department of agricultural Economics, Nagaland University, SASRD, Campus: Medziphema – 797106

* Department of Agricultural Economics, Assam Agricultural University, Jorhat 785013, Assam, India.

showed an inverse relationship with the farm size. The main determinants of marketed surplus for paddy were size of operational holding, total production, farm level consumption and family size. An increase in the area under the crop and total production would resulted in increase in the total amount of marketed surplus whereas increase in the amount of farm level consumption and family size reduced the quantum of marketed surplus of paddy in Assam.

Introduction

Cereals come under the food grains in India and it plays an important role in the national economy contributing about 32.40 per cent of the GNP during 1994-95 (Anonymous, 1996). Rice is the major cereal in India contributing about 47 per cent to the total cereal production in the economy and occupies about 23.29 per cent of the total cultivated area during 1995-96 (Anonymous, 1997). In Assam also, cereal plays a significant role in the dietary system and economy of people. It is closely linked with Asaamese culture. The production of cereal in Assam increased from 191730 tones in 1951-52 to 3505360 tones in 1995-96. Rice, wheat and maize are the major cereal of Assam. Among the cereals, rice alone occupies 70.5 per cent of total gross cropped area (Anonymous, 1997).

The marketed surplus is the quantity of production that is actually sold out in the market. The marketed surplus varied according to the size of holding i.e. more is the size of holding, more is the marketed surplus (Lavania *et al*, 1966). Mandal and Ghosh (1968) reported that there is a positive relationship between marketed surplus and farm size. As the production of commodities expands, the market sales increases proportionately more than the increase in output and if the output of commodities falls, the decrease in the market sales is proportionately more than the fall in output (Acharya and Agarwal, 1996).

Marketed surplus of food grains constituted the basic source of earnings in the agrarian economy. The commercialization process sets up physical flows of commodities of which marketed surplus is an indicator in monitizing the economy. The administrator's plan faced several difficulties because of shortfalls in production and restriction on the flow of the surpluses in the market. This leads to inflationary pressure and frequent shortage of food grains. Therefore, an attempt is made here to estimate the marketed surplus of rice and factors effecting marketed surplus of rice in Assam with the objectives of (i) Estimation of marketed surplus and (ii) Factors affecting the marketed surplus.

Methodology

The study was conducted in Assam covering all the six agro-climatic zones, viz., Upper Brahmaputra Valley Zone (UBVZ), Lower Brahmaputra Valley Zone (LBVZ), Central Brahmaputra Valley Zone (CBVZ), North Bank Plain Zone (NBPZ), Barak Valley Zone (BVZ) and Hill Zone (HZ) Respectively, covering a total sample of 300 from three size groups *viz.*, 82 small (1.01-2.00 ha), 95 medium (2.01-4.00 ha) and 123 large (above 4.00 ha) being selected through multistage stratified sampling procedure. The data related to the year 1996-97. Marketed surplus was calculated as the quantity of production that was sold out in the market. For analyzing the factors effecting marketed surplus, multiple regression analysis was done. The relation can be expressed as follows:

$$Y = B_o + B_1X_1 + B_2X_2 + B_3X_3 + B_4X_4 + B_5X_5 + U_t$$

Where,

Y = Marketed surplus of rice in quintal

X_1 = Size of operational holding in *bigha*

X_2 = Area under paddy in *bigha*

X_3 = Total production of paddy in quintal

X_4 = Farm level consumption in quintal

X_5 = Family size in adult equivalent

U_t = Error term

Results and Discussion

Table 1 represents the area, production and amount of marketed surplus of paddy. The analysis was carried out for different categories of farmers in Assam. The table revealed that the average size of the operational holding under paddy was 1.65 ha, 3.05 ha and 4.47 ha for small, medium and large group of farmers respectively. The per hectare marketed surplus was highest for the small group, the amount being 7.26 qt followed by 5.14 and 2.99 qt respectively for medium and large group of farmers. This shows that per hectare marketed surplus is inversely related to the farm size. The per farm marketed surplus was found to be 12.01, 15.69 and 13.34 qt respectively for small, medium and large farmers.

Table 2 represents the regression co-efficient of marketed surplus for rice in small size group of farmers across various agro-climatic zones of Assam. Most of the equations gave good fit as the co-efficient of multiple determination (R^2) was found higher. Also, the co-efficient are having the expected sign. The co-efficient of multiple determination was ranging between 0.88 to 0.98 indicating that 88 per cent to 98 per cent of the variation in the total quantity of marketed surplus of rice for small farmers was explained by the explanatory variable included in the model. Among the explanatory variable total production of paddy (X_3) had positive and significant influence on total marketed surplus of rice in all the six agro-climatic zones of Assam. Farm level consumption (X_4) had negative effect on marketed surplus but it was significant only in LBVZ and UBVZ. Size of the family (X_5) was found negative and significant in UBVZ of Assam. The co-efficient for total production was 0.506, 1.087, 0.766, 0.767, 0.743 and 0.691 for different zones implying that one unit change in the total production will result in 0.506 unit changes in the total amount of marketed surplus for LBVZ. Similarly 1.087, 0.766, 0.767, 0.743 and 0.691 unit changes in the marketed surplus for CBVZ, NBPZ, HZ, UBVZ and BVZ respectively will take place due to one unit change in the total production. On the other hand, one unit increase in the farm level consumption will result in 0.746 and 0.421 unit decrease in marketed surplus in LBVZ and UBVZ. The table also shows that one unit increase in the family size will result in 1.011 unit decrease in the amount of marketed surplus for paddy in UBVZ of Assam.

Table 3 represents the regression co-efficient of marketed surplus for medium group of farmers in various agro-climatic zones of Assam. In this group also, the co-efficient of multiple determination (R^2) was as high as 0.77 to 0.96. This implies that 77 to 96 per cent of the variation in the marketed surplus for medium farmers was explained by the variables included in the model. For medium farmers, area under paddy (X_2) had an positive and significant influence on marketed surplus in CBVZ and UBVZ. The co-efficient for area was 2.150 and 6.167 for CBVZ and UBVZ respectively implying that one unit change in the area under paddy crop will result in 2.150 unit and 6.167 unit increase in the marketed surplus for CBVZ and UBVZ respectively. Total paddy production also has got positive and significant effect on the total amount of marketed surplus in all the agro-climatic zones of Assam for medium farmers. Farm level consumption was negative and significant in LBVZ, CBVZ and BVZ. Family size was significant in LBVZ and NBPZ.

Table 4 represents the regression co-efficient of marketed surplus of paddy for large group of farmers. The co-efficient of multiple determination (R^2) was ranging between 0.36 to 0.98 indicating that 36 to 98 per cent of total variation in the marketed surplus for large group was explained by the explanatory variables included in the model. Size of operational holding (X_1) was positive and significant in LBVZ. The co-efficient was 0.601 implying that one unit increase in the size of operational holding will result in 0.601 unit increase in the total amount of marketed surplus for the large farmers in LBVZ of Assam. The variable total production was also positive and significant in all the zones except NBPZ. Farm level consumption was negative and significant (-1.355) for HZ implying that one unit increase in the farm level consumption will result in 1.355 unit decrease in the total amount of marketed surplus for this group.

Conclusion

From the above analysis, it can be concluded that the main determinants of marketed surplus for paddy were size of operational holding, total production, farm level consumption and size of the family. An increase in the area under the crop and total production will result in increase in the total amount of marketed surplus whereas increase in the amount of farm level consumption and family size will reduce the quantum of marketed surplus of paddy in Assam.

REFERENCES

Acharya, S.S. and Agarwal, N.L., 1999. *Agricultural Marketing in India*, 3rd Edition. Oxford & IBH Publishing Co. Pvt. Ltd., New Delhi. PP 316-335

Anonymous, 1996. *Basic Statistics for Agriculture*, Govt. of Assam, Guwahati.

Anonymous, 1996. *Hindu Survey of Indian Agriculture*, Ministry of Agriculture.

Lavania, S.B. and Singh, B.N., 1970. Marketed and Marketable Surplus of Paddy in Chinpur Block of Arrah District, Bihar. *Proceedings of second All India Marketing Research Conference*. pp. 23-25.

Mandal, G.C. and Ghosh, M.G., 1968. A Study of Marketed Surplus of Paddy of the Farm Level in Four East Indian Villages. *Indian Journal of Agricultural Economics*. 23(3): 21-36.

Table 1. Area, production and marketed surplus of paddy across various farm categories of Assam during 1995-96

Farm category	*Area (ha)*	*Production (qt)*	*Average area under*	*Productivity (qt)*	*Marketed surplus (qt)*	*Per hectare marketed surplus (at)*	*Per farm marketed surplus of paddy*
Small	135.59	3581.09	1.65	26.41	984.64	7.26	12.01
Medium	290.02	4165.55	3.05	14.36	1490.45	5.14	15.69
Large	549.83	7565.27	4.47	13.76	1641.25	2.99	13.34
All farms	975.44	15311.91	3.25	15.70	4116.32	4.22	13.72

Table 2. Regression coefficients for marketed surplus for rice in small size group of farmers across various agro-climatic zones of Assam

Variables	*Symbol*	*LBVZ*	*CBVZ*	*NBPZ*	*HZ*	*UBVZ*	*BVZ*
Constant term	a_0	-2.185	-9.643	-5.349	-0.562	-5.874	8.131
		(4.037)	(5.589)	(5.589)	(3.3963)	(4.916)	(13.921)
Size of operational holding	X_1	0.019	1.347	0.169	0.003	0.657	0.075
		(0.033)	(1.070)	(0.374)	(0.514)	(0.670)	(0.326)
Area under paddy	X_2	0.601	1.195	0.130	0.200	0.592	0.082
		(0.372)	(1.055)	(0.500)	(0.564)	(0.739)	(0.655)
Paddy production	X_3	0.506*	1.087*	0.766*	0.767*	0.743*	0.691*
		(0.090)	(0.575)	(0.196)	(0.085)	(0.065)	(0.162)
Farm level consumption	X_4	-0.746*	-0.345	-0.577	-0.418	-0.421*	-1.154
		(0.263)	(0.296)	(0.625)	(0.331)	(0.173)	(0.760)

Family size	X_5	-0.570	-1.441	-0.460	-1.727	-1.011*	-0.512
		(0.759)	(1.134)	(2.425)	(1.238)	(0.546)	(1.415)
Goodness of fit	R^2	0.95	0.98	0.88	0.96	0.97	0.98

(Figures in parentheses indicate standard error), * Significant at 1 per cent probability level.

Table 3. Regression coefficients for marketed surplus for rice in medium size group of farmers across various agro-climatic zones of Assam

Variables	*Symbol*	*LBVZ*	*CBVZ*	*NBPZ*	*HZ*	*UBVZ*	*BVZ*
Constant term	a_0	-2.282	6.530	3.287	58.915	27.822	6.437
		(14.919)	(8.548)	(11.486)	(31.65)	(16.706)	(14.548)
Size of operational holding	X_1	0.582	1.980	0.515	4.884	3.757	1.056
		(0.294)	(1.156)	(1.074)	(2.648)	(2.224)	(1.287)
Area under paddy	X_2	0.756	2.150*	0.219	3.974	6.167*	1.858
		(1.165)	(1.192)	(1.148)	(3.078)	(2.338)	(1.421)
Paddy production	X_3	1.220*	0.895*	0.967*	0.753*	0.115*	0.673*
		(0.246)	(0.127)	(0.108)	(0.255)	(0.051)	(0.145)
Farm level consumption	X_4	-0.896*	-1.084*	-0.019	-1.222	-0.828*	-0.770*
		(0.218)	(0.245)	(0.108)	(0.927)	(0.634)	(0.163)
Family size	X_5	-5.089*	-0.530	-4.302*	0.667	-1.703*	-0.439
		(1.231)	(0.833)	(707)	(6.476)	(1.916)	(1.432)
Goodness of fit	R^2	0.77	0.89	0.94	0.87	0.93	0.96

Table 4. Regression coefficients for marketed surplus for rice in large size group of farmers across various agro-climatic zones of Assam

Variables	*Symbol*	*LBVZ*	*CBVZ*	*NBPZ*	*HZ*	*UBVZ*	*BVZ*
Constant term	a_0	-3.379	-15.043	126.680	-22.484	98.268	26.657
		(16.835)	(6.647)	(74.989)	(0.712)	(60.686)	(42.148)
Size of operational holding	X_1	0.601*	0.452	1.070	0.063	1.002	1.788
		(0.213)	(0.248)	(2.426)	(0.061)	(4.489)	(1.257)
Area under paddy	X_2	-0.461	-0.037	0.177	0.756	-2.837	-0.342
		(0.548)	(0.124)	(0.223)	(0.460)	(4.289)	(0.799)
Paddy production	X_3	0.635*	0.930*	0.001	0.997*	1.131*	1.254*
		(0.189)	(0.056)	(0.010)	(0.121)	(0.372)	(0.311)
Farm level consumption	X_4	-0.428	-0.450	-0.940	-1.355*	-1.543	-0.092
		(0.823)	(0.394)	(1.402)	(0.639)	(1.078)	(0.930)
Family size	X_5	-0.498	-1.857	-1.381	0.671	1.990	-1.522
		(2.068)	(1.527)	(5.281)	(1.730)	(2.741)	(2.526)
Goodness of fit	R^2	0.65	0.98	0.36	0.91	0.60	0.63

33

Role of Biofertilizers in Crop Production

R.P. Singh

ABSTRACT

Agriculture is the mainstay of the economy of our country but unfortunately more than 85 per cent of this vital industry is in the hands of small and marginal farmers who do not have access to the present day agricultural technology because of the financial constraints. Biofertilizers have recently attracted the attention of scientists as they have been shown to add as much as 140 mt of biologically fixed nitrogen to the soil. This is important because the entire industrially fixed nitrogen amounts to only about 40 mt with an investment of US $ 15 billion and daily consumption of 2 million barrels of crude oil. Initially the term biofertilizer was coined to embody all such organisms, which specialized in metabolizing the molecular *nitrogen from the air.* Biofertilizer contains live or latent cells of efficient strains of nitrogen fixing, phosphate solubilizing or cellolytic micro-orgsni£ms used for application to seed, soil of composting areas with the objective of increasing the number of such micro-organism and accelerate there microbial processes

* Department of Agronomy, SASRD, Nagaland University Campus: Medziphema—797106.

which augment the availability of nutrients that can be easily assimilated by plants.

Introduction

Soil is the home of hundreds and thousands of different types of organisms including microorganisms such as bacteria and fungi. These microorganisms play very vital role in mobilization of different nutrients from organic and inorganic non available forms to available forms and vice versa. To sustain the fertility status of soils, maintenance of appropriate status of micro flora is very essential. Increased use of chemical fertilizers, fungicides and pesticides has badly affected this micro flora which is being reflected in continued loss of soil fertility. In this heterogenous soil micro flora complex, there are certain group of microorganisms which play very vital and significant role in mobilizing the availability of nutrients from their inert elemental or complex organic or inorganic forms to simple available forms. For example *Rhizobium, Azotobacter, Azospirillum, Acetobacter,* Blue green algae etc, fix atmospheric nitrogen.

Organisms like *Bacillus, Pseudomonas, Aspergillus, Penicillium* etc solubilize fixed insoluble phosphate in soil to soluble primary and secondary orthophosphate ions. *V. Mycorrhiza not* only help in better availability of phosphorus but also enable the plants to absorb more nutrients and water from deeper and far-off soil sections through their ramifying hyphae. Similarly, other microorganisms such as *Aspergillus, Trichoderma, Chaetomium, Myrothecium* etc act on complex organic matters and release a wide range of micronutrients from their captivity.

Biofertilizers are ready to use live formulations of such beneficial microorganisms which on application to seed, root or soil, mobilize the availability of nutrients by their biological activity in particular and help build up the micro flora and in turn the soil health in general. Biofertilizers are usually available in either moist powdered form (carrier based) or in liquid form. Each gram of this product must contain a minimum of 10 to 100 million live microbial cells at the time of manufacture and a minimum of 1 to 10 million within 15 days of expiry.

Different estimates are available for the total potential of biofertilizers in the North Eastern Region, if the entire cropped area of the region were to be inoculated with biofertilizers then the total requirement of bacterial biofertilizers would be around 7163 million tonnes and blue green algae biofertilizers of 19185 million tonnes. As per the estimates, if only 50 per cent of the total cropped area is brought under biofertilizers use then there will be a total requirement of 2540 million tonnes of bacterial biofertilizers and 1901 million tonnes of blue green algae biofertilizers. State wise requirement and pattern of different biofertilizers use in the states of North Eastern Region is given in Table 1 and 2.

Table 1. Potential of different biofertilizers in North Eastern Region as per different estimates

State	Expected potential of bacterial biofertilizers					Expected Potential of
	Rhizobium	*Azotobacter*	*Azospirillum*	*PSB*	*Total*	*BOA*
Ar. Pradesh	0.56	25.98	71.87	98.41	196.82	726.6
Assam	58.08	3134.88	1794.46	487.0	5474.42	14319.4
Manipur	—	4.17	113.94	118.11	236.22	974.4
Meghalaya	2.15	23.13	60.8	85.36	171.44	626.4
Mizoram	0.10	3.89	35.68	39.67	79.34	318.0
Nagaland	6.12	12.44	109.31	127.87	255.74	721.20
Tripura	10.08	206.24	160.14	376.46	752.92	1501.0
(Potential demand for 50% of the total cultivated area)						
Ar. Pradesh	3.0	13.0	36.0	52.0	104	.367.0
Assam	13.0	130.0	756.0	899.0	1798	7510.0
Manipur	—	40.0	39.0	79.0	158	405.0
Meghalya	1.0	43.0	36.0	80.0	160	307.0
Mizoram	1.0	3.0	19.0	23.0	56	197.0
Nagaland	3.0	10.0	41.0	54.0	108	420.0
Tripura	2.0	5.0	71.0	78.0	156	695.0

Anonymous, (2003).

Table 2. Pattern of different biofertilizers use in the states of NE Region

State	Biofertilizer consumption in quintals during 1997-98				
	Rhizobium	*Azotobacter*	*Azospirillum*	*PSM*	*Total*
Assam	38.0	58.0	29.0	28.0	153.0
Arunachal Pradesh	11.30	20.0	8.50	2.0	41.8
Manipur	16.7	16.0	2.20	28.0	62.9
Meghalaya	0.8	0.4	—	—	1.2
Mizoram	8.04	27.0	15.0	55.0	105.04

Nagaland	14.3	45.2	2.04	57.5	119.04
Tripura	12.04	—	—	—	12.04
Total in NE	101.18	166.6	56.74	170.5	495.02

Anonynaous, (2003).

Types of Biofertilizers

Basically biofeertilizers can be grouped into three categories:

1. Nitrogen fixers
2. Phosphate solubilizers/mobilizers
3. Compost accelerators and enrichers

1. Nitrogen fixing biofertilizers

It has.been estimated that approximately 250 million ton of nitrogen is being fixed per year on the entire earth. Out of this about 50 million ton of nitrogen is being fixed by industrial means, 30 million ton by natural electrical lightening and other natural means and about 170 million ton by tiny microorganisms present in soil and water (biological nitrogen fixation). This is indicative of massive potential of these microorganisms. In nitrogen fixing biofertilizers highly efficient and high nitrogen fixing microorganisms are being used, dependirw on their requirement for a particular type of crop in a given soil environment. Among them *Rhizobium, Azotobacter, Azospirillum* and *Acetobacter* are the most widely accepted biofertilizers.

Rhizobium

Rhizobium biofertilizer is a carrier based product contains 10 to 100million live bacteria. On seed treatment these bacteria multiply rapidly in soil along the developing roots and enter into the developing roots through root hairs. There inside the roots in due course of time they develop large number of nodules. These nodules are the actual site of biological nitrogen fixation, and the growth and yield of the plant are directly dependent upon the nodules. More the nodules, more shall be the yield. In this system it is only the right partnership between legume and *Rhizobium* which results into nitrogen fixation. Both the partners i. e. *Rhizobium* and legume while living alone cannot fix atmospheric nitrogen.

Legume—*Rhizobium* system of nitrogen fixation is one of the most promising system of biological nitrogen fixation and it accounts for approximately 35-40 million tons of nitrogen fixation on the entire earth, which is almost equivalent to total industrial nitrogen fixation. The contribution of this system under different crops is given in Table 3. Large number of field trials conducted over years in India and abroad have proved that the crops inoculated with specific strains of *Rhizobium,* yield 10-30 per cent extra yield over their inoculated control (Table 4).

Table. 3. Estimates of total nitrogen fixation (kg/ha per season) by different legumes under natural conditions

Name of crop fixation	*Quantum of fixation*
Groundunut	50-60
Lentil	90-100
Gram / Black Gram	50-55
Pea	52-77
Soybean	60-80
Alfa- alfa	100-200
Red gram	168-200
Clover	100-150
Gram	85-110
Cowpea	80-85

(Biofertilizers, A training manual).

Table 4. Response of Rhizobium biofertilizers on yield of different legume crops in field trials at fanner's field

Crop	*Control (q/ha)*
Moong (kharif)	11.20
Moong (rabi)	7.42
Black gram	6.24
Chickpea	12.73
Beans (green pods)	70.80
Pea	37.85
Arhar	10.00
Cowpea	5.30
Groundnut	19.75
Soybean	17.29

Trials conducted at All India level

Treated (q/ha)	*% increase in yield due to Rhizobium*
12.60	12.50
9.12	22.99
7.39	18.42
15.40	21.00
78.60	11.50
43.22	11.10
12.50	25.00
6.90	30.00
23.50	26.98
20.76	20.00

Table 5. Effect of legume-*Rhizobium* association on companion non-legume crop in intercropping

Crop	*Dry matter yield (q/ha)*		
	Straw	*Grain*	*Total*
Maize alone	59.20	34.20	93.40
Cowpea alone	38.91	8.60	47.51
Maize in intercrop	56.80	34.90	91.70
Cowpea in intercrop	18.75	4.17	22.92.
Maize+Cowpea	75.54	39.07	114.61

(Biofertilizers, A training manual)

N-content %		*Total N uptake*
Straw	*Grain*	*Kg/ha.*
0.73	1.04	78.78
2.24	3.71	118.60
0.73	1.04	76.75
2.47	3.72	62.45
		139.20

34

Alder-based Jhum Cultivation in Nagaland

Sentinungba Longchar*

ABSTRACT

Most of the farmers in Nagaland practice Jhum cultivation that results in the degradation of land. Nowadays, a traditional method of farming, Alder based Jhum cultivation is getting more popular in Nagaland. It can be integrated into Jhum and agro forestry system that would not only save the environment but also give economic return to the farmers.

Alder is a fast growing nitrogen fixing tree. Important spices *viz.* ginger, cardamom, black pepper and cash crops like tea and coffee could be well grown under the cultivation of Alder trees.

Introduction

About 17,000 sq km of the land is subjected to 'Jhum', known

* School of Agricultural Sciences and Rural Development, Nagaland University, Campus: Medziphema Nagaland-7971 006

as the practice of slash and bum agriculture, in Nagaland. But due to heavy cutting down of trees and deforestation, the rich flora and fauna flourishing in the state are being endangered, thus, effecting on the ecological balance of the society. Landslides and loss in fertility of the soil gives rise to state transportation problem and low productivity in the agricultural field. Therefore, development of forests is essential not only to earn revenues but also to prevent soil erosion and maintain ecological balance.

Area under Land uses in Nagaland (1995-96):

1.	Geographical area	: 16,57,900 ha
2.	Reporting area for land utilization statistics	: 15,45,640 ha
3.	Forests	: 8,62,532 ha
4.	Area under non-agricultural uses	: 57,430 ha
5.	Cultivable waste land	: 73,920 ha
6.	Land under misc. tree, crop like orchards, etc	: 1,29,980 ha
7.	Fallow lands other than current fallow	: 2, 96, 500 ha
8.	Current fallow	: 1, 14,090 ha
9.	Net area sown	: 2, 11,298 ha
10.	Total cropped area	: 2,27, 828 ha
11.	Net irrigated area	: <52,100 ha
12.	Gross irrigated area	: 71,600 ha

Source: *Nagaland Agricultural Guide Book,* 1997

Alder-based Jhum Cultivation

Now days, alder-based jhuming system has been adopted by man) traditional farmers and is becoming very popular in Nagaland. This system which satisfies the ecological principles, provides the basic needs for food fuel and housing material to the farmers. The ability of the alder tree t< develop and retain fertility of the soil has been fully tltilized by the farmer: in Angami, Tuen$sang and Mon areas.

The Alder Tree

Alder *(Alnus nepalensis)* is a deciduous tree, belongs to the famil Betuloceae. It is widely distributed in the northeast region of Indi; Malaysia, South Asia and other cooler temperate regions of the world.

This, fast growing, nitrogen-fixing tree can grow in an altitude of about 1,000 to 2,000 meters and is moderately shade tolerant. It thrives well even in less fertile soils but prefers permeable soils. It is oft~n found growing along watercourses, gullies and shady ravines.

Life Cycle of an alder tree:

The life cycle of an alder is like that of other flowering plants. Both male and female flowers bloom on the same tree. In the months of September and October, during pollination, the female flower changes to fruit green, dark brown and black in colour. The catkins (pendant clusters of unisexual flowers) mature by the month of December.

Seed selection and sowing:

Cone-like woody seed bearing structures are collected from the nurser: or seedlings from the wild. Usually, alder ripens in the months of Novembe to January. A kilogram of catkins yields about 125 grams of seeds with aJ equivalent of 1 gram containing about 570 seeds.

The best time for sowing alder seeds, is the month of February, just afte a shower. A spacing of 3-4 (m between plants and 5-6 ..:m between rows j maintained. The seeds are sown evenly spread over the beds, and a thin lay~ of fine soil is spread evenly over the seeds. The seedlings, if transplante when they are about twelve months, grow into healthy trees. The trees aJ planted in lines that may run roughly in the north-south direction to gl better sunshine.

Pollarding:

Usually, alder is pollarded during the months of December and Janua when its bark develops rough fissures in 6-10 years. Subsequently, it pollarded once after 4-6 years, that is, 2 years of cropping and 2-4 years fallow period.

a height of about 6 meters and diameter of about 15 em in 2-4 years when i is pollarded again. After pollarding, the fresh cut is plastered with mud t~ prevent it from drying and cracking.

Steps involved in Alder-based Jhum system:

Ist year: Alder trees are pollarded, during December and January, at height of 2 meters from the ground before or after the slash and bun operation. Pollarding minimizes the insect pest harbouring in the tree ani also the pollarded trees are used as fuel for burning. In the burnt field-mixed cropping is practiced by growing rice, maize, millets and other grai. crops as main crop. Vegetables like colocassia, beans, chilies, cucurbits an, leafy vegetables are grown as secondary crops. Seeds of both primary an secondary crops are sown, during the months of February-April, with the seeds of secondary crops in between the rows of primary crops.

2nd year: The cropping operation is repeated. Then, the field is lej fallow for 2-4 years allowing the alder trees to grow for pollarding an cropping in the subsequent cycle.

Merits of Alder-based systems:

1. This system has the potential to increase food production and can be adopted on a wider scale in villages having scarce land areas suitable fc alder. Small and marginal farmers can easily adopt this type of system.
2. This is sustainable and productive system that provides good timber, food and fuel.
3. Alder tree is fast growing and can be easily propagated.
4. Reduces fallow period.
5. Prevents soil erosion.
6. Fallen leaves of the tree are used as mulching material and thus retain moisture in the soil.
7. Fixes nitrogen from the atmosphere thus adds to fertility of the soil and minimizes use of chemical fertilizers.
8. Increase the production in a wide variety of crops' like cereals, legume:

Conclusion

Alder-based systems follow the ecological principles and are profitable that can be widely adopted in fallow Jhum fields. Farmers can cultivate cash crops like tea and coffee in alder systems.

REFERENCES

Anonymous (2000). *Nagaland Horticultural Book 2000.*

Anonymous (1999). *Building upon Traditional Agriculture in Nagaland,* India.

Anonymous (1998). *Tree farming through Jhum cultivation in Nagaland.*

Robbie, T.A. *Forestry.*

Ziliang, D.K.; Kevichusa, R.; Angami, T. (1985). *Nagaland the use of alder trees.*

35

Status, Constraints and Prospects of Farm Inputs Marketing in Manipur

*S.B. Singh and I.M. Singh**

ABSTRACT

The necessity of farm inputs in Manipur state is of vital importance for increasing food productivity to feed the ever-increasing population in the state.

The changing world trade scenarios and demand for horticultural products also accelerate their importance. However, farm inputs are produced countryside and thus, production can be enhanced if they are reached to the farmers in time at the least cost.

Dynamic and efficient channels for marketing of farm inputs are required for the popularization of knowledge about modern inputs among the farmers.

This paper analyzes the status, constraints and prospects of farm input marketing in the state. Till August 1992, there was existence of three-tier system of distribution of fertilizers

* ICAR Research Complex for NEH Region, Manipur Centre, Lamphelpat – 795004.

in Manipur i.e. government purchase through Manipur Apex Cooperative Marketing Society and distributed to wholesalers, retailers and farmers. Since then, the system was privatized through direct business between manufacturer , dealers and retailers. There are 34 dealers and 500 retailers operating in the state. Untimely and Inadequate supply, high prices, lack of adequate sell centers, lack of knowledge of salesman are the problems and constraints in the marketing of fertilizers. The projected seed requirement of rice, rapeseed and mustard, potato and tomato for the year 2005-2006 in the state was estimated as 301.4 tons, 4.8 tons ,1266 tons , and 0.16 tons respectively. There existed a deficiency of 292.3 tons (rice), 3.36 tons (rapeseed and mustard), 379.8 tons (potato) and 0.01 tons (tomato) indicating a huge gap between the requirement and availability of quality seeds in Manipur. A study on status of seed use, diffusion and adoption of quality seed of four major crops, viz. rice, rapeseed and mustard, potato and tomato reveal that 97.10%, 86.18%, 25.8% and 2.81% of the total seed used in rice, rapeseed and mustard, potato and tomato was retained from previous year crop. About 1.95%, 12.77%, 70.95% and 95.94% of the seed requirements of rice, rapeseed and mustard, potato and tomato was fulfilled through the supply of certified seed by the Department of Agriculture, ICAR and seed dealers. Study on source of information on use of quality seeds showed that fellow farmers in the village played a major role in diffusion of quality seeds use in rice (92%) and mustard (80.23%). For potato (48.08%) and tomato (46.25%), existing seed dealers exerted a leading role in the dissemination of information on quality seeds. Extension departments played an insignificant role of 1.95%,-10.77%, 12.75% and 2.81% in rice, rapeseed and mustard, potato and tomato respectively which need to be looked upon. Non-availability of seeds of desired variety was found to be the most hindering factor for low adoption of quality seeds in rice, rapeseed and mustard while in the case of potato untimely supply due to late transportation was reported to be important. Lack of fund and high price of quality seeds are the least hindering factors in all the selected crops. For pesticides and insecticides, the system of distribution is totally privatized through dealers and retailers. Failure to distribute suitable types of chemicals and high price are the main problems in the distribution of insecticides and pesticides. Private dealers, Government and Banks played a vital role in distribution of farm machinery and implements. High prices of farm machinery and maintenance cost hinders efficient delivery system of farm machinery. The above findings necessitate suitable policy options to bring efficient marketing system of critical farm inputs in the state. Improvement in transportation, warehousing and storage system, provision of credit and subsidy, promotion of balance fertilization through efficient distribution and effective extension systems, organize effective training programmes for private, wholesalers and retailers, personnel of cooperatives and institutional agencies the use of chemicals and fertilizers.

For seeds two possible options, viz. establishment of seed farms either state or private party owned and improvement of production of own saved seed are available to solve the quality seed problem in the state. In case of potato and tomato, most of the requirements are met by supply from outside through seed dealers. Although the state having potential for potato seed production, lack of market infrastructure particularly cold storage constrained the system. State government's intervention in this regard is necessary. The other option may be alternative arrangement through seed dealers well in time as per requirement. The fellow farmers played a leading role in diffusion of quality seeds thus targeting progressive farmers in selected areas through training and FLDs may result effective diffusion. Establishment of plant health clinics may further supplement the system of quality seed and right type of chemicals and fertilizers dissemination as shown by the effective role played by them in information diffusion.

36

An Analytical Study of Almond Marketing and Problems of the Almond Growers in Kashmir Valley of J&K

Jaspal Singh, Tyagi, D.B.[1] & Sharma, A.[2]*

ABSTRACT

The analysis of price-spread, marketing cost and margin is an important method of examining the efficiency of the market. In the present investigation the Almond growers made up the supply side while the wholesaler and Arhatias in the market represent the buyer side to establish prices. On producer's side, there was absolute dearth of market intelligence, consequently forced to sale most of their produce in the absence of pure competition and tied to establish price for their mutual benefit. The high marketing cost and excessive profits of traders are signs of marketing inefficiency.

With the producer's view point the direct sale of almond was most beneficial but this channel handles very less amount

* Raja Balwant Singh College, Bichpuri, Agra (UP).

1 Shri M.S. Degree College Abidgarh Agra (UP)

2 Department of Agricultural Economics, Nagaland University, SASRD, Medziphema: Campus (NL).

of marketed surplus of almond. Producer's share in the consumer's price in channel II, III and IV was 82, 72 and61 per cent respectively while the highest marketing cost incurred in channel IV. Absence of regulated market and producer's organization, undeveloped market infrastructure, lack of market vigilance and the most important lack of knowledge and technical know-how are the main problems of almond growers in the study area.

Introduction

Having achieved self-sufficiency on the food front, the focus in Indian agriculture, in the last decade or so, shifted to their fields of commercialization. One of the areas that emerged as a viable diversification option, which offer immense scope for the cultivation of various kinds of horticultural crops. This provides an excellent platform for the country to emerge as leading producer of horticulture crops. The horticultural sector has established its credibility for improving their economic conditions of farmers and entrepreneurs, enhancing exports and above all, providing nutritional security to people. Diversification and value addition will be the key words of Indian horticulture. However, there are many challenges. These include increasing irrigation facilities, improving productivity and quality of produce to be globally competitive, creating infrastructure and resources for post-harvest technology and giving priority to exports. What is required is the creation of proper infrastructure and incentive policy. There is a need to create proper facilities for value addition on horticulture crops. According to a food ministry, the country wastes more fruits and vegetables than what the UK consumes every year.

After the green revolution, blue revolution and yellow revolution, we now have yet another revolution called the "Golden Revolution". With the advancements made in the horticulture sector is terms of rapid increase in fruit production like *Almond*, the dollars earned through cut flower exports, the employment generated and the tremendous potential it promise for the future, it is apt to call it a "Golden Revolution". The horticulture sector has given an altogether new dimension in striving towards nutritional security.

Jammu and Kashmir is world wide famous not only for its scenery and beauty but also for it's plenty of fruits (dry or fresh) of various varieties. Almond is a favorite fruit in our country. It is concentrated source of energy due to its high oil content. As production of almond is very much limited in India, bulk of the almond is imported from foreign countries. Almond cultivation has been in progress to some extent in the hilly areas of Jammu & Kashmir and Himachal Pradesh. The almond is native to hot and arid region of western Asia, from where it was probably carried to Greece, North Africa, Europe, Australia and America.

In Kashmir, almond fruit is ready for harvest in July to August; its harvesting is done by climbing on trees and beating fruits with the help of sticks. After harvesting, it is left in open sunshine for a few days to reduce moisture, shells are removed manually which is a labour consuming work but local people are only acquainted with this method. The almond has to be dried properly otherwise any moisture within the almond can cause the decay of its kernel. These are stored in gunny bags in ventilated rooms free from excessive humidity. Almond is send to market in two forms, viz. one with shell and the other without shell (kernel). At present, there is no agency to regulate the pricing of dry fruits. Worldwide fame of Jammu and Kashmir is not only for its scenery and beauty but also for its plenty of fruits (dry and flesh) of various varieties. Almond is most important dry fruit of Jammu and Kashmir State grown on an area of 18817 hectares producing 9672 metric tonnes annually.To provides market cover to small and marginal fruit growers at doorsteps, 17 satellite markets, one terminal market and grain mandi are being developed in the state at an estimate cost of Rs. 44.26 crores. As state earns revenue of Rs. 1300 crores annually from fruit industries, a comprehensive plan has been formulated to develop this industry on modern lines to fetch more income to the state. The plan envisages setting up of more fruit markets, packing of fruit on scientific lines, cold storage facility and providing other incentives to the growers.[3]

Since the modern agriculture is progressively replacing the subsistence one. The changes could be observed more on the production end, as in the use of improved farm machinery, varieties, pesticides, and fertilizers etc., the positive trend in the income generated from Almond cultivation has attracted more land to be diverted for Almond cultivation. On the other hand the growers fear that the Almond cultivation is going to be less remunerative owing to the costly potential productivity of Almond in mind, it is worthwhile to look into the Almond business in the valley. So as to highlight the unfavourable factors responsible for the inefficiency in the business. An efficient marketing system as the farmer visualizes, is one which maximizes his net returns form a given transaction and helps in expanding the market in respect of grading packing etc. The preparation of Almonds for market involves picking, drying, scraping, grading, packing, transportation etc. As all these functions are important determinants of price the Almond will fetch in market, require great care at every step. Any carelessness at any stage in the marketing channel will result in lower prices and hence would miss the target of higher net returns.

This study was, therefore, undertaken to find out the various costs and margins in the marketing of almond and problems faced by the almond growers of the J&K.

Objectives of the Study

The specific objectives were *(i)* to work out the marketing cost, marketing margin in different marketing channels of almond, and *(ii)* to analyze the problems faced by the almond growers.

Research Methodology

Out of fourteen districts of J&K state, Kashmir valley consists of six districts, Budgam is an important district with respect to almond cultivation as it occupy a large proportion of the total area under almond cultivation in Kashmir valley. Therefore, district Budgam was selected purposely for the present study. Out of 9 blocks of Budgam district, one block Budgam was selected randomly and 5 villages were also selected randomly from the list of Almond growing villages of the Budgam block. At the final stage of sampling a pooled list of Almond growers from all the selected villages was prepared and were classified into three categories viz. Small growers having less than 50 almond trees, Medium having 50 to 100 almond trees and Large growers having more than 100 almond trees and a sample of

20 percent growers was selected randomly in proportion to their number in each size group The data on costs and margins by various functionaries at different levels of marketing channels were collected by survey method for Batmallo (Srinagar), an unregulated primary market and Kanck mandi (Narwal), Jammu secondary/terminal markets from where the produce is supplied in local, national and international markets.

The price spread was, therefore, worked out at a point of time. Simple tabular analysis was used to present the data. The total marketing cost has been worked out by following formula.

$$C = C_p + C_{m1} + C_{m2} + C_{m3}$$

Where,

C = Total cost of marketing of the almonds.

C_p = Cost paid by the producer from the time of produce leave the farm till he sell it

C_m = Cost incurred by the middlemen in the process of buying and selling the product.

The producer's share in consumer's rupee has been computed as follows:

$$FS = \frac{(RP - MC)}{RP} * 100$$

or

$$FS = \frac{RF}{RP} * 100$$

Where

FS = producer's share in consumers' rupee expressed in percentage.

RP = Retail price of the almonds.

MC = Marketing cost

RF = Price received by the producer.

Marketing channels:

The most common marketing channels involved in the marketing of Almond in Budgam district of Kashmir valley are as follows

i. Producer – Consumer

ii. Producer – Retailer – Consumer

iii. Producer – Wholesaler – Retailer – Consumer

iv. Producer – commission agent – Wholesaler – Retailer – Consumer

Price-Spread for Direct Sale between Producer and Consumer (Channel- I)

This channel is not much common and handles only about 5 per cent of the marketable produce in the primary market. The transportation charges mentioned here are the expenses incurred by the producer to carry the produce from orchard to the house for value addition.

Table 1: Price-spread for Almond through channel-I (Producer-Consumer)

Particulars	*Amount (Rs./qt)*	*% of Consumers' rupee*
Net price received by producer	8750.70	97.23
Marketing cost paid by producer		
Transportation charges	26.10	0.29
Grading and cleaning charges	147.60	1.64
Loading/unloading	5.40	0.06
Weighment	3.60	0.04
Cost of bags	62.10	0.69
Other charges	3.60	0.04
Total	249.30	2.77
Consumer's price	9000.00	100.00

Through this channel producer sells his produce directly to the consumers and earned handsome (about 97 % of consumer's rupee) money by spending only Rs. 249.30 per quintal as marketing cost.

Channel II (Producer – Retailer – Consumer)

In channel-II producer farmer sells a part of the produce at farms directly to the local retailers. But this system is not very common and handles hardly 10 percent of the total marketed surplus. All the expenses incurred in the movement of eggs from farm to retailer are born by the retailer.

Table 2: Marketing Cost and Margins in the Marketing of Almond in Channel II

(Rs./Quintal)

Particulars	*Amount*	*% of consumers' rupee*
Producer's share	8671.70	82.59
Marketing cost paid by producer		
Transportation charges	27.30	0.26
Grading and cleaning charges	153.30	1.46
Loading/unloading	6.30	0.06
Weighment	4.20	0.04
Cost of bags	63.00	0.60
Other charges	4.20	0.04
Total	258.30	2.46
Retailer		
Producer's sale / Retailer's purchase price	8930.00	85.05
Marketing cost paid by retailer		
Transportation charges	54.60	0.52
Packing	52.50	0.50
Storage	31.50	0.30
Loading/unloading	6.30	0.06
Weighment	21.00	0.20
Other charges	4.20	0.04
Total	170.10	1.62
Retailer's margin	1399.90	13.33
Consumer's price	**10500.00**	**100.00**

Table further reveals that in this channel total marketing cost of Almond was 4.08 percent of consumers' rupee, out of which producers and retailers spent about 2.46 and 1.62 per cent respectively.

Channel - III (Producer – Wholesaler – Retailer – Consumer)

This channel is more prominent in the marketing of almond. In this channel wholesaler contact themselves to the producers at their place either during pre-harvest period or at the time of harvesting and ensure the purchase of almond by advancing some payment in advance. Some times producers bring their produce to the wholesalers in the primary market. Both types of transactions were considered in the estimation of marketing cost and margin through this channel.

The total marketing cost incurred by producer, wholesaler and retailer was Rs. 260.40, Rs. 743.40 and Rs. 136.50 per quintal respectively. The burden of high marketing cost up on the wholesaler was due to payment of various taxes.

Table 3: Marketing cost and margin in the marketing of Almond in channel III

(Rs./quintal)

Particulars	*Amount*	*% of consumers' rupee*
Producer's share	7614.60	72.52
Marketing charges paid by producer		
Transportation charges	29.40	0.28
Grading and cleaning charges	153.30	1.46
Loading/unloading	6.30	0.06
Weightman	4.20	0.04
Cost of bags	63.00	0.60
Other charges	4.20	0.04
Total	260.40	2.48
Wholesaler		
Marketing charges paid by wholesaler		
Transportation charges	174.30	1.66
Road tax	14.70	0.14
Loading/unloading	10.50	0.10
Wightman	4.20	0.04
Sales tax @ 4.5%	354.90	3.38
Mandi tax @ 2%	157.50	1.50
Storage charges	21.00	0.20
Other charges	6.30	0.06
Total	743.40	7.08
Wholesaler's margin	621.60	5.92
Retailer		
Marketing charges paid by retailer		
Transportation charges	21.00	0.20
Packing	52.50	0.50
Storage	31.50	0.30
Loading/unloading	6.30	0.06
Weightman	21.00	0.20
Other charges	4.20	0.04
Total	136.50	1.30
Retailer's margin	1123.50	10.70
Consumer's price	**10500.00**	**100.00**

Producers shared 72.52 percent of the consumer rupee through this channel while 16.62 per cent occupied by the intermediaries (wholesaler & retailer) and rest 10.86 per cent was accounted for total marketing cost at different stages through this channel.

Channel – IV (Producer–commission agent–Wholesaler–Retailer–Consumer)

Producer's share in consumer's rupee was 61.62 per cent by selling the almond through kachha arhatia and rest about 39 per cent was accounted for marketing cost and margin of intermediaries (Table 4).

Table 4: Marketing cost and margin in the marketing of Almond in channel IV

(Rs./quintal)

Particulars	Amount	% of consumers' rupee
Producer's share	6470.10	61.62
Marketing charges paid by producer		
Transportation	21.00	0.20
Grading and cleaning	151.20	1.44
Loading/unloading	6.30	0.06
Weighment	4.20	0.04
Cost of bags	63.00	0.60
Other charges	4.20	0.04
Total	249.90	2.38
Kaccha Arhatia		
Marketing charges paid by K. Arhatia		
Transportation	18.90	0.18
Loading/unloading	8.40	0.08
Weighment	4.20	0.04
Other charges	4.20	0.04
Total	35.70	0.34
K. Arhatia's margin	762.30	7.26
Pacca Arhatia		
Marketing charges paid by P. Arhatia		
Transportation	16.80	0.16
Loading/unloading	6.30	0.06
Weighment	4.20	0.04
Other charges	4.20	0.04
Total	31.50	0.30
P. Arhatia's margin	443.10	4.22
Wholesaler		
Marketing charges paid by wholesaler		
Transportation	174.30	1.66
Road tax	14.70	0.14
Loading/unloading	10.50	0.10
Weighment	4.20	0.04
Sales tax @ 4.5%	359.10	3.42

Mandi tax @ 2%	159.60	1.52
Storage charges	21.00	0.20
Other charges	6.30	0.06
Total	749.70	7.14
Wholesaler's margin	497.70	4.74
Retailer		
Marketing charges paid by retailer		
Transportation	21.00	0.20
Packing	52.50	0.50
Storage	31.50	0.30
Loading/unloading	6.30	0.06
Weighment	21.00	0.20
Other charges	4.20	0.04
Total	136.50	1.30
Retailer's margin	1123.50	10.70
Consumer's price	10500.00	100.00

The total marketing cost incurred by producer was Rs. 249.90 per quintal while kachcha arhatia, pacca arhatia, wholesaler and retailer spent about Rs.36, 31,750 and 136 per quintal and earned about 7, 4, 5 and 11 per cent margin in the consumer's rupee respectively.

Problems faced by Almond Growers

Marketing in widest sense, compressing all the relation involved in the movement of Almond from producer to final consumer, unfortunately the present system of marketing of Almond in the study area was not only indicates marketing inefficiency but feasibility of ensuring proper share to producers was engrossed with numerous marketing problem. The major problems faced by producer have been described here under following headings.

Absence or regulated market:

In the study area, there is no regulated market for marketing of almond Therefore most of the almond growers have to sale their produce to the middlemen and consequently receive less share in consumer's rupee.

Lack of producer's association:

There is not any kind of collective organization among the producers to guide, protect, organized and to operate on large-scale basis to safe guard the interest of the producers.

System of Village Arhatia:

This investigation revealed that the system of Arhatia was not only suicidal to producers, but made them enable of getting the reasonable margin of their produce.

Absence of cleaning, grading and standardization:

Cleaning, grading and standardization are important principles of modern commence. It provides a base for a system of trading in which internal inspection of the packages prior to purchase because unnecessary, there by effecting considerable economy in labour, time and money at all stages of marketing. No systematic cleaning and grading was being practiced by any grower engaged in the distribution of Almond.

Inadequate Transportation facilities:

Transportation and communication facilities posed another problem for marketing of almond. Trucks are lacking the facilities for the quick and safe transport of the product. The absence of railway system, from Srinagar to other markets is also a major problem.

Undue deductions:

In the marketing of Almond there are many kinds of arbitrary deductions at each level, which reduces the producer's share.

Superfluous middlemen:

Since the producers sell their produce to middlemen intervened between the produce and final consumer. Middlemen enjoy cream of the cake at the cost of producer who toiled and moiled in the dust from down to dusk. In this context, the measures like organization, producer's cooperative and cooperative marketing societies are necessary.

REFERENCES

Bhat, M.S. and Alam, S.N. (1987) "Agricultural growth performances in Jammu & Kashmir state". *Agriculture Situation in India*, Vol. 42:9, pp. 701-705.

Economic survey of India (2005)

Tripathi, R.S. "Economics of production and marketing of fruits in the Garhwal hills of Uttar Pradesh", *Annals of Agricultural Research*, 1999, 18: 1, 5-11;

Wani, M.H; Mattoo, M.S.; Sofi, A.A. "Resource-use and economic efficiency of various marketing cost components in apple" *Agricultural-Marketing*, 1995, 37: 4, 38-40.